THE WORD GOD SENT

THE Word
God Sent

PAUL SCHERER

BAKER BOOK HOUSE
Grand Rapids, Michigan

Paperback edition issued 1977 by
Baker Book House Company
with permission of Harper & Row, Publishers, Inc.

ISBN: 0-8010-8102-5

PHOTOLITHOPRINTED BY CUSHING - MALLOY, INC.
ANN ARBOR, MICHIGAN, UNITED STATES OF AMERICA
1977

TO MY COLLEAGUES AND STUDENTS
ACROSS THE YEARS
AND TO MY WIFE AND DAUGHTERS
ALL OF WHOM HAVE IN MANY THINGS QUESTIONED ME, BUT IN
EVERYTHING GENEROUSLY GIVEN ME THEIR SUPPORT

Contents

PART II
THE WORD IN SEARCH OF WORDS

Preface

The first part of this book, committed now to whatever future it may have, has had already a rather long and varied past. Much of its basic material was first used in lectures at Union Theological Seminary in New York City; then at a number of seminaries and institutes in the East. Most recently, in their present form, though considerably abbreviated, three of the chapters were delivered as one segment of the Earl Lectures for 1964 at the Pacific School of Religion in Berkeley, California. There is nothing I want to do more than to acknowledge at once my deep indebtedness for the many kindnesses shown Mrs. Scherer and me on that occasion by President Anderson, by the faculty and students, and by those who were in attendance on the Convocation. The only thing that could possibly have forestalled such a cherished memory was the rather intimidating list of distinguished former lecturers which was sent me as an inducement to come!

Perhaps just here I may be allowed a brief word about the *how* and the *why* and the *what* of this that follows. There was a time when all of us more or less assumed that if you could determine any given Bible author's specific point of view, and discover the particular purpose he had in writing, you could safely discount a great deal of what he said: simply because of everybody's tendency, whether or not designed, to uphold his own opinion and further his own aim. To some extent you could almost expect him to tamper with the facts, taking care to make them fit, which was a very serious matter indeed; certainly he would interpret them, and that might quite well turn out to be all the more misleading the less he intended it to be. If only someone, somewhere, from Genesis to Revelation, had provided us with a bit of straightforward reporting, with an account of what really happened!

And of course no such thing is possible. You may choose to write of a certain event: but already the choice of event is itself your choice, not necessarily mine; and the account, when it is written, is not my account, but yours. Before you start, you have left behind the myth of scientific objectivity. Witness the manifold distortions of even the current scene which find their way into newspaper articles, and by nothing more deliberate many a time than just that choice of event which the complexity of modern life renders inescapable. The dilemma is with us in every generation. The only way to manage is to grasp it firmly with both hands. To be open to as many facts as you can is good; to be wide open to all of them is impossible. Neither choice nor interpretation can be avoided. But let it be remembered that to take a position is not to leap into it or try to impose it on another. Nobody should be asked to conceal a purpose in order to keep from thrusting it on somebody else.

There is no use trying to dodge it: these pages are written from a specific point of view, are designed to serve a particular purpose, and are as a result chock-full of interpretation. More than that, there is a strong tendency noticeable in most of them to uphold my own opinion and to further my own aim. That aim, without further ado, is to take stock of the hazards we face whenever we make bold either to speak or to hear what offers itself to us as the Word of God: not to take stock of all of them, but of those that seem to constitute the greatest threat; and to say what can be said about the common effort we have to make— layman and preacher alike, for the hazards are of as much concern to one as to the other—in some measure to overcome them; if not that, at least to be aware of them, lest we continually be caught off guard.

My own initial acquaintance with them came out of a quarter of a century in the parish ministry.[1] After that, everything I thought I had learned fell under the often discerning and always somewhat disconcerting eyes of my students at Union Seminary in New York City. Nor has there been any considerable letup since my retirement to the status of visiting professor.[2] All the way along, what I kept finding out was subject to that constant scrutiny, and beyond any ability of mine to express my gratitude was being deepened and enriched—I hope so; I know they tried—by the scholarship and generosity of many colleagues. In addition, such notions as I brought from the parish with regard to the preacher's task in the preparation of sermons was for the first few years of teaching running headlong, week after week, into the information I was gathering for the next two or three lectures. I was poring over textbooks, and going back to original sources whenever I could, to learn more about theory and practice, but especially about the history of preaching. It was in the effort to familiarize myself with a little of the vast literature of the Christian pulpit that two of my firmest convictions came into sharper focus.

One of them is that to the ever-changing panorama of the years the Word of God, properly understood, never has to be made relevant. Too much honest, misguided toil has been devoted to that. The Word of God is already relevant. It was relevant before we arrived on the scene. The honest toil is called for as one seeks to understand it, and by understanding it to apprehend its relevance. All it asks is that instead of being adjusted to the modern situation, or exploited to ends it never had in mind, it be allowed to address, at this time and in this place, what is most deeply characteristic of human existence.

The other unshaken conviction is that there is not today, there never has been, and there never will be any adequate substitute for preaching. The correspondence between the greatness or the wretchedness of the whole Christian enterprise, when one rightly conceives of them, and the fidelity or faithlessness of the Christian pulpit is from age to age altogether too obvious for anybody to miss it. You may read the sequence as you like: the one as cause, the other as effect—or you may turn the tables around. In any case what you have on your hands seems to be more than a phenomenon; it looks like a pattern.

So it was that canons which do not often appear in print, and are rarely if ever raised in discussion, began to emerge. As they grew more and more insistent, I had to turn with them to my own preaching; then to the sermons I heard or read, in student groups or churches, in books or in periodicals. Increasingly I found myself impressed, and I speak now primarily of the first half of this century, by the well-nigh unfailing but often contrived relevance of what was being said. Most of it did succeed in making some meaningful contact with human life and human experience, though frequently, it seemed, at rather superficial levels. The content was largely of the hard-nut-to-crack variety. The structure was usually clear and logical, the style concise, direct, concrete. There was a wealth of illustrative insights and applications— everywhere a keen awareness of the social implications of the gospel, and everywhere a busy feeling around for the imperatives of the Christian ethic: but not very often any notable concern for the indicatives of the Christian faith, where all the imperatives are born.

Little by little a number of quiet misgivings as to what I myself was about began to slip into the picture. Soon they decided to get noisy. First they stayed at home, then they wandered abroad: only to come back and stir up more trouble at home than ever. The adjectives for what seemed to be happening in the pulpit could not now wear very bright faces. Some of the more manageable aspects of that disillusioning story, and such suggestions as I should like to make with regard to them, I have tried to write out in the four chapters that follow: after which the only thing left was for me to undertake, rightly or wrongly, to do myself what I was finding it necessary now to talk about to others. The sermons I have added were the result of that. They are largely expository and doctrinal. The topics, which I like to assume are not altogether unrelated to the content, have been arranged under captions borrowed from Christopher Fry's *A Sleep of Prisoners*.[3] These, it seems to me, not only carry their own meaning with them, but indicate as well the direction in which the Christian gospel is forever intent on moving, whatever the obstacles we set in its way. Numerals above the line in all cases indicate notes—printed for greater convenience and less hindrance at the end of Part I—which I hope will prove useful to such as wish to pursue further some of the points that are raised. An index is added, partly with the thought that in some measure it may facilitate comparison of Part I with Part II, of creed with conduct, of theory with the painful and time after time frustrating attempt at performance. Repetitions where they occur stand at times in different contexts— which may itself have some significance. I need scarcely say that such preaching is not likely to prove popular and I am not using the word in any pejorative sense. To many in our day—by whose failure?— it may not even seem intelligible. No other claim is entered for it except that it wants to stretch itself out toward ends which I believe have dropped too consistently from view. In the effort to state those ends and to show how far short of them we are all liable to fall, I may well appear to be presumptuous. If so, one may be sorry for it, I suppose, as indeed I am, without knowing how to remedy it.[4]

I shall not forget what I owe Professor Samuel L. Terrien of the Faculty of Union Seminary, New York City, for his careful reading of these lectures, and for all he did as scholar and friend to pull me out, not always on the Sabbath, of the pits into which I had fallen. The faults that remain, after much rewriting, are mine, not his. Among other changes, somewhat extensive notes have been added.

Let me add with appreciation that Princeton Seminary has generously provided secretarial assistance. Mrs. Bernard K. Bangley, Miss Helen Brock, Miss Mebane Harrison, and Miss Margaret Payne have prepared large portions of the manuscript for the printer. I certainly want to record the fact, too, that Eugene Exman, Melvin Arnold, Hugh Van Dusen, and Beverly Lancaster, of the staff of Harper & Row, have shown me many personal courtesies, and now as in the past have given ready assistance. I do so gratefully acknowledge my indebtedness to them all.

PAUL SCHERER

Princeton Theological Seminary
Princeton, New Jersey
October, 1965

THE WORD GOD SENT

PART I

Not as the Word of Men

Not as the word of men, but as . . . the word of God. . . .
—I Thessalonians 2:13

I

A Great Gulf Fixed

People . . . said . . . it thundered: others said, An angel . . . JOHN 12:29

Before the Word of God can get itself lived, it needs to get itself believed—and what is believed is not always lived. But before it can get itself believed, it has to get itself heard—and what is heard is not always believed. Farther back than that, however, is the hurdle which is to be our chief concern: before the Word of God can get itself heard, it must get itself said—and what is said is not always heard.

1. WHO CAN HEAR?

A Roman Catholic author is on record as having expressed the opinion that if ever Protestantism should be found dead of an assassin's wound, the dagger in its back would be the Protestant sermon. Whether or not the field of coverage could be extended beyond the confines of Protestantism is beside the point: what we do have to admit is the relevance of such an indictment wherever it can be shown that the good news of Jesus Christ has been largely depleted of its content in the effort to render it somewhat more acceptable or measurably easier to understand. Without attaching any premium to unintelligible profundity, or taking any refuge in the "offense" of the gospel, as if that alone in our case accounted for the emptiness of our pews, it has nevertheless become necessary to point out not only that the sermon most readily understood and heartily approved is likely to have in it relatively little of what brought the New Testament into being, but also and as a corollary that the church most depressingly crowded often hears least of what that New Testament, almost bursting at the seams, is straining so hard to say.

In one of the contests sponsored some years ago by *The Christian Century Pulpit* in order to select "the Seminarian preacher of the year," I protested the choice which was made on the ground that it was bad pedagogy to print as a sort of model, under the imprimatur of the judges, a sermon with but one casual reference in it not to Christ but to Jesus, as on the whole a good example to follow. The editor agreed, but explained that unfortunately those who could say what they had in mind did not apparently have the gospel in mind, while those who had the gospel in mind could not seem to say it. The comment was not only perceptive: it fairly begs for wider application. Sermons that have nothing distinctively Christian about them, and so have no right in the Christian pulpit, can be made to sound so good—and indeed they are good, except for the one sense in which they are bad; while sermons that do all they can to stand up in the high tradition of the Christian faith at its best may be simply bad sermons, except for the one sense in which they are good.

That dilemma confronts the man who enters the ministry with a choice which in many cases turns out to be quite tragic. He may well leave the seminary much impressed by what we have come to regard as the recovery of theology, and he may well try manfully to preach what he has learned; all too often, however, weighing it down with exegesis and doctrine—convinced that there has been much too little of both; disagreeing with Cullmann on "time," quoting Tillich on "nonbeing," expounding Bultmann on "myth": whereupon, like a Boeing 707, or 727, or whatever the number is this week, with far too heavy a load, he finds it quite impossible to get off the ground, and disaster waits for him at the end of the first runway. Businessmen and physicians, members of the Ladies' Aid and the Couples' Club take to asking, "What on earth was he talking about this morning?" As *The New Yorker* once said of poets, "what they mean by what they mean" seems so much "tougher than it's ever been."[1] Before too long it may well begin to dawn on him that he is not on speaking terms any more with his people. The words he uses and relies on, *sin, grace, rebirth, kingdom,* have become "undecipherable hieroglyphs." Inevitably he grows discouraged. The pressure of pastoral duties increases. What is called for is an administrator or a counselor. For Sunday there can always be "Helpful Hints for Hurtful Habits," or a few positive thoughts about negative thinking— maybe even vice versa; followed by one or two recommendations on the subject of God's will for the brethren.

So it is, according to Theodore Wedel, that a whole generation has grown up among us which has actually never heard the Christian gospel: only the *Reader's Digest* version of it, the success-story rendition, log cabin to White House; whereas, of course, the Incarnation is quite the other way around, from White House to log cabin.[2] A number of years ago, under a title which was arresting enough at any rate, *The Message and Silence of the American Pulpit,* Sabapathy Kulandran, a Congregational Bishop of South India, summed up what he believed had come to be the sad condition of affairs in the United States: the message had largely to do with playgrounds and plumbing, patriotism and labor, Mother's Day and the United Nations; the silence had to do with what the New Testament calls the *kerygma, the word of reconciliation and life.*[3]

It is therefore by no means a surprise that preaching has fallen into some disrepute, not only in much of our Western civilization, which is still nominally Christian, but even within the Church itself; and what is worse, increasingly in many of the theological seminaries that provide the Church with her ministers.[4] Writes Herman Melville in *Moby Dick,* as Father Mapple climbs the ladder to preach his now famous sermon from the lofty perch, so like the prow of a ship, in the little chapel at New Bedford, "The pulpit is ever this earth's foremost part. . . . The world's a ship on its passage out . . . and the pulpit is its prow."[5] Strangely enough, that was in the middle of the last century, when there was already a growing public thoroughly persuaded that the preacher with his "platitudes, his truisms and untruisms," was "the bore of the age, the old man" whom the Sinbads could not "shake off, the nightmare" that disturbed one's "Sunday rest, the incubus" that overloaded religion and made "God's service distasteful"![6] Today is there any one at all who will dare to enter the claim that the pulpit is the world's prow? It would scarcely be even pathetic; it would be ridiculous. Group dynamics, pastoral counseling, the theory and techniques of nonverbal communication—what in Heaven's name is the continued use of preaching when there is so much else which promises to prove so much more effective?

No wonder there is endless talk about the secularization of religion! Christianity belongs to this world, not to some other; but it's in deadly peril when it comes to be "understood as an intellectual and moral ideology of culture."[7] Martin E. Marty, in his book on the *New Shape of American Religion,* has traced through the last four hundred years the evolution of what he considers to be now not so much a religion in any truly Christian sense of the word as a sort of national observance masquerading as Christianity, to which, in a world which seems about to be overrun by Communism, it is almost treasonable not to adhere.[8] Peter Berger has given us a sociological analysis of its cultural, political, and social forms. It adds up to something like this: Have faith in faith— it is of great therapeutic value. Get up every morning and stand erect in front of the open window, head thrown back, breathe deeply three times, every time with the words, "I believe, I believe, I believe." Be a loyal husband, a good father, a responsible citizen, an energetic lawyer, broker, merchant. Live the American way. "Our government makes no sense," said President Eisenhower, "unless it is founded in a deeply felt religious faith—and I don't care what it is."[9] Go and listen to Billy Graham when he comes to town: he will use all the right words, eternal life in heaven, sin and damnation in hell; but be assured that the words are quite harmless.

2. CULTURAL INTERPRETATIONS OF THE GOSPEL

Whenever in history such a condition, or anything like it, has prevailed, the fault has certainly not been all the fault of preaching: if it were so now, the remedy might perhaps be applied with relative promptness and ease. The difficulty lies there, but it lies deeper too, in the very patterns of our thought and of the society in which we live. As specialization and diversification go merrily on, men and women in all walks of life seem to find it more difficult than ever to communicate with each other—and in a day, ironically enough, when the means of communication have been developed beyond the wildest flights of the imagination. Walt Whitman is said to have asked a workman who had just put the last finishing touches to the first telephone line ever strung between Maine and Texas, "But what if the people of Maine have nothing to say to the people of Texas?" I thought of that in July, 1962, when we on this side of the Atlantic, for the edification of the French, bounced off a satellite which we had thrown out into orbit a picture of the American flag, with a number of self-congratulatory remarks. The French bounced back a bit of music from a nightclub. *The New Yorker* satirized it in a cartoon. A man was sitting in his easy chair viewing a line of can-can dancers on his television screen, while underneath ran the caption, "What wonders God hath wrought"! Meanwhile, as areas of common concern grow smaller and smaller and dialogue dies down, groups form: literary, philosophical, professional, social, national, gathered each around its own center of shared interest, each isolated, esoteric, cut off from every other—the only dialogue of which it is capable, a dialogue solely for the initiated.

Obviously the man in the pulpit cannot tolerate that. He wants to speak so as to be understood by all of them; only to find that he is separated from them by a barrier which he seems comparatively helpless to surmount. More helpless, I am afraid, than he thinks. Certainly no headway can be made by resorting at last to the historic faith of the Christian Church.[10] If only we had never wandered so far away from it, everything would be all right. But of all tongues else that tongue now is most foreign. Neither does the secret lie in using the language of the man in the street. Too often his language is the wrong language. Nor in addressing him where he is. Too often he is in the wrong place. It is simply not true that all the preacher needs is to find out what people want, or think they must have, and give it to them—a strategy which has achieved very nearly the proportions of a cult. Young and old ask their questions, and as week follows week the sermon tries to get together an answer. But what are the questions? "How can I find a little peace?" they would like to know in the midst of the turmoil. When they lose their money, or a job, or somebody they love, it's "Where then should I turn?" Does it make any sense to advise such bewildered folk, in one way or another, to have faith in God? If we could hold on to any distinction at all between the religious and the secular, would it be fair to say that as a rule what they are looking for is a "religious" answer to a "secular" question? And there are no such answers. Whatever correlation may be possible has to take place at profounder levels. In the New Testament peace is relevant not so much to secular as to religious anxiety. If there is no trace of that to begin with, down where the ultimate questions are asked and the ultimate answers are given, then the only thing possible for anybody is the counterfeit of peace which is sentimentality, a kind of "premature sanctification," as a friend of mine has called it, the illusion of security.[11] As for faith in God, that is always a priority and a preventive, never a prescription!

And so, over and over again, there is no meeting between the problem and the solution: partly because preachers preach as they do, but largely also because people think as they do. In the pulpit the preacher speaks of freedom, equality, brotherhood, that great trinity of the French Revolution; and everybody nods his head, heirs as we all indeed are of our own American Revolution. Man, woman, and child, they are sure they know what he means; and unfortunately maybe they do. But they are not thereby excused from understanding what the New Testament means. There is a cultural apprehension of a culturally conditioned freedom, equality, brotherhood—a democratic notion of the worth and dignity of the individual—which is marked by little or no apprehension of any of these things as they are Christ-conditioned. The New Testament sees them, not in the context of our Declaration of Independence, or of our textbooks on sociology, or even of the conferences which bring together on the same platform Protestants, Catholics, and Jews; the New Testament sees them in Christ.

Take the very clearest of illustrations. Over the door of many a library, as over the gate of more than one university, are inscribed the words, "Ye shall know the truth, and the truth shall make you free." Is there anyone who reads them without thinking that they mean something about the freedom which we enjoy either as scholars or as citizens, certainly with a few moral overtones thrown in, but nevertheless a freedom which issues at its source from the pursuit and discovery of truth: the truth about man, or history, or science, or literature, or Russia, or the H-bomb. And nothing, of course, could be farther from the mark. Eugene O'Neill once wrote a grim play called *The Iceman*

Cometh, in which he is said to have concerned himself primarily with the Freudian struggle between the elemental forces of life and what was thought of then as the equally elemental death-wish; but in the course of it he destroyed with devastating thoroughness the glib contention that any sort of "truth," about himself or the world he lives in, can strike the shackles from a man's soul. Rob people of the lies they tell themselves, he contended, and you do not make them free; you simply ruin them.[12] And in the flat horizontal of human existence, what he said is true.

In the Bible, on the other hand, truth has to do, not first and foremost with philosophy, or with any pursuit or proposition; it has to do first and foremost with the sum total of the revelation which God has made of himself in Christ. And knowing has to do, not so much with any intellectual grasp of matters as they really are; it has to do far more significantly with entering into that obedient communion which Christ has made it possible for any man to have with God. And freedom has to do, not with the Bill of Rights or with the unfettered exercise of the human will, but with release from the bondage of sin and death. What kind of freedom is it that may drive you into the arena to face lions, or land you behind bars in prison? Suppose it sets you down in the midst of a Christian community where the strong are to bear the burdens of the weak? What kind of freedom is that? What kind is it that stands day and night under the final threat of death? What kind is it, when everything that seems to hamper and negate it most serves most to enhance and enrich it? Besides, if indeed we are to listen to the New Testament at all, there is that other little matter of the *if* and the *then* which precede our entirely too familiar quotation: "If ye continue in my word, then are you my disciples indeed; and ye shall know the truth, and the truth shall make you free." Where can be found a better measure of the extent to which a prevailing cultural situation can distort into falsehood what Scripture has to say? Men have heard the interpretation which their culture has provided, but they have not heard the gospel: and when they like what they have heard, they like it because they can live with it, and live with it comfortably; they can on occasion even use it to bolster the economic, social, or political status quo.

In short, science and industry, politics and trade, the seething leaven of nationalism, the power struggle, racial tension, conflicting ideologies, kaleidoscoped by jet planes and kinescoped for TV, have provided not only a strangely new world for the molding of thought, but strangely new minds for thinking: minds that are learning to accept as normal the threatening nightmare of a society held together by scarcely more than the precarious balance between self-concern and mutual antipathy, living day by day in the kind of security which is provided by nothing but an almost unbelievable potential for the annihilation of all and sundry by next Wednesday week—unless the United Nations can prevent it, or radar, DEW or SAC, or anti-missile-missiles. Perhaps religion would help. Perhaps we ought to return to it. But there are so many. Which one shall it be? David H. C. Read describes the issue: total bewilderment, moral relativism, mental imbalance, nervous exhaustion, and apathy, unparalleled it may be in history.[13]

How shall we speak to such a situation? We are in the middle of it and cannot get out. Little use to try that. There is no overlooking it, though we may be unaware of it precisely because we are a part of it. But worst of all, to say to it what the New Testament has to say is to tell it what Abraham told Dives: "Between us and you there is a great gulf fixed: so that they which would pass from hence to you cannot; neither can they pass to us, that would come from thence" (Luke 16:26). Impossible as it will seem to be, the guide in King's College Chapel, Cambridge, whose business it is to know what he is talking about, in explaining to visitors the two tiers of magnificent windows there along the aisles, one above the other, and each related to each up and down, when he comes to the pair depicting at the top the fall of Adam and at the bottom the agony in Gethsemane, is recently reported to have said that as far as he had been able to make out there was no discernible relation between them; they must have been set that way by some strange mistake. If by any chance he was himself a college man, it is safe to say that his grandfather may very well never have seen the inside of a college; yet his grandfather would without any question have understood why they had been set that way.[14]

It is to this reorientation of the mind that Protestantism seems all too readily to have succumbed. The whole aim of the Reformation was to get human life back on center. Man was not in the middle, where the Renaissance was trying so hard to put him; the Church was not in the middle, as the Roman hierarchy insisted on having it: the Word of God was in the middle, and that Word was Christ. To him all men everywhere might have access, straight and unimpeded, strong in the faith which only God could kindle, in a fellowship which was the body of Christ, where no man was master and no man was slave; all men were citizens on earth of the Kingdom of God. But one by one the generations that refused to be bound by the Pope, and refused to be bound by the Church, decided in an ecstasy of freedom that they would not be bound by anything—not by the Bible, not by conscience, not by God himself. From believing too much that never did have to be believed, they took to believing so little that for countless thousands human existence and the world itself no longer seemed to make any sense. Poets began talking at last about the "wasteland," with "ghostly lives," as Stephen Spender put it, "moving among fragmentary ruins which have lost their significance."[15] "Nothingness" became a subject of conversation, nihilism a motive, frustration and despair a theme for novelist and dramatist, and "the edge of the abyss" as much of a nautical convention among the intelligentsia as it was for explorers in the days of Columbus![16]

But none of this is so disconcerting as the fact that Protestantism apparently has to be assigned the leading role in the drama which brought it about. Not since the sixteenth century has the real power of an expanding civilization flowed through the Roman Church. The nations that have done most to determine the history of the Western world have been Protestant nations. What then if the upshot of it is an order that has grown more and more self-destructive, where the Christian faith and the Christian community have slipped away from the functioning center of human life toward the circumference; where good and evil seem no longer related to eternity, and man is well along the road to moral anarchy; where rugged individualism has run riot to such an extent that all sorts of substitute communities have to be manufactured, from fraternal orders to the kind of remedial social regimentation on a national scale which we must both in some measure undertake and perhaps in even greater measure desperately fear? An order where the Church tends almost insensibly to become a club which you may join or not as you see fit, come or stay at home, tinker with its ritual, abandon its creed; and where in a thousand pulpits the gospel is reduced to a plaintive warning, with a vague promise, held together with a bit of advice? If that indeed is the outcome of an era during which Protestantism has exercised a decisive influence, it may well be that we are standing this day before the bar of God and of human history to render an account of our stewardship.

Nobody would wish to do away, even if he could, with the Renaissance and the Enlightenment—so influential over the years in the shaping of Protestant thought; but it might be interesting to set down how nearly they have come to doing away with us! There are five salient angles along which they have made their assault on the human mind. Given the first, the others followed. The process began with the whittling down of man's faith in God. Gradually that undermined the very notion he had of himself, his sense of right and wrong, his status in community—all he had left was jerry-built, not divinely fashioned—and at last his conception of life's meaning and purpose. For the knowledge of God he was persuaded to get along as best he could with a little knowledge about God, which proceeded at once to move from little to less, and from less to the vanishing point; until today, as the cynic has it, there is no God, though it may be wise to pray to him now and then. For any knowledge at all of himself as a creature, with undreamed of possibilities both above the line of his creatureliness and below it, man was inveigled, in his now no more than two-dimensional world, into a view of himself on Mondays, Wednesdays, and Fridays as "the master of all things," with his hand on the wheel of destiny; on Tuesdays, Thursdays, and Saturdays as "a cosmic accident," "an itch on the epidermis of a pygmy planet," the first cousin of an ape that had learned how to shave! So that on Sunday quite clearly there was little need for him to go to church. He could spend the whole day with the newspaper, or in front of the television, shuttling back and forth between helmsman or "master" and "accident" or "itch," to his heart's content—like a colt lost on the plains, whinnying now at the mud, now at the stars.

It was the schizophrenic form which our culture had given to the New Testament view of man as both sinner and saint. For his knowledge of right and wrong, once rooted in eternity, the question he was now asking had become "Is it expedient?" The same question was raised just prior to the downfall of the Greek city-state. One may follow the line of disintegration on through the centuries. For corporateness and solidarity he took to manufacturing separateness and rivalry. He no longer even thought of himself as one of the predatory pack; he was the lone wolf. Free enterprise was his slogan, the cockpit was where he lived, the skin game was his vocation. Every man was obsessed with himself and with his rights. If he was a white Anglo-Saxon Protestant, a WASP, he no doubt still had an occasional yearning to worship God; but he could massage his soul now where it hurt by going out into the wide open spaces and frying bacon and brushing away the flies, "alone with the Alone." When something happened to him that he could not understand, it took on immediately the character of a religious problem. Why ever should God treat him that way? Indeed most of the hymns he knew had taught him to look for something quite different: something that could properly be called a kingdom, with a kind of personal salvation at the end of it, if not by heaven's main entrance, then by way of some hidden postern gate. "Jesus Savior pilot me": there was the crew of one, with one passenger. "When I tread the verge of Jordan": with no hint whatever of all the others who were surely subject to the same necessity. He became more and more like the old 'cellist who quit moving his fingers because he had found the right note. And the note was not *do,* not *re,* only the *mi, mi, mi* of a broken record. When he had to stroke his desire for "togetherness" and "belonging," he did it by way of conformity to some pattern, in a fellowship integrated about something less than God, where the only issue there could be was something less than man. For his awareness of meaning and destiny, if any, he had to fall back on getting ahead. Having fled from that point where alone an understanding of self and duty, of neighbor and purpose, was possible—the point where the vertical line of a man's relationship to God meets and cuts across the horizontal line of his relationship to his fellows—he had grown afraid of any costly loyalty to the absolute of God's will, afraid of the responsibility to human life with which it confronted him, and so afraid of that high calling toward which every muscle had to be strained if his life was to have any ultimate content at all: "That ye love one another, as I"—those terrible words!—"have loved you" (John 15:12). What was there at last for his emptiness but the death-wish, his atom bomb and world war?

These are the areas par excellence with which the modern pulpit is under the most insistent obligation to concern itself. It cannot be without

significance that both of the "genuine mental diseases" of our *Zeitgeist,*
Nazism and Communism, have each in its own fashion held out some
spurious substitute at every stage along the way of that Pilgrim's Progress in reverse. One is startled to think of how thoroughly in our world
every Christian doctrine has been assigned its secular counterpart. For
God as the transcendent loyalty Hitler gave his followers the *Volk;* Communism says the State. For the realization of selfhood, in Germany "I am
an Aryan"—as if we should boast "I am a white man"; in Russia the
proletariat, the worker, the revolutionary, the common man. For conscience, with Hitler whatever was to the advantage of the Third Reich;
in Russia whatever is to the advantage of the Soviet Republic. For
community the Party—"Heil Hitler!"—"Long live Brezhnev!" For
love, the conquest of the world. Both Nazism and Communism have
to be regarded as "religious" readings of life; and so both are demonic
religions, neither is an accident, together they are the upshot of humanity's bankruptcy. To try writing off either of them by the simple
expedient of building more air bases and manufacturing more effective
nuclear weapons is sheer nonsense. We need something other than the
time we can buy with larger military budgets.

3. THE THEOLOGICAL ASPECT

And here we come within sight of the deepest, farthest source of our
embarrassment. It is not simply that we have been provided with different minds. If communication is, as it has been called, "the funda-
mental human fact," then the kind of widespread breakdown with which
we have to do, writes Hendrik Kraemer, is more than a temporary de-
viation, a passing psychological phenomenon, a sociological footnote to
some political or economic crisis; we have on our hands an anthro-
pological problem, which is a theological problem in disguise. In his
book *The Communication of the Christian Faith* he properly begins
with the "Biblical Perspective."[17] There in Genesis God speaks, and
creates man for that communion with him which never can be fashioned
by communication, but is the only matrix in which communication becomes possible, the foundation of all true relationships, "the fulfillment
of human existence." "The fact that our humanhood is not normal . . .
is the evil source of a corruption which becomes manifest in all rela-

tionships. . . . Defectiveness in communication is a sign as well as a consequence of the distortion of the divinely willed order of existence . . . filling human life with anxiety, fear, and frustration. . . . Man, fallen out of his partnership relation with God, flees from God, and immediately all relationships are affected and in disorder." Hostility enters, communication becomes combat, not intimacy, ears are deafened, dialogue becomes monologue, and ineffable loneliness follows, alienation from God and man. The record of God's initiative in the restoration and re-creation of that primal relationship is the history of salvation. In Jesus Christ, and in him alone, is the manifestation of "the unbroken relationship of man with God, and of men with each other."

And these are precisely the aspects of the Christian gospel which seem least congenial to the mind of the twentieth century. We speak of the good news, and to multitudes it is neither news nor particularly good. It is the old, old story of what happened two thousand years ago. We mention faith, and are understood to mean by it the believing of something for which there is little or no evidence. If we answer that in the New Testament faith is not so much an activity of thought or will as a being-in-right-relationship with God and man, once broken, now restored, the answer is unintelligible. How can you get the cart before the horse that way? What people want to know is whether or not there is a God to begin with. And to that the Bible never does address itself! We mention hope, and everybody assumes we are talking about something we should like very much to have happen, and maybe it will, though the chances are against it. Roget's *Thesaurus* lists the synonyms: castles in Spain, illusion, will-o'-the-wisp, counting your chickens before they are hatched—a very valley of dry bones, the burying ground of everything that might have been and never was. The Biblical word for hope is as far away from all that as anybody can well get. Listen to it in Israel's dark history, singing its way along on the lips of prophet and psalmist. Watch it blossom like a flower all over the landscape of Paul's letters. It has nothing on earth to do with wishful thinking, or with the projection of some normal human desire on the future. We mention love, and the man in the pew smuggles into it his own ideas and is exceedingly glad that he knows at last what the sermon is about. He even has some vague idea now of what God is, for God is love— with an *o* three syllables long that drips with sweetness. But in the

New Testament the symbol of love is a gaunt cross on a little hill out-side the walls of Jerusalem. It would take a lifetime to pace off the distance from one to the other! We insist that God acts, and he says "How do you know?" We want him to understand that God speaks, and he would like to have the name and address of anybody who has heard anything at all. We try to tell him that Christ has won the final victory over sin and death; and he begins looking around for the evidence. Nothing could be more unreal, more imaginary. It is legend, fiction, myth—call it what you will.

The trouble is not only that we are addressing the child and heir of the last four centuries. That makes the task difficult enough. The trouble is that we are addressing "fallen" man. And he lives in a strange world of his own. For him God no longer occupies the center of the picture; he does: which is what the Fall means. He regards himself as the victim of forces beyond his control; but he has to do the best he can on the assumption that he can master them singlehanded and shape his own destiny: which is what the Fall means. So he thinks of himself as standing over against nature to conquer and exploit it; and for the most part over against his fellow man as well: which is what the Fall means. He has to handle things, and deal with facts, and come out as near the top as may be. He has his own ideals and standards, moral, intellectual, aesthetic, cultural, and you will please allow him to operate under his own articles of self-government. This is where he lives, this is his frame of reference, this is what the Fall means. His is not alone the mind of the twentieth century; his is the mind of Adam. If you can give him something he can use right now, where he is, to his own advantage, well and good; but please, no more of this double talk about the foolishness of God which is wiser than men, and the weakness of God which is stronger than men—things which are not, and yet bring to nought things that are—an eternal Word revealed in a historical event—a faith which is within history, yet transcends history. What has any of that to do with him? He has been driven out of the Eden for which he was made, to cast about for it now, in his lonely search, every day he lives, without ever finding it.[18] Its imagery is quite alien to him, its language is scarcely any more to be called language! If *agape* does not mean "having one's mouth open," then you have to set it down as gibberish.

4. Preliminary Approaches

If we had to leave the whole business right there, we could try to content ourselves with sitting still, just where we are, and waiting for the "apocalyptic smashup." But we have other options. There is much to be said, and there is perhaps even more to be done. Suppose we get that clear before we go any farther, and call it our first preliminary approach to the problem. Communication by word of mouth is not the only means the gospel has of finding its way into this common life of ours. The Word is in search of more than words: it is forever in search of lives. It gets itself said not only in preaching. It gets itself said in the realization by God's grace and gift of that fellowship which is the Church of Jesus Christ, with its uniqueness of belonging and participation. Such a fellowship cannot be fashioned. It is already bestowed, and has only to be translated into the brick and mortar of daily human relationships. Here is the context out of which the Christian gospel came, and must continue to come. Jean Paul Sartre in *No Exit* wants us to believe that "Hell is other people."[19] Not for anybody who has found his place among the "people of God." For him there is no other heaven. The Word that comes to him in that fellowship comes to him there as in no other place. It comes to him in the mutuality of forgiving and serving love, battering down the walls of his loneliness, shattering the terror of his isolation. And it comes to create what it says.

Obviously the difficulties it encounters are not just difficulties of language. If they were, we could iron them out by the mere, if indispensable and certainly none too simple, process of restatement and retranslation. But we can't. There are those who seem to think that getting rid of the archaic forms of the King James Version—addressing David and Jesus, the centurion of Capernaum, the woman of Samaria, and God himself, quite indiscriminately, as "you" instead of "thou"; saying "precede" and not "prevent"; having God threaten to "spit" the lukewarm church at Laodicea out of his mouth—that such a manipulation of words will accomplish wonders. The barrier at Laodicea was not a language barrier. Why should it prove of itself such a never-ending source of embarrassment in our case? I am reminded of the page in *The New Yorker* where everybody is reading *The Philadelphia Bulletin* except one poor soul, hopping about in ecstasy as he points with alarm to something which he is sure calls for more attention than it happens to be getting. "Spue" need not have occasioned so much excitement!

Besides, it does not mean to "spit." Paraphrases often serve better than translations to convey not so much the meaning of a word as the situation out of which the word derived its meaning. When a thing is neither cold nor hot (Rev. 3:15-16), God does not spit. We do not require in that connection a symbol of contempt. He vomits! It "makes him sick"! The arbitrary manipulation of words can distort whole patterns of thought. The plays of Shakespeare would prove rather startlingly unimpressive if done in modern speech. In a revised standard version of *Othello*, something more significant than the poetry would tend to dissolve. Is it of no significance at all that both Shakespeare and the King James version of the Bible were nearer than we are by more than three hundred and fifty years to the thought-forms of our Hebrew inheritance? During those years our very language has been increasingly hammered out on the anvil of scientific and technological objectivity, becoming more and more functional, denotative not connotative, and so, I suggest, less and less capable of expressing the "mythical structure" indigenous to the New Testament—a structure, as we are coming now to understand, that can never be presented "discursively"; it "can only be shown."[20]

The second preliminary approach we can make to the problem of communicating the gospel in our day is by way of the simple realization, as I have already indicated, that the Word which seeks to crowd itself into the words we speak and the lives we live, pushing its way through, has indeed a power of its own. The gospel is not so utterly dependent on us, in respect of either language or freshness and originality of insight, as we are sometimes inclined to believe. Altogether too often the preacher assumes that he has to hit on something quite novel or sensational. He has to discuss current events. He has to use the idioms of exceedingly common speech. He has to entice people to listen by telling stories, particularly at the beginning of the sermon. If his stories were like the parables of Jesus, sweeping up from fields and ovens and village squares right into the Kingdom of God, nobody could object; but for the most part they are no more than bait for the unwary, and the sleek old veterans in the pool either refuse to rise to it, or dislodge it and take it away with them, leaving the hook utterly alone. But no matter: follow the mode. Try not to mention the Bible too soon. Avoid beginning with a text—so we are told. Sneak up on the congregation, and slip in an apostle when nobody is looking. Use the inductive method. Maneuver everybody into a corner—and who among them will not resent being cornered?—where there is nothing else for them to do but to turn to the fourteenth chapter of John or to the tenth of Isaiah.

Meanwhile, and all the while, the Word of God is a living Word; and it has its own ways of addressing the human soul. Understand it and represent it at once in its relevance and urgency, stripped of all theological jargon and piously meaningless clichés. There is no need to shift about at the start from one foot to the other, hoping to arrive at some point of contact, when all you have to do is to tell a man that his house is on fire! It may well be a genuine disservice to preface the news with a long introduction, simply because you have fallen into the habit of taking it for granted that the only highway which can possibly be made ready must lie through a wilderness of incident and anecdote.

What we shall actually find it possible to do will best be done when we realize what it is that the Word of God does, and begin quite consciously, by way of a third preliminary approach, to lend ourselves to the same strategy. The Word of God lays hold on the stuff of human existence and reshapes it. It first appropriates: there is scarcely a key word anywhere in the letters of St. Paul that had not already been current coin in the pagan world. But it does more than appropriate: it transforms. It takes the things that are, and with them brings to birth the things that are not. It adopts some known pattern, and by standing over against it fashions the new.[21] It comes upon an old barrel top, as Raphael is said to have done, and leaves it a Madonna of the Chair.[22] It borrows a folk song and writes a symphony. It takes the conflicts which tear human life apart, and speaks to them of wholeness, which is the strange peace of God. It takes the realities of guilt and death, of anxiety and despair, and speaks to them of bondage and of salvation— "Thou hast set my feet in a large room"; of captivity, and the deliverance which is the Kingdom of God. It takes a man's estrangement from himself, from his fellows, and from God, and speaks to it of isolation and separateness: only then does it speak of "sin," holding out in both hands the word of forgiveness, which is the word of acceptance, and the word of justification by grace, which is the word of belonging and of that restored relationship which is faith.

Professor Cyril Richardson, of Union Seminary in New York, writes of the "many themes of catacomb painting which illustrate the spirit" of the early Church. Most characteristic of "the youthfulness which this art expresses," is "the figure of Christ, who is always depicted as a beardless young man, generally in the guise of the Good Shepherd. When one has walked through miles of catacomb corridors and met this figure again and again in the frescoes, it leaves an indelible mark on the mind." It keeps insisting on

the fact that the salvation of the world was accomplished in a young man scarcely thirty years old—something which the dominant symbol of Christ in Christian art obscures, and something which, as one grows older, one finds a source of uneasy amazement. . . . The origins of the . . . figure are undoubtedly to be found in the idealized portraits of Alexander the Great and of such gods as Apollo and Orpheus—types taken from Greek art with its concern to express the divine in terms of the beauty of youth. We should, however, be deceived were we to let the matter rest there, and to claim (as has sometimes misleadingly been done) that we have here nothing but a Christ in the guise of Dionysus or Antinous. The symbol to be sure comes from the art of the Early Empire: but its meaning is entirely different. Where the Greek ideal is concerned with physical beauty and even with sensuousness in the features of its gods, the early Christian is quite otherwise. Not only is the painting crude, unstudied and impressionistic, so that the concern for beauty in itself is lacking, but the ideal of youth in the figure of Christ is a symbol of the creative newness of the Christian gospel. This is the impelling thing about early Christianity, the sense that the world has been made new in the Person of Christ, that antiquity has at last been overcome by the freshness of young life. When we consider how the classical world regarded what is old as ideal, and viewed the return to antiquity as the path to renewal, we can the better appreciate the revolutionary nature of the gospel: that in a moment of time late in the history of the world, God's decisive action for man's salvation had occurred. . . . Here was "the proclamation of The New Event, The New Creation, which was to stand in contrast to a world grown weary with antiquity."[23]

So did the New Testament, bringing with it all the richness of its inheritance from the Old, use the language and the thought-forms of its day, shaping them to its purpose even as it confronted and contradicted them: commandeering what it found, making the Greek serve the Hebrew purpose; hammering, bending, and under God creating. What emerges is not a mixture of Hebraisms and Hellenisms, with a bit of Stoicism and a dash of Gnosticism thrown in, all melted down into an alloy of the mystery cults. What emerges is distinctively Christian. Interpretation of the Gospels and Epistles errs when it runs off in some preconceived direction. The impact of the whole, God's saving deed "when the fulness of the time was come," establishes a direction of its own. It probes far and deep toward the bedrock of human life; then casts its line across the gulf, as the engineers did when they built the great bridge from Washington Heights to the heights of Jersey. There is no "by your leave" or "if you please" about it. It lays hold on everything and appropriates what it will. It leaves nothing unchanged. It fashions and transforms. And the name of its ceaseless activity is revelation.

II

The Nature of Revelation

The word that runneth swiftly. . . . PSALM 147:15

It should be comparatively safe to say that through most of the eighteenth and nineteenth centuries man's knowledge of God was by overpowering odds regarded as intellectual knowledge. It was to be arrived at as the last stage of a long process. Protestant Christianity, on the whole, seemed to be busy building its own Tower of Babel, setting up its own Jacob's ladder. A host of philosophers and preachers were going up, not many coming down: only a few here and there gave evidence of having listened and heard something. Whereupon, one would suppose largely under the pressure of historical events, a change came about in the theological climate. Between the two world wars there were already those who had grown suspicious of the Christianity commonly being preached and currently being accepted, if somewhat casually. Its major concerns were the Jesus of the Synoptics, the Sermon on the Mount, and the Kingdom of God, with technicolor by Ritschl. Confidence in the Bible as the inspired Word of God had been rudely shaken. Nor could one be so sure that the Christian faith was as eminently reasonable as it was reputed to be. Would it indeed—did it in fact—commend itself to every serious and thoughtful person? "Biblicism" was gradually seen to be impossible, and Modernism was discovered to lack something: after that, the conflict between the two became increasingly sterile; until it would seem at last to have turned into the whipping of a dead horse, the only justification for which was that some people apparently still needed the exercise.

The clue to such confusion, whenever you come upon it, is to be found in the answer given to the question about revelation. For the pulpit, I am brash enough to believe that here, without any under-rating of difficulties or underwriting of techniques, lies the crux of the whole matter. It is possible that we have begun now to move toward a better understanding than we have ever had before of what we mean when we speak of the self-revealing God, of the Word in which he both confronts and addresses us, and of the unique function at that point which the Bible serves. Partly because of the spiritual, social, and political upheaval which was taking place during the first four decades of the present century, there was a highly significant shifting of interest. It was not so much any more the philosopher's problem that seemed of primary concern—"Where is thy God?" Instead, all the way from novelists and poets and dramatists to the editorials in *Life* magazine, it was rather the problem which God put to Adam in the Garden of Eden that assumed priority: "Where art thou?" There was a turning away from a primarily speculative, philosophical theology in the direction of a theology more specifically Biblical which began to take with utmost seriousness not so much the discovered God as the revealed God, not so much man's account of the God he had found as his account of the God who had found him.

1. WORD AND EVENT

When today we say that God has revealed himself, what is it that we are trying to put into words?[1] Perhaps the briefest, most straight-forward suggestion I can make is that we are attempting in that way to represent his relentless moving in upon our lives, individual and corpo-rate, whatever form it takes. You cannot spell it out simply. It cannot be reduced to some weird and deathless intuition of a Presence that inhabits Eternity. That is to set man at the center again. Our being conscious of God is not what matters, or our being unconscious of him either. The Bible spends precious little time on the way we feel about anything. It never equates the divine self-manifestion with those ideals and aspirations which haunt the human heart and make it restless until it finds its rest in God. That, too, sets man at the center. To open the Bible is not to discover either being or the ground of being: it is to run the risk of becoming involved with someone in the long-continuing and God-shaped epic of life and death. The God of the Bible acts, and the story of his dealing with us, which is the drama of his redemption, becomes his Word. Because the prophets saw and understood what he was doing, they heard and proclaimed what he was saying. There was a word that Isaiah "saw concerning Judah and Jerusalem." In the speaking was the acting. Said Habakkuk, "I will watch to see what he will say unto me." In the acting was the speaking.

From the Garden of Eden to the garden of Gethsemane, from the place where Adam hid to the place where Jesus prayed, all the way along that drama goes forward and the Voice comes: as it comes now in this place, where we too are trying either to hide or to pray—for our lives are always there, somewhere between Eden and Gethsemane, between hiding and praying. There are many who like Thomas Hardy hear only what seems to them like the dim-witted utterance of a god who is half asleep and has forgotten his creation. To others, as to Francis Thompson, who lived when Hardy lived, and was considerably worse off, it all seems quite different.

> Still with unhurrying chase,
> And unperturbed pace,
> Deliberate speed, majestic instancy,
> Came on the following Feet,
> And a Voice above their beat—
> "Naught shelters thee, who wilt not shelter Me."[2]

But mind you, that Voice is forever associated with the act by which God confronts us, in Bible or in church, in worship or history or person. He is not intent on sharing conceptual truth. That must come later. It is not some saving measure of information he wants to impart; it is himself he wants to bestow: that not having seen him we may yet meet him and know him and trust him and live our lives in him, freely and for love's sake. In just such fashion to Israel, through evil fortune and good, in tragedy and triumph, by prophet and priest, psalmist and scribe, captivity and deliverance, he revealed his holy will; but never in any way to stultify theirs. Their will, like our will, was the risk he had to take. He laid on them his claim, but compelled them to no obedience. Through his very judgments he brought them his loving-kindness.[3] By his tender mercy he established among them his justice. Always and only that in their listening he might utter his name, and in their seeking find them. Yet not so as to be laid hold on and possessed—as if you should be able to meet him in space, or establish by the evidence of your own senses his sovereignty in time. He was not to be had in a Book or housed in a Creed. He would not conform to the "measure of man's mind."[4] It was between Israel's knowing and her not-knowing that he spoke, when she least expected to hear. Between her having and her not-having he was silent, when she most expected him to speak. "Verily," cried the prophet, "thou art a God that hidest thyself" (Isa. 45:15). But in the very hiddenness was the revelation. It was in the revelation that he was hidden.

Clearly then at the core of Biblical theology there is what G. Ernest Wright of Harvard once called the theology of recital.[5] Because our thinking has been shaped into the molds of an empirical, technological, and "post-Christian world," we are prone to begin in matters religious, if not with the facts of human life and human experience, then with what we can gather from the world of nature about the God who surely must have fashioned it. A sunset, a rainbow, some flower in the crannied wall, a butterfly—do they tell us nothing about him? But add a shark to a tiger, throw in an octopus, a hurricane, cholera, and cancer—what now does that look like? "Tongues in trees," Shakespeare would have us know;[6] but what do they say when the tree falls on you? "Books in running brooks"—but how does the book read when you stumble flat on your face in the running brook and drown? "Sermons in stones"—except for the one that struck Goliath squarely between the eyes! From start to finish the Biblical writers are concerned first and foremost with the mighty and saving acts of God. The historian records them, the prophets proclaim them, and the psalmists celebrate them. When Isaiah and Jeremiah tell of what God has done and will do they are more than interpreters of some event; they are the heralds of a Word which itself fashions the event. To speak of the God who acts, which was what they understood preaching to be, was for them one of those acts. As a result, what they have left us is not just God-centered.

Anybody can sit where he is and think, with God at the center of his thought. What they have left us is rather the thought that moved in upon them from God and took precedence of their own. They were sure of it. (Cf. p. 236.)

You see at once how remote that is from the way in which we operate. Said Descartes, *Cogito, ergo sum*, "I think, therefore I am." For prophet and evangelist, there was another Thinker in the universe whose thinking mattered more. Descartes thought of him as the conclusion to an argument; the Bible thought of him as a prior fact: it was he indeed who had thought Descartes, and there was Descartes! It would amuse you, if it were a somewhat less sobering business, to transpose bits of American history into the pattern of the Biblical record: And it came to pass in those days that the Lord God spake unto George Washington and said, "Get thee up out of thy tent, and from among thy fellows, and gird thy loins, and get thee over the river which is called Delaware, and smite thine enemy hip and thigh, at the place called *T'ir-hassār*, which being interpreted is Princeton. What troubles me is the feeling I have that it should have been written that way! At any rate this is precisely what characterizes the Hebrew-Christian tradition, and differentiates it from all others.[7] In the Bible we do not begin with nature. The psalmist does not consider the heavens; he considers "thy heavens": he has already been somewhere before he starts (Ps. 8:3). Neither do the Biblical writers take off from history. The Egyptians wrote history, and saw in it more than any mere human agency; so did the Greeks. The difference is that the Bible begins, continues, and ends with the God of history, as he ceaselessly works out his gracious plan of salvation.[8]

2. THE MEANING IN EVENT

There can be nothing static, therefore, about revelation. You cannot cut it all in stone, or print it all on paper, and expect it to stay there. God kept on talking, as someone has put it, after his book went to press. His word may be something spoken or something done. He says by doing, and he does by saying. Events become words; which in a manner of speaking is to hold that facts have meaning. Certainly meaning without fact is insanity: as when the patient in the hospital wants you to believe that he is Napoleon, because God has told him so, and the man in the bed next to his replies at once, "I did no such thing!" And so, by the same token, is fact without meaning only another kind of insanity. For the "beat generation" it used to go by the name of life in the twentieth century: and they were not altogether mistaken.[9] Revelation is the fusion under God of fact with ultimate meaning, event with Word.

Could it be that no true reading of history is possible on any other premise? That if events have significance at all they have to be seen as the underside of that huge tapestry which on God's side is his dealing with human life to redeem it? The two sides do not stand to each other in any simple relation of cause to effect: no metaphor has to be pressed against the wall until all the life is squeezed out of it! The will of man and the will of God, in conflict and correspondence, weave the pattern of the centuries. Perhaps it is because we here in the West see so little meaning in our history as a people that we flounder around so awkwardly in the face of Communism.[10] We have a Bible because Israel was brought by her prophets to see the "true" meaning of her history. At their hands she knew herself to be a people covenanted to the Lord: standing as the object and the instrument both of his judgment and of his redemption. What less than that twofold knowledge of our life can keep our own American dynamism from becoming demonism?

But is there any guarantee at all that such a reading of history is justified? When God acts, as indeed he does continuously, by what alchemy does his act become for us a Word? The children of Israel are said to have made their way out of Egypt. How ever is that to be read as the righteousness of God, which is his deliverance? There is an old legend to the effect that a tribe of Indians, driven by their enemies to the brink of a deep canyon, found a way of escape which was so unexpected as to seem miraculous: it lay across what is now known as the Natural Bridge in Virginia. Were they so utterly wrong to think that their gods were somehow involved?[11] Facts are bound to "take on" meaning: is superstition the only word we have to describe the faith of those for whom facts "take on" divine meaning? A man was put to death on a cross. How ever shall it be for us a deed of lovingkindness, the answer of One who from heaven which is his dwelling place had heard the cries of his people? Nowhere does the quarrel rage so much nowadays, not as it once did, about the events themselves. The historical and literary critics, for example, cannot reconstruct in detail the life of Jesus,[12] or determine exactly what were his very words—no need to hide the fact away in sheer terror of it!—yet they have nonetheless provided us with a firmer footing in history than our fathers had. They have shown us that into our hands has come, and we recognize it at last for what it is, the sober testimony of those for whom Jesus was not only a remembered reality but a living Presence;[13] and the sheer texture and quality of the remembrance, often in the very convincingness of nuance and context, bear witness to the fact of the Presence in which the remembrance had its source. The quarrel is not so much with events. The quarrel is with interpretation.

And at that point one thing urgently needs to be said, and just as urgently needs to be taught: we have to be content in the matter of our Christian faith with something other than the kind of certainty which so many seem to covet—lest our faith turn into knowledge considerably ahead of schedule.[14] The Christian is pretty much suspended in mid-air. He cannot get his feet on the solid ground of what anybody will allow to be verifiable fact. We are told, as you know, by one school of philosophers that the word "God" actually has no meaning. Conceivably, they insist, everything would be precisely as it is if there were no God. What we say of him is subject to neither proof nor refutation. Therefore our language about him can have no content.[15] But does it not have as much content as our language about any person can have? What is decisive is not simply the facts about a friend or an enemy: what is decisive is the faith or the lack of it that interprets the facts. The facts are of course relevant, but not because they are determinative. We should insist that the only meaning which can ever be associated with the word "God" derives not from demonstrable propositions or from the weighing of evidence, but ultimately from personal relationship and witness.[16] Doubt will have its place. Jesus was never panic-stricken by doubt. The story in the Fourth Gospel (John 20:24-29) seems to do little more than to extend that unearthly poise of his mind with which the Synoptics were so familiar: "Thomas, Reach hither thy finger. . . ."

There are, then, events recorded in Scripture which to some extent can be verified by our methods—but not any of the interpretations. I remember hearing Dr. John Baillie contend, in one of his Bampton Lectures, that if there were about any interpretation the coercive authority of fact; if there were no ambiguities involved in our reading of history; if there were no quality of anonymity about God and his gifts—if he signed his sunsets, as Turner did; if there were no hidden-ness, no possibility of rejection, no possibility even of heretical opinion with regard to that revelation of himself which God has made in Jesus of Nazareth: then we could no longer talk of freedom, we could no longer talk of persons. Revelation is event plus interpretation, where the event and the interpretation are mutually interactive. When the interpretation is under constraint, above all when it is compulsive, there can be no revelation; there is then only some form of totalitarian dictatorship.

It follows that the act of apprehending is of absolute importance. We are to say that with our lips, and quit plucking at it with our fears. Apprehending is by faith. "Who on earth," asks Dr. Baillie, "could this carpenter of Nazareth have been, that his undistinguished birth could have achieved cosmic significance for these men who coupled his name with God's and were sure that it was no blasphemy? That a felon's death between two thieves should for them have marked the final defeat of both sin and death? That the life of a humble Galilean should come to be known as God's life among men?"[17]

Here are the facts, insists the New Testament. Every man's inter-pretation of them is at cost. What the apostles and evangelists meant by what they said is often conveyed to us by way of pictures, metaphors, stories:[18] but all truth, even twentieth-century truth, has to be conveyed that way when it is ultimate truth; when it is the truth which lies beyond mere sequence and causality, within history and beyond it; the truth which is deeper than fact, which unlike the truths of natural science cannot be said so much as shown, and has therefore to speak in para-bles.[19] The Bible is faith's witness by fallible men to the infallible truth which is sovereign over history and gives history its meaning: and it is a witness borne in order to reconstitute in every separate and believing life, by means of that very deed itself which the Bible is, the saving fact of God's redemption.

The other thing that cryingly needs to be said, of course, is that in

the interpretation no man is left to his own devices: he has the un-
ceasing testimony of the Holy Spirit, not simply in the individual life,
and not alone in Scripture, but in that ongoing community which is
the Christian Church. This is not to say that we can find our way
across the threshold of the house of faith from the portico of some
doctrine of inspiration, verbal, plenary, or dynamic. I am not to
believe in God simply because the prophets and apostles have spoken
of him—that would be to believe primarily in the prophets and apostles;
or simply because the Church bears witness to him—that would be
to believe primarily in the Church; or simply because I am told that
their witness and hers is inspired—that would be to believe primarily
in inspiration. I am to believe in God because God himself speaks
of himself; and through his witnesses and by his Spirit, in the family of
his people, will work in my life the same faith that was wrought in
prophet and apostle. To that end not an infallible record but an infallible
God is required: not to compel, but to confront and persuade; to face
me not with the necessity of accepting but with the necessity of choosing
—which is all that even God can do, unless he means to dissolve both
love and faith in the process.

Is it not obvious then that this faith by which we apprehend, in the
Church, through the Spirit, is something more than knowledge coupled
with assent, as in the Middle Ages it was understood to be? "The devils
also," says James, "believe, and tremble" (2:19). Knowledge they have,
and to assent they are compelled. Shall we go beyond that and say
that faith is reliance? If we do, we shall be coming closer to its meaning;
because we shall be coming a shade nearer the world of persons, where
we belong. But in that world, since it is God's very self that he not
only reveals but imparts, faith becomes more than knowledge, more
than assent, more than reliance, more than obedience—though all of
these are alike involved. There between persons, as between a man and
his wife, not one of the words we have used thus far could define it.
Rather is it the sum total of a creative relationship between God and
the human soul: a relationship lost in the Fall but now restored in
Christ, and under the bare constraint of his love to be lived out only
in love for others.[20] Alexander Maclaren once said that if Christianity
had ever taken this truth seriously, it "would have been delivered from
mountains of misconception, and many a poor soul would have felt that

a blaze of light had come in upon it. . . . The object of trust is a living person, Jesus Christ, and . . . the trust which grapples us to him is essentially a personal relation entered into by our wills and hearts far more than by our heads."[21]

To lose sight of that is to assume either that God has not provided us with the gift of faith or that we ourselves have failed in the exercise of some faculty of our own which could have provided it. There is nothing about Christian faith that resembles an Operation Bootstrap. Our being once more in right relationship with God, and so with our fellow men, is his doing, not ours. It is in this sense that faith is a gift, and in no other. It is not the believing which God gives—how on earth could he? There are too many who will tell you that they simply were not there when it was handed out. One does not enter upon faith by being brought to divine "a profounder meaning in certain encountered events."[22] To be saved "by grace . . . through faith" (Eph. 2:8) is in Christ to have the alienation which sin introduced into God's creation overcome, so that "the glory of God," as Paul calls it, which is his image in us, may by his handiwork be fashioned anew.[23] And in that is more than the offer of himself: in that is God's downright bestowal of himself made possible. Revelation is more than disclosing, more than communicating: revelation has to do with the imparting of oneself.

3. COMMON QUESTIONS GROWN IRRELEVANT

If this is what happens, a goodly number of our questions about revelation become strangely irrelevant. Says a friend of mine, for instance, who I am afraid does a bit of posing as an agnostic, "All right; if you want to find the meaning of your life in the story of a particular and unique and none too savory segment of humanity, namely the history of Israel, go ahead. You have that privilege, but you will please excuse me. What have I to learn from a horde of nondescript, wandering, dirty, and for the most part illiterate Orientals who were nothing but slaves in Egypt, then swarmed across the desert into Palestine? I much prefer the Greeks. You waste your time. I am not inclined to waste mine!" How relevant is that? What is said to be the shortest bit of rhymed verse in the English language puts it quite bluntly:

How odd
Of God
To choose
The Jews![24]

Odder still is the acute awareness of that problem in the Old Testament itself. "Thou art a stiffnecked people" (Exod. 33:3; Deut. 9:6). Isaiah called them "a seed of evildoers" "a rebellious people, lying children" (1:4; 30:9). Moses had once tried to figure it out and had had to give up. "The Lord did not set his love upon you, nor choose you, because ye were more in number than any people; for ye were the fewest of all people: but because the Lord loved you. . . ." (Deut. 7:7-8). The only reason was a "just because" kind of love: the kind of love which will not spend its time reckoning up accounts, debit and credit; the kind that turns questions around, so that we have to answer them ourselves, or do the best we can at it. If choosing the Jews was odd, so was choosing Abraham. He was a liar, and Jacob was a thief, and Moses was a murderer, and David was an adulterer. And you? How odd is God's choice of you? So does he keep his immemorial silence. It may be only within the circle of his uncalculating love that we can arrive at any of the answers about his revelation or about ourselves.

Or take the familiar problem, "Why did this have to happen to me?" Another friend asked it of me in the agony of his grief. And I had not the vaguest idea. By no farthest reach of the imagination, if you stretched it until it broke in two, could you have called the wretched thing fair. There are answers we have to live out, not spell out. No theodicy is possible. One cannot justify the ways of God to men. Milton wrote *Paradise Lost* to make the Almighty's conduct of affairs seem a little more reasonable; and that was more than two thousand years after the Book of Job had launched its great polemic against all such enterprises. Thornton Wilder came much nearer the mark in *The Bridge of San Luis Rey*. There Brother Juniper, the young Franciscan, after he had spent six years trying to show that every person who perished in the apparently fortuitous and senseless collapse of that bridge had perished at what for each of them was exactly the right time, was himself burned as a heretic![25] There are thoughts which are not our thoughts and ways that are not our ways. When that ceases to be the case, God will have ceased to be God. If we understood him we should do well to doubt him! His inscrutable providences, embracing both the good that he wills and the evil which runs contrary to it but cannot defeat it, will not lay themselves open to our inquiry.[26]

The nearest we can come to any of the answers is the knowledge we may have in Christ of God's unfailingly gracious purpose, and his readiness and power to clothe his purpose with our own flesh and blood. The one profoundly religious and truly relevant question is the question Saul asked on the road to Damascus: "Lord, what wilt thou have me to do?" (Acts 9:6) To hear the voice of God is to hear him seeking for someone: "Whom shall I send, and who will go for us?" And a sword leaped from its scabbard: "Here am I; send me" (Isa. 6:8). The why may remain a mystery: the what is never past finding out. Life can divine the purpose and do without the reasons. What matters first is the response; and nothing else matters last, because nothing else is decisive.[27] Israel's tragedy lay in her failure to realize that. She knew herself as the chosen people of God; but she thought it was for her sake, and God cast her off: it was for the world's sake. If we will stop asking about causes and start thinking about results, there is a hand that can shape them, in victory and in defeat, in triumph and in tragedy.

4. The History That Becomes History: Preaching from the Old Testament

With such an understanding of what is meant by faith, we are in a better position to try out some definition of what the Bible is. It is more than a record. It is that witness to God's saving deed which in the witnessing becomes his deed. By it and through it the incarnate, crucified, and risen Word finds his way into your life and mine. It is the history that becomes our history. It is the proclamation which brings about what it proclaims. It not only offers liberty, it sets men free. It does more than promise sight; it "opens blind eyes."[28] It speaks as Life speaks, and Death. It binds you, and yet leaves you free in that freedom which men find so dreadful that they can scarcely tolerate it, are forever attempting to flee from it to the shelter of some external, ecclesiastically validated, or self-validating authority. Its authority is not subject to evaluation. It is not the authority of a code or a system. It is not the authority of a

tradition or a rule. Its authority is the authority of One who stands at
the door and knocks. You open the door at your peril. To treat the
Bible as the source from which we are expected to distill some doctrine,
some permanent law—some shining ideal which everybody can romanticize without having it make one penny's worth of difference, some
guiding principle—is tacitly to assume that the Almighty has gone off
and left his world to be governed by doctrines, laws, ideals, and guiding
principles. From beginning to end, from Genesis to Revelation, echoes a
Word which refuses to be dismissed as what God said once, and insists
on being heard as what he is saying now, and to you. The Bible is
the history that becomes history.[29] "The Lord made not this covenant
with our fathers, but with us, even us, who are all of us here alive this
day" (Deut. 5:3).

But there we run headlong into one of our most serious difficulties.
How in the name of common sense can that great body of literature
which has to do with Israel's history before the dawn of the Christian
era be understood still as a living Word? If we are able and willing at
all to think of the Old Testament as revelation, must we not use the
term only in the vaguest sense? Granted perhaps that here indeed may
be an account of what God said once and did once, must we not nevertheless insist that it all took place among a people who except for that
one fact have little spiritual kinship with us?[30] And in times so far
removed from our own that we would seem to be justified in setting their
history aside, over in the files where it belongs, and taking for granted
that what really matters for us is to be found, if it is to be found
anywhere, in the last two hundred and fifty pages of the thousand
pages of the Bible? Which would of course, if it were true, involve a
tragic loss of time on God's part, and on ours a sad waste of printer's
ink!

But what if it were not all back there while we are all up here!
Surely our chances of hearing any Word at all, whether in the New
Testament or in the Old, are not a bit improved if we are habitually
intent on hurrying back somewhere to listen. The sense of immediacy
has to be seen as indispensable to any adequate understanding of what
revelation means, or of what proclamation involves. Always the past
has to move across the frontier and become present. And this is precisely
what takes place in Scripture! One finds there a constant *re-presentation*
and reinterpretation of historical events: the renewal of the covenant,

the Passover, the giving of the Law, the journey "round about by way of the wilderness." The very record itself seems to struggle with the context of the changing years, and so becomes vastly more than a record.[31] Moreover, seen from our vantage point as Christians—and how else can we see it—history, poetry, prophecy are all quite startlingly open-ended, reaching out on almost every page for what is yet to come: so that standing where Amos stood, or Hosea, Isaiah, or Jeremiah, is no longer possible for us. We cannot take up our address any more within the community of those who were still looking forward to the coming of God's Messiah. Even to try doing it now with no thought of Christ, no mention of Christ, as I have heard some preachers try, without ever telling me why they had to, is I submit a betrayal of both prophecy and history. It is not even to see the door that God forever keeps open toward the future. On such terms the whole long drama of his dealing with Israel seems strangely bereft.

On the other hand, to read Christ into any book of the Old Testament, or into any part of any book, as into the fifty-third chapter of Isaiah, or the twenty-third Psalm, is to sacrifice authenticity for the sake of relevance, at the expense of all responsible dealing with the text. That is to see what we want to see. It is to do what the satirist says we do: to seek our own opinion and find it. Any serious reckoning with the historical situation and with the author's sober and conscious intent will at once rule out, as neither honest nor in the long run meaningful, such facile solutions. The all too avid quest for "analogies" and "types" and extraordinary "correspondences"—though they are indeed to be found, simply because God is always doing the same thing!—must nevertheless be measurably suspect, as any attempt at careful elaboration will readily show. This is to run the risk of making oneself "master of the text and its context instead of entering" into its service.[32] So with the quotation of Old Testament passages in support of New Testament doctrine. If you remind me that the New Testament itself provides us at this point with all the precedent we need, I can answer only that in every instance what is produced in our minds is likely to have somewhat less than the desired effect.[33] Whenever and wherever the attempt is made, its very lack of cogency for the modern reader not only exposes the dilemma itself but may help to indicate the way in which we have to set about resolving it.

As we undertake that task we shall have relatively little guidance from the textbooks, and not much more from the modern pulpit.[34] The so-called "character" approach, which is often recommended and often employed, as a kind of footnote to our widespread personality cults, just as often misses the point entirely, whether the suggestion be to emulate or to avoid. The Bible is not primarily concerned with character and personality. It is interested in the purposes of God. Nothing else gives any of its "heroes" his proper place in the scheme of things. Even Abraham, "the father of the faithful," as Paul describes him in the fourth chapter of Romans, is not acclaimed there in order that we may go and do likewise; his story is singled out because of itself it makes manifest God's continuing intent.[35]

Further still: the delight which so many of us seem to take in those brilliant passages which strike off with such accuracy some one or other of life's moral ambiguities and pitfalls turns out to be equally wide of the mark. The Bible is not a peg on which we can hang a few modern ideas of our own. It is not an armory from which we may select whatever weapons we choose, provided only that they are well suited to our needs. The preacher's use of it as a picture book of vivid stories and dramatic incident from which to plunge into the Christian gospel as from a kind of springboard is wholly without excuse. In all such cases it seems to be assumed that lying around somewhere in the history, almost everywhere, in poetry or prophecy, is a hidden treasure of Christian meaning: and that is precisely what there is not. Here is a text which fairly invites us to preach a sermon on Christian evangelism: "We do not well: this day is a day of good tidings, and we hold our peace." It is taken from the ninth verse of the seventh chapter of Second Kings, and has nothing in the wide world to do with any such thing. Four lepers had taken a chance on finding a bit of food in the tents of the Syrian host that was besieging Samaria, and to their utter amazement had discovered that from one end to the other the camp had been deserted: "Behold, there was no man there." They did not stop to ask why. We are told that the Lord had frightened the Syrians by making them hear a noise of chariots and horses, so that they left everything and fled for their lives. At any rate the whole army was gone. That was the glad news which had to be passed on immediately to the king of Israel: nothing less than that, and nothing more. If either the Sunday-School lesson or the sermon wants to apply it to our stewardship of the gospel, we ought to be told in all fairness that the author meant nothing of the sort. There is not a great deal of relevance in picturesqueness alone.

Or turn to the Song of Solomon, chapter 4, verse 16: "Awake, O north wind; and come, thou south; blow upon my garden, that the spices thereof may flow out." Here the preacher is likely to throw off all the restraints of fact and let fancy have its way. He leaves out the south wind and plays around only with the north, while he discourses on the rigors of life and their hardy influence in the molding of stalwart manhood. The only trouble is that frustrations and disappointments of themselves do not have that effect. Life is all too often shriveled up by them. Besides, what more does the passage mean than it says? The bride would like to have the sweet perfume of her presence wafted away to her lover: "Let my beloved come into his garden." She tells us herself what the winds are to do! Perhaps we should take her at her word. If you will glance at the sixth verse just above, as in the seventeenth verse of chapter 2, you will come upon that other favorite, cut into tombstones as if it were a promise of the resurrection: "Until the day break, and the shadows flee away." There we may smuggle in a comment or two on the life everlasting, and so make of the Bible a kind of Merlin's code book of reference for the weaving of magic spells. If a man is really committed to this import business in the matter of Biblical interpretation, determined to get in what was never there, the honest thing to do is to open up his satchel for the customs officers, and let all and sundry see his wares—what he really has, not what he wishes he had—what he is actually bringing in with him on this trip. All the poet meant by the daybreak and the fleeing shadows, if there is anywhere any interest at all in what he meant, was that the lover and his beloved were planning to linger with each other the whole night through, from sunset to dawn. It is difficult to construct gorgeous palaces and insubstantial pageants out of that!

What then is left for us? Is it enough to follow the advice of some and the practice of many by suggesting to ourselves on every page of the Old Testament that none of this ever actually came to its fulfillment except in Christ? The preacher either points that out as he goes, or holds it back for more specific development in the last section. In no case is it conclusive, often enough it is not even very impressive.[36] The New

Testament is not simply built on the primitive foundations of the Old. Both are fashioned from the same stuff. It is not added to the Old, as an ell might be added to a house. It is not an afterthought. It is not one of God's desperate expedients when everything else had failed. What has to be said is that the Old Testament and the New, together, not separately, constitute the pattern of God's redemptive dealing with his people. The relationship between the two is an integral relationship.[37] It cannot be represented in terms of any "before" and "after." The Old Testament is not a kind of preliminary study in the "common spiritual experience" of the race. If it were, all we should have to do would be to learn the gentle art of "spiritualizing" its "timeless truths": to analyze accurately some condition of affairs to which God addressed himself in a more or less preparatory way, as one would deal with children, many and many a year ago; and then item by item to point out the similarity between that state of things and this that we face ourselves—making it very clear, whenever we get a chance, how strangely contemporaneous the text seems. We do not stand between an ancient situation and a modern, pulling at a Levite with one hand and at some deacon with the other, trying to get them for God's sake and humanity's to meet, so that some verse of Holy Writ may come alive like Jairus' daughter! Oddly enough, one is sometimes asked, and even by veterans of the pulpit, how we can make God himself come alive, make him seem real to our generation. That, they tell us, is our problem. If they are right, then our problem is not to be mentioned in the same breath with God's, which is how to make *us* come alive and seem real!

We have to begin by laying hold on the fact that the Biblical situation is not just "like our situation." We are not engaged in antiquarian research, with a notebook in front of us for the jotting down of a few inferences here and there. John Knox writes of the Church, "My primary experience is not that of *learning* something about the past, but of *recognizing* something in the present."[38] I am unable to recall any Biblical situation of which that cannot be said. Far from being "like," in a very real sense every Biblical situation *is* our situation—though the two may in no instance ever be identified. It is the saving acts of God that are in every instance to be re-presented. The tension is never so much between the now and the then: always it is rather between the old as human life perpetually makes it, and the new in every generation as God perpetually wants to shape it, setting his seal on all that has been to make room for all that still can be.

Certainly we are to do what we can to reconstitute the past: to hear what God said at that time, in that place, to that person; but not to compare it with anything, and not to haul it up bodily and chuck it down in the present, as if there were no differences worth taking into account. The historical event happens but once. You cannot rush the rich young ruler cap-a-pie into the drawing room of your millionaire friend and expect the injunction of Jesus to do anything but fall flat on its face: "Go and sell that thou hast, and give to the poor" (Matt. 19:21). There may be something here that even a tramp, without a penny to his name, needs to have the gospel say to him.

Yet under all the discontinuities, under all the differences which render every situation unique, under all the contingencies which change with the passing of the years, it is not some similarity we are seeking; it is rather a massive and profound identity which makes even the similarity seem irrelevant. In what is past God speaks to what is deeply present. The authenticity and the relevance belong together.[39] The story of the Fall in the garden of Eden is not *like* something, it *is* something: it is the sad and minor theme running through the whole of that swelling symphony which crashed out its discords on Calvary. In the words of St. Augustine, all of us are what Adam did. By the same token the deliverance from Egypt becomes the contrapuntal major theme which like the great music of Beethoven finds its only echo before "a throne . . . set in heaven" (Rev. 4:2). All that went before the Incarnate Word has happened since. Back toward the dim beginning, and on down the lengthening years, falls the shadow of the cross.

The unity which binds the Old Testament with the New, therefore, is the unity of God's purpose in history. It is an organic, dynamic unity which draws very simply from the fact that God always means the same thing. It is a unity which cannot be discerned in mere resemblances, or in coincidences of event, or in function, or in language. It is to be discerned in the deep and underlying patterns of "salvation history": Fall, Exodus, Judgment, Mercy, Sacrifice, Atonement. The very listing of these dominant motifs—and the list could be almost unbelievably drawn out: Fatherhood, Kingship, Messiahship, the People of God, Repentance, Forgiveness—the very listing of them should be in itself not only evidence enough that there can be no profound understanding of the New Testament apart from the Old, or of the Old apart from the New, but also warning enough that the differences between the two may never be reduced simply to contrast. The God of the Old is not a God of wrath, as distinguished from the God of the New who is a God of love; nor does the rending of the veil of the temple at the crucifixion mean, as one very distinguished preacher put it, that now because of the death of Jesus men have direct access to God. They had had that for untold generations before Calvary. The Epistle to the Hebrews, however unsatisfactory its argument may sound in our ears, treats more meaningfully what the Gospels had in mind, and far more responsibly. The author at least gives some evidence of understanding that the unity of Scripture can be apprehended only when we take up our position where we are historically, in this present time, and look back at the Old Testament through the New, in order to see the Old in perspective, in sharp relief, to explore it in its true dimensions, to grasp in all its fullness what God once did by taking our bearings from what God has since done.[40]

There is an analogy which seems almost ready-made for the occasion. Fifty years ago, in nearly every parlor there was a stereoscope, with its hooded lenses, its long wooden tongue, and the little slide that moved back and forth to bring the twin photographs into focus. The dictionary says that the purpose of the stereoscope is to combine "the images of two pictures taken from points of view a little way apart" so that they may seem to merge at a point farther beyond and so disclose the depth in an object which the camera of itself had flattened out.[41] In some such manner did the evangelists look back through the resurrection and crucifixion at the life of Jesus—and wrote for us what has to be seen now as the gospel in retrospect! Birth, baptism, ministry, the Sermon on the Mount, the "mighty acts," the "triumphal entry"—all were set out in different perspective. Meaning which may not have been deliberately or even consciously conveyed at the moment was in the issue conjoined with fact. The unity of the Old Testament with the New can be discerned only in the unity of God's completed design.

In the briefing session arranged between a rabbi, a priest, and a Protestant minister who were to appear together on television, the hope was expressed that no controversial matter would be introduced. Whereupon the rabbi asked, "Would it not serve to make clear what is indeed our common aim if we simply stood with the prophet? 'What doth the Lord require of thee, but to do justly, and to love mercy, and to walk humbly with thy God?'" (Mic. 6:8). The minister answered at once, frankly, but I hope without arrogance, "No; and if you ask me why, I shall have to say, 'Because the Lord has done something since.' And if you ask me over the air what that something is, I shall have to put it just as clearly and forcefully as I can." It was precisely the requirements of the Law that revealed man's inability to do justly, to love mercy, and to walk humbly with his God—a failure for which he himself could make no sacrifice (Mic. 6:6-7). God had to provide that. And he provided it in Christ for a people "not circumscribed by birth or ritual as were the Jews," moving through the Old Testament and the New, not "from a narrow particularism to an undifferentiated universalism," but from "an exclusive particularism" toward a particularism which "exploded" at last into "a form more obviously the measure of his loving-kindness."[42]

To read the Old Testament, then, or to preach from it, is to see it from the place where we know ourselves to be as Christians, looking back to what God once did through what God has since done. There was a day when the Lord confronted Moses in the wilderness, as the bush burned but was not consumed; and there arose between them a conflict, long drawn out—"Who am I, that I should go?" "What shall I say when they ask 'Who sent you?'" "But, behold, they will not believe me." "O my Lord, I am not eloquent." "Send, I pray thee, by the hand of another." (Exod. 3-4) Until at last, but only with the greatest reluctance, that ancient leader of Israel undertook the commission which was laid on him. It is not possible now for any Christian to read the story without an awareness of how this same God confronts us in Christ, to trouble us still out of our cowardice and our sloth; and of how the conflict surges up around us, raging its way along in our lives toward a cross—death for him (Heb. 6:6) or death for us (Rom. 6:6); coming finally to this: "As my Father hath sent me"—all the rough road along from Bethlehem to Golgotha—"even so send I you" (John 20:21). Inexpressibly deepened, heightened, broadened, lengthened—away toward "the spires on the world's rim"! And that is not to read Christ in. It is in Christ to read a meaning there far greater and more poignant than any the Old Testament knew. But we know it. Luther would have it that the Christ of the Old Testament is *Deus ipse loquens,* God speaking in his own proper person! To betray that knowledge by ignoring it is to dam the stream of God's revelation at its source. "By him were all things created. . . . he is before all things . . . by him all things consist" (Col. 1:16-17). And to dam that at its source is to wade flat-footed through shallower water than ever God intended.

In such fashion, by its ceaseless invasion of all our lives, does this living Word of God create its own situations. It does not merely reconstruct or simply reproduce: it creates. And without exception the situations it creates are more than contemporary. And they are more than timeless, having indeed everything to do with time. We need never have any fear that what the Bible fashions today will be outdated tomorrow. Because the words which were written on those pages, although they are the words of fallible men, are the words which God has found; they are taken up in every generation by the Holy Spirit of God to become that Word. In setting down the long and varied story of God's intervention, they are his intervention. In recording the history of revelation, they are revelation. We do not have to apologize for them, speak well of them, put the most charitable construction on all the most embarrassing facts, circumvent the troublesome passages, present in modern dress their naïve and primitive accounts, clothe them with slang to make them popular, throw around them the philosophical mantle of Wieman or the psychological mantle of Freud to make them respectable. We should never have had to attempt that if we had not been stuck fast in the flypaper of our own unfaith. It is not our business to keep something alive which we are afraid is dead—as motion pictures try to keep alive the dead romance of the pioneer West. There was a man once who thought it was his function to steady the ark of God, and died of it! Which seemed to convince everybody that it never had been his function, and that God himself had said so emphatically and unmistakably! (II Sam. 6:6f.) The Bible is intent on creating what it records: and when that happens, nobody has to bring it up to date, or keep it from stumbling over its own feet.[43]

To know what it is we are dealing with is to have all the false props of tradition knocked out from under us, though not its support. The Bible is what Protestantism calls it, the only rule of faith and practice.

But since history is a one-way street, and the clock cannot be turned back, and the Spirit of God has not been unemployed since the closing of the canon, there is no call to be either primitivistic or literalistic. A rule is not a yardstick, exacting of everybody this measure of assent or that measure of forgiveness—a kind of straight-edged conformity all around. A yardstick is a dead stick. There is a rule because there is a God who rules. His is the Kingdom and the power and the glory; and that Kingdom and power and glory are over the Bible, they do not proceed from it; they come by way of the Bible, but they are not in it. The Word of God cannot be contained in any of the words that channel it, like apples in a basket. Your words and my words may go far to reveal us; but they do not contain us. God's Word is God's self: not to provide anybody with answers, but to create faith; not to teach truth, in so far as I will condescend to believe it, but to give life, in so far as I will receive it. And Christ is that life. He is God's Word. It is he, says Luther, who is the judge of Scripture. All things must be in conformity with him, and he is alive. Writes P. T. Forsyth, "Christ did not come to bring a Bible but to bring a Gospel. The Bible arose afterwards from the Gospel to serve the Gospel. We do not treat the Bible aright, we do not treat it with the respect it asks for itself, when we treat it as a theologian, but only when we treat it as an apostle, as a preacher, as the preacher in the perpetual pulpit of the Church. . . . The Bible, the preacher, and the Church are all made by the same thing— the Gospel."[44] And with that gospel no record can be identical; of it no record alone can be the source.

Moreover, to know what it is we are dealing with is to be rid of all slavish dependence on reason and history, though not of our relation to them. The Scriptures do not commend themselves to every reasonable person: many who are of the highest intelligence will not submit to any of the claims which we all too often make for the Bible. There is here something more than gentle reasonableness, something more than sweetness and light. The Christian faith, like the heart in Pascal's saying, "has its own reasons"; and they are beyond reason. There is something here also which transcends historical fact. It would not necessarily be all right with us if only we could validate the miracles and establish the Resurrection beyond all gainsaying. "If they hear not Moses and the prophets, neither will they be persuaded, though one rose from the dead" (Luke

16:31). Abraham said that in Jesus' story of the rich man whose name God forgot, and Lazarus whose name everybody else had forgotten. But no matter. Whoever said it, it happened! There was one who was raised—unless indeed the life of the Church sprang out of a fiction, and has to be written down now as a senseless enigma. The Christian faith is rooted in the kind of history that becomes our history; not in the history that lesser things are buried in.

What we have, then, is not old. Yesterday is old. As much of this year as has already passed, that is old. Last century is old. But this is not old: "There the Christ stands!" In everything we say, we are to say that. There are times when we have to say it knowing quite well that what we say is to the soul's despair; but despair is the only cradle which Christian hope has ever known. We have to say it because Christ is forever compelling us to choose: not in Pilate's judgment hall, but here, as he keeps eternally judging Pilate and us. How far from reason alone is the peril of his love! How far from history alone are the goodness and severity of God, made for us in Christ flesh of our flesh and bone of our bone! How far from believing alone is the pressure of a Word which has never been bound by the words, but forever moves through them to meet us where we are and to deal with us as only a living Presence can deal—in unsearchable judgment and endless mercy. Maybe God in his compassion should tell us that none of it is true! Or maybe, because of his compassion, if it were not true, he could no longer be God!

III

The Credibility and Relevance
of the Gospel

That they may hear, and . . . learn and . . . observe to do. . . .
Deuteronomy 31:12

Dr. Herbert Farmer, in an address which he delivered at Union Theological Seminary in New York shortly after World War II, set out the three main indictments which were then, and are still, being brought against the Christian gospel—often enough by those who in a manner of speaking accept it, certainly "in the sense that they do not actively reject it." He told us that in England there were many who regarded it and outspokenly described it as incredible, irrelevant, and cheap. It will be seen at once that while such strictures may well lie in almost any generation against what is said in the pulpit, they do not therefore and necessarily lie against the gospel. The fact is that as far back as 1938, though in a somewhat different way. Dr. Farmer had himself already so characterized the preaching to which the first quarter of the century had grown accustomed. In his Introduction to a volume of his own sermons, *The Healing Cross,* he had contended that the pulpit needed first of all to recover the cosmic note. The gospel had to be presented and understood in terms "not incommensurate with the great forces sweeping through the modern world"—lest one conceive of it as something "too small to be true." Is that perhaps why some have learned to dismiss the gospel as "incredible"? In addition, there had to be "a strongly agnostic note" running through our apprehension and proclamation of God's good news, in order that "the mystery of God's purpose in the world" might have the emphasis it needs; that the light of the gospel might be "a Light which shines out of darkness, not one that banishes" the darkness—lest we conceive of it as something "too confident to be true." Is that, in part at any rate, why some think of it as "irrelevant"? And one thing more: through it all "the note of austerity" had to be "clearly heard." There had to be demand as well as succor, succor because of the demand, and demand because of the succor lest we conceive of it as something "too easy to be true."[1] Is that why multitudes of young people, who might otherwise have been drawn to it, have learned in our day to call the gospel "cheap"? Let me suggest that we try here to pursue these indictments to their source. It is possible that we may help to write what the lawyers call a *nolle prosequi* across their face, so that if what we believe and presume to advocate must stand trial, as indeed it must, with our world for judge and jury, it may not have to be tried any longer on such counts, not at least by reason of anything we think or do or say about it.

1. Too Small To Be True

The charge "incredible," "too small to be true," may derive from the fact that the gospel has been represented with such startling consistency in our time as something other and therefore less than it is. Anders Nygren, in the course of an illustration which I had always thought was mine—the ancients, as someone has remarked, have appropriated all our best ideas!—calls it a message: one of our favorite clichés for introducing the visiting preacher! Writing for the *Scottish Journal of Theology*,[2] he says:

In order to show what it signified that the Gospel comes to us as a message, let me take an illustration which . . . almost seems created to bring clearness into this problem. During the last world war, one country after another was occupied. . . . Many of the citizens had to go underground . . . or else they would languish in prisons and concentration camps. . . . But then one day . . . comes the message: "Your country is *free*. The occupying power is beaten and must abandon the field." . . . It signifies that an objective change has occurred. . . . Something . . . has happened . . . : a power has come which is stronger than the occupying power, and has deprived it of its dominion. . . . The whole life takes a new form. The period of the violation of justice . . . has passed away. The law, which was unable to function, . . . returns to power.

Freedom, where it had been only a memory or a dream, had become a fact again.

Note if you will several salient features of this. We already know, do we not, at even deeper levels, and even in the so-called free world, what it means to be occupied by an alien power. It is this that the theologian calls Sin, with a capital *S*. For all our democratic processes, we are still in a position to understand what Paul is driving at when he says that we are possessed, ruled over (Rom. 6:14, 16-17, 19-20). And we know something of the effect it has on us: the endless obsession with self-interest, the feeling of inferiority and futility, the not being ourselves. Nor do we have to be reminded that others are in the same situation. There is no reason why we should not begin to spell that out in our very thinking, instead of forever seeking refuge in such abstractions as sin, and evil, and wrongdoing, and the subtlety of temptation.[3] Moreover, we know that if the "occupation" were lifted, the inward character of our very existence would be changed. Not necessarily the outward. The enemy troops would still be around. The cruelty would no doubt, with desperation, become even more cruel—as indeed it did in France and Holland and Belgium during the last years of the war. But a new purpose, a new joy, a new endeavor, would take the place of the old frustration. The very atmosphere and climate would be different.

That indeed is what "salvation" means.[4] It means to be whole again, to be delivered in the midst of peril. Far back toward the Hebrew root of the word, it may even suggest that no matter how closely the evil hedges you about, God will yet clear for you all the space you need to move around in. He will "make room," *Lebensraum*. The fences, away out on the western plains of the United States, which the cowboy in the song wanted to get rid of—"Don't fence me in!"—are all quite gone, really. The psalmist has his version of it: "Thou hast known my soul in adversities; and hast not shut me up into the hand of the enemy" (Ps. 31:7-8). "I called upon the Lord in distress: the Lord answered me, and set me in a large place" (Ps. 118:5). The ambiguities which

you find in the seventh chapter of Romans, and under the surface of
the eighth chapter too, will all be there, perhaps more insistently than
before; but you can conclude them now as Paul concludes them: "We
are more than conquerors through him that loved us" (Rom. 8:37). It
is not enough to say that we have been given a new start, another
chance. We usually do with the new start and the other chance what
we did with the first and the second and the third. Something more
radical has happened. Another dominion has moved in. Another al-
legiance has been offered us. Sin and the law which reveals it and the
death which issues from it may think that they are still in control,
and behave as if they were; but what is actually on the throne now is
the grace of God. And that makes it possible for us, even as we are, to
be "one body in Christ." The new age has come, the new creation.
Everything in the gospel stems from that conviction: its ethic, its
authority, its urgency, and its assurance.

Yet even this, we must be bold to say, is something less and other
than the gospel. In *The Divine-Human Encounter* Emil Brunner writes:
"In His Word God does not deliver to me a course of lectures in dogmatic theology. He does not submit to me or interpret for me the content of a confession of faith." Nor, we may add, does he send me a
message. "He makes himself accessible to me . . . an exchange takes
place here which is totally without analogy in the sphere of thinking.
The sole analogy is in the encounter between human beings, the meeting
of person with person."[5] It is not in an *I-It* relationship that we stand
any more, the *I* over here and the *It* of God's good news over there.
The relationship now is between an *I* and the *Thou* of God's good news
in Christ—which incidentally would seem to provide sufficient justification for holding, without being an obscurantist, that metaphysics, whatever else it is, is not the way to the Holy. Philosophy no more inevitably
leads to faith than it does to marriage: though very conceivably it can
in both cases help those who have already crossed the frontier! And one
may say that without being cynical with regard to either! To say it is
simply to say that persons have priority in both matrimony and Christianity. I have often sat at my desk, as Martin Buber somewhere
describes it, with books and paper and typewriter before me, if not
master then manager in that realm of things; when all at once the
telephone would ring at my elbow, and a voice which I have never con-

fused with any other voice in the world would say that dinner was ready. On the instant the whole situation was transformed. A higher order of reality had cut across my existence. What was called for now was not so much reason as response. So is the Christian gospel more than a message: it is "a message with a messenger . . . not one without the other; but both together."[6] It is the dramatic encounter between God in Christ and the human soul.

Now it is precisely the betrayal of this, in one form or another, the betrayal of its deep and inward nature, that has made the gospel again and again all through Christian history seem incredible. The good news has been represented as other and less than it is. It has been identified in the popular mind with the true, and its truth is under no bond to be our truth. It has been identified with the good, and its good forever challenges and upsets our good. It has been identified with the beautiful, and its beauty is the beauty of holiness, which on the record is not altogether what we mean by the word beauty. The God of the Bible who allowed his people to be led away into captivity and looked on while men and women and children were driven into the arena will not lend himself to our decoration: he is "naked God"![7] There are no devices by which we can make him over into our image and get him to fit in with our plans.[8]

As one specific instance of the attempt to identify the gospel with the "true," let me quote a sentence from an exceedingly well-written article—of all things else on the communication of the faith!—in an exceedingly reputable religious journal by an unusually able preacher: "Jesus and his disciples accepted the idea of the supremacy of God without question." With what that intends to say one would have no quarrel: but mark what it actually says. A worse sentence could scarcely be framed. "Idea" is a Greek word that in some sense has to be set over against the deeper Hebrew understanding of the knowledge of God as intimate communion.[9] To "accept" an idea means to appropriate it as one's own, primarily by intellectual assent to it. One scarcely needs to be reminded that in the New Testament faith means vastly more than the acceptance of an idea. But as if this were not enough, Pelion is next piled on Ossa: the "idea of the supremacy of God" is to be "accepted," apparently, "without question." Nowhere does Jesus ask of anybody that kind of weak-minded compliance. How on earth can you manage it in a world which so often seems to make such a good job of canceling God's supremacy entirely? Where was that supremacy when you lost all you had? When someone you loved died as Camus died, as President Kennedy died—so wastefully? Where was God's supremacy when soldiers drove great spikes through the hands and feet of Jesus? Surely in order to know where it was you will have to have some idea of what it means! Could it be that we have to begin listening to the gospel by clenching our fists and closing our eyes and setting our jaws and "accepting" something, which is to say "believing" something, which is to say "swallowing" something that sticks in your throat every time you try? Said the queen in *Through the Looking-Glass*, when she saw how bewildered Alice was, "I daresay you haven't had much practice. . . . Why, sometimes I've believed as many as six impossible things before breakfast." One may recall Thomas Carlyle's story about the boy from the country who was one of the guests at a formal dinner and got a large piece of hot potato in his mouth. Much to the embarrassment of everybody he took it out in the palm of his hand and laid it on his plate. As they all cleared their throats and refused to meet his eyes, he looked calmly around and said, "You know, some fools would have swallowed that!" Acceptance is hardly the word for the kind of attitude we should be taking toward the sovereignty of God. If I am to understand myself as one known and loved by the Almighty, I should look around for some other way of describing my response. I should not make use of the language of acceptance. You would not try it on your wife: "I accept the idea of your supremacy without question"! I never try it in my prayers.

Neither is the gospel a way of feeling, or a way of thinking about things in general. It is not a way of looking at life, seeing it steadily and seeing it whole; not a *Weltanschauung*. I remember a sermon in which the suggestion was made to some seven thousand people that they think of a vast Oriental rug of many colors spread out on the floor of an auditorium. A butterfly flutters in through a window and settles on what to her is a broad expanse of blue. As far as her eye can see, everything is blue, as on some "blue Monday." After a while she slowly makes her way on foot to the wide reaches of the red, and grows strangely short-tempered and choleric. Then to the green, where a deep serenity seems to come over her spirit. Next, the sunshine brightness and vivacity of the yellow. Until at last she launches out on her wings again, this time perching on the great chandelier high overhead, where she looks down at the lovely pattern for the first time. She sees it now steadily and sees it whole. That, we were told, is what Christianity is for: in the home, in the community, in the church, and in the world—the easy categories of a weary mind!

The trouble is, the Bible is not particularly interested in the way we look at things. It does not put to you before anything else what G. K. Chesterton once said was by far the most significant question a landlady could possibly put to a prospective tenant: "Sir, what is your total view of the universe?"[10] The Bible, without consulting you at all as to your views in the matter, announces a universe with God at the heart of it; and will not stop even for a moment to inquire how you feel about such a situation. Neither the way they regarded the catastrophe that had overtaken them, nor the way they felt about the breast stroke or the Hawaiian crawl for long-distance swimming, was what saved Noah and his family: the ark saved them. Viewpoints are important; they largely determine what you see: they can never determine what there *is* to be seen. So too it has to be said that feeling does indeed have a cognitive function. Thank heaven it often tells the truth! As John Macquarrie points out, a tiger in the zoo behind bars is one thing, a tiger loose on Fifth Avenue is another thing altogether; and you feel quite differently about it![11] But observe that the "feeling" cannot be deliberately whipped up. You may not ask, "Go to, now: how can I feel that something happens when I pray?" Prayer is not intended to light a fire and bring human life to the boiling point. Sometimes whole services of worship seem to have been designed to that end. The organ swells to an almost intolerable volume as the offering is brought forward, and the congregation rises, giving cry to "Praise God from whom all blessings flow." Or after the sermon the choir sings quietly with bowed head, "O Lamb of God, I come, I come." The gospel is not primarily concerned with thinking or with feeling; certainly not with logic or the weighing of evidence. It has been said that you cannot discuss the problem of the existence of God in the same way in which you might go about inquiring if there are any "one-eyed cats"! God's good news is not concerned with anything which in the common sense of the word is verifiable. It is concerned with response to a Person!

The greatest of all the obstacles, however, is none of these. The greatest obstacle in the way of any man's hearing is to have the Christian faith presented to him as a way of life. It is that, certainly. "A distinction between religion and morality is . . . wholly absent from all ancient thought, being a most doubtful product of later philosophical rationalism."[12] But there is something else which takes precedence. The Good and the True are related to the Holy, but not as a means to an end. The unholy man cannot acquire enough truth or enough goodness to make him holy.[13] It is frequently urged upon us that Jesus was an ethical teacher; and so he was. But it is not likely that he saw less clearly than Paul saw; and Paul saw that the ethics and the theological context belong together. Already in the Garden of Eden the devil tried to drive a wedge between the two. God had said of the tree, "Ye shall not eat of it"—that's the ethic—"lest ye die"—that's the theology! The serpent said, "Ye shall not die." There the theology is cut away. "Your eyes shall be opened, and ye shall be as gods." There is the ethic misshapen and distorted. In the breach between faith and action, between theology and ethics, life becomes demonic. Give the Golden Rule no more than a secular context, and it becomes immoral. "Do unto others as you would have others do unto you." That is to say, you are to share your heroin with others, if you would have others share their heroin with you. The Great Commandment is sometimes quoted as if it were the sum total of religion. It is nothing of the sort. It is the sum total of the Law and the Prophets. Without the gospel in front of it, it is nothing but an imperative without any visible means of support. The imperative must have its indicative. "God so loved the world": therefore, "thou shalt love the Lord thy God, and thy neighbor as thyself."

Jesus was an ethical teacher because the Jewish religion had ceased to be a truly ethical religion. Not so with us. Quite the opposite. Our ethics, in so far as by and large we can still be said to have any, have ceased to be religious. Too many of us have been trying too long to live on the ethical capital of our forebears, without replenishing any of it at the level of faith: caring in some measure about the fruits, while allowing the roots to look out for themselves. The result is that what we have on our hands is a "cut-flower" civilization.[14] The ultimate dimension of the task that lies before us is not to make a religion ethical so much as to make an ethic religious! And that is not done simply by affirming a truth about God, then adding to it a truth about man, after which you expect people to lay down their knitting, recite the Apostles' Creed, and give themselves over to the good life. The good life is the sharing of God's life. Behind the willing to do God's will is the ministry of God's Spirit. Behind the imperative of his will lies the indicative of his saving act, which is the giving of himself. This he has done, and as someone put it not long ago, we are supposed to do a good deal more than simply to say "Oh?"[15] To do or not to do is by no means the choice in front of us: the choice is to be or not to be—not as Hamlet meant it, but as the New Testament means it—in the grace of our Lord Jesus Christ, in the love of God, and in the communion of the Holy Ghost. To be and not to do, however hard it is to relate them in practice, is a contradiction in terms. The being is sonship. The not doing is idolatry.

In short, then, God's good news is simply that we are invited to meet him in the intimacy of that restored relationship in Christ which is faith: where requirement goes hand in hand with rescue, and mercy goes hand in hand with judgment; where love, if it is experienced only as law, ceases to be love, and law, when it is experienced primarily as love, ceases to be merely law. The Christian gospel is about that relationship, about nothing more, and about nothing less. The Church is about that relationship. Worship is about that relationship. The Bible is about that relationship. Said Jacob at Bethel as he awoke from sleep, with the memory of the vision he had had and the voice he had heard, "Surely the Lord is in this place; and I knew it not" (Gen. 28:16). There is the sacrament of meeting, and it had been vouchsafed to a man who was not particularly skilled in discerning the presence of the Lord anywhere: he had been too busy with other things. Little wonder that he added, "How dreadful is this place! this is none other but the house of God." It was not the happiest moment he had ever had. Why should it have been? Why should it be for any of us? But beyond it stretched the unimagined vistas of God's purpose: "this is the gate of heaven" (verse 17). For one moment, over against what he knew of his own warped and twisted life, he saw the picture of that life which was in the heart of God; over against his poor Bethel of stones, he saw a house not made with hands. But never could he have dreamed what it was going to cost him to travel the road that led toward it.

There in the years ahead, so the story runs, was to be his dark and desperate wrestling with an angel on the banks of the river Jabbok; and the issue of it: "As he passed over Penuel the sun rose upon him, and he halted upon his thigh" (Gen. 32:24-31). It was the dawn of a new day, but he had to limp into it. What else is there here but the poignant and continuing epic of human life, face to face with the austere and holy love of God? See that in the context of the Word made flesh, of the vast reconciling work of Christ, and you have the whole sweep of the gospel.

See it in that context, and you will understand how utterly beside the point, once more, are the sorry little questions people insist on asking. Is the Bible true? What is the use of prayer? Why do we have to go to church, and listen to preaching? "You'll feel better," read a sign in the New York buses some years ago. Or will you feel worse? Will it "do you good" to meet God? Will it give you a lift after a hard week at the office? Because the gospel is the place of meeting between God and the human soul, these are precisely the wrong questions, to which therefore there can be no right answers.

Could it be this that explains in greatest measure why the Bible sounds to us like such a strange book? Not so much because of its language[16] as because of its underlying assumptions. From Genesis on the West to the Revelation of St. John on the East lies a place instinct with God: never empty; never like the place in which we live, where big is big, and little is little, and 90 per cent of almost everything amounts to nothing. In the Bible, down every highway, at every turn of the road, you are met and challenged by an infinite mind and the yearning of an eternal heart. Take any page and strip it of God, as we strip our lives, down to the bone, until that infinite mind is away somewhere, and the yearning of that eternal heart is only a grand Perhaps, and you will be back in the world with which you are already too familiar. A sower sowing his seed will be just a sower sowing his seed; that it is and nothing more. A dead sparrow by the side of the road will be just a dead sparrow by the side of the road, and who in hell cares, or who in heaven? And all of it is stale, flat, and unprofitable; it makes people sick! What the Bible keeps saying is that we can swap our world for that other, where there are three dimensions, and everything is a parable of the Kingdom of God; and we can swap it whenever we like. The Bible is about that. Christian worship is about that. The gospel is about that. And we had better not read it down to any other level.

2. Too Confident To Be True

But the charge "incredible," "too small to be true," is only the first of the charges which are being brought against the Christian gospel. The second is that it often seems quite "irrelevant," as something altogether "too confident to be true."[17] It seems too small, and therefore incredible, when it is conceived of or proclaimed as less or other than . it is. It seems too confident, and therefore irrelevant, when the tragic sense of life is allowed to drop out of it. And that happens with astonishing rapidity whenever we allow ourselves to be obsessed, as we readily do, with the notion that somehow the gospel ought to "work." The pulpit assures everybody that it will, and here and there in the pews there are those who nod their heads in agreement; the only trouble is that disillusion on that score is never very far off from either the pulpit or the pew: and whoever has sense enough to know it should have courage enough to say it. The gospel works; but works what? There is, for instance, no guarantee anywhere that the good news will make good neighbors, cowardly people brave, selfish people compassionate, irritable people patient, or decent people happy. There is not any guarantee anywhere, either in the Old Testament or in the New, that God's promises will be fulfilled—except when and as it pleases him. The Bible is constantly looking forward not to something but to someone, and that someone acts in sovereign freedom, incalculably.[18] There is no guarantee anywhere that God answers prayer—except when and if and as he sees fit. Most of the time we would prefer to have matters turn out some other way: and so we either talk with great solemnity about the problem of "unanswered" prayer, sometimes we sing about it, when of course there is no such thing—there goes that solo!—or at the peak of such piety as we can muster we pray for the patience we want God to teach us. Whereupon, said Henry Ward Beecher, God set out to do it in his case by sending him a green cook! The gospel works, but works what?

At one end of my private and intimate gallery of portraits is the memory of a man whose face had been half-destroyed by cancer. When a friend came to see him and faltered at the threshold, terribly shocked by his appearance, he said, "Never you mind, my sword is still in my hand." In hidden corners of the world, behind closed doors, alone or on crowded streets, there is always someone who no matter what happens will go soaring

> Like an eagle to meet the sun:

> no talk of problems, little talk of patience; deep inside, if you will listen for it, a shout of triumph,

> Lord God, thy will be done![19]

At the other end of that same gallery is a man who told me one day that he hated God. His partners, leaders in the church, had cheated him out of his business, and at his age the only opportunities left for him were miserable little jobs hardly worth his time; and he had found his wife dead on the floor that evening when he came home. God was forever promising what he either could not or would not deliver. People kept telling him that faith would do for him what it obviously was not doing for them. He hated God! No preacher should ever write a sermon until the sound of that is in his ears: somebody walking up and down wringing his hands, with tears coming loose, starting, stopping, and starting again unnoticed down his cheeks.

Back of such an experience, more often than not, are the glittering generalities so lavishly thrown out from many a pulpit, beatitudes turned into platitudes, a paring down of life to make it fit the gospel, fifty-seven different varieties of do-it-yourself techniques, a wrapping up of the tragedies of human existence into neat bundles tied with a blue ribbon. No strong "agnostic" note: only confidence, and too much of that for any of it to be genuine.[20] No light that was content to shine in the dark: only a light which had tried to banish the darkness; and it could not, so it had gone out. A security so insecure that a bad cold could dispel it! It was not God my friend hated; he hated his picture of God: and that likely enough was the most discerning, the most truly "pious" thing he could have done. He had not stopped being a Christian, as he said he had; he was simply a better Christian than most: as Job the blasphemer was far more deeply religious than any of his orthodox friends—a point, by the way, which Mr. MacLeish, in his play *J.B.*, quietly ignores.

The Christian faith in our time could well take its cue from Graham Greene's novels and set about caricaturing its own caricatures. The gospel fairly begs to be held up beside the toughest lot a man can encounter, without offering in the least to provide "the answer." It wants to travel the hardest road a man can travel, share the most disillusioned life a man can imagine: fairly pleading with us to let it maintain itself under such circumstances without alteration or adjustment. "Our hearts rejoice in the knowledge and love of God." So said the young preacher in a recent sermon. Do they indeed? Wrote another, "We are bowed down before the Lord in humility and thanksgiving." The wish that we might be found in that posture kept begging the question on almost every page, and never did catch up with the facts!

Suppose we bring now under some sharper scrutiny this "strongly agnostic" note which runs through the New Testament. Nobody there ever tried to shut himself away from the ominous discords which resolve themselves at last into such majestic harmonies. Not to hear them is to listen to the Siren's song: death is at the end of it. The music of life is stern music. And nowhere does it come through more clearly than in the four gospel lessons which the traditional liturgy of the Christian Church has associated with the first four Sundays of the Church year— the so-called Advent season.[21] Each in its own way looks forward to Christmas, and each in its own way records the deep undertones of misgiving and conflict. Against the background of the great deliverance which God had wrought for his pilgrim people as he led them out of Egypt, and had wrought again seven hundred years later as he brought them back home from their weary and bitter exile in Babylon, the same story of his desperate intent never willingly to let anybody go is set down in its new dimension, which is Christ. If you take the four lessons together, you would almost say that they are a transcript of Christian experience: the tug of war between the *Yes* and the *No* that goes on forever in the human soul, issuing in the confidence which never can be born except on the field of battle at the heart of all of life's mysteries.

The first of the four is the familiar, dramatic account of what we know as the Triumphal Entry into Jerusalem (Matt. 21:1-9). But what a triumph! I dare say it caused less stir than we are accustomed to think it did. Here was a defenseless preacher of righteousness who had set far too many tongues wagging: the brief disturbance of his coming ended in a crucifixion. To the people who really mattered in Jerusalem the whole business must have seemed an irrelevance. And it would be an irrelevance still if it had not been longer and broader and deeper than even the disciples realized as they followed him down the Mount of Olives and into the city. So much vaster that with profound insight the earliest Reformation tradition, looking back, found a place for it both on Palm Sunday and at the beginning of Advent too:

> Ride on, ride on in majesty!
> In lowly pomp—what kind of pomp is that?—ride on to die!

Is it any wonder that we should turn our faces as we remember it not only toward a cross but toward Bethlehem as well, and the shepherds, and the star, and the wise men, and the manger? This is not an event that can be pinned down anywhere. It tells a story; but what is more, it brings us up short in front of a fact which keeps repeating itself. There is One who in every generation, never to be discouraged, year after year, day after day, humbly, unobtrusively; hidden away somewhere in our homes, among our friendships, back of the things we have done and the things we have left undone; contradicting what we have learned to expect; so often not where we look, but where we fail to look and are sure he is not to be found—One who keeps moving in on your life and mine.

What tragedy there is still in his triumph, and what triumph in the tragedy of his coming! Where in all this world of laughter and of tears will you tell me there is no sound of it? No imperious hand laid on you when you thought you were alone, having your own way? When you supposed that the "riddle of life" could be "more easily solved down below than up aloft,"[22] and found yourself saying "Nobody need ever know. It can never possibly make much difference": no presence there, no eyes that met yours, so that you could find no cover from them? "And the multitudes . . . cried, saying, Hosanna to the son of David"—while underneath, the rotten traffic went on: he had to drive it out of the temple itself! And you have never wondered about what there is deep down in you, as you trail along with these others—what pride, or willfulness, what deep resentment at his probing? The moment stretches itself out endlessly as he continues to assert his strange sovereignty over the human heart—which never has belonged to him! We may not like the crown he wears, but he wears it: the centuries have put it where it is; and it rests on his head most securely when you twist and turn and try your best to pull away. Every day you live, there is the *No* you say to him—to him and to his terrible words, as they toil desperately up the stairs out of the cellar where we have tried to lodge them; but no matter: still they flout the wrong you do, with not a shred torn from their banner. "Ye have heard that it was said by them of old time. . . . But I say unto you. . . . (Matt. 5:21, 27, 31, etc.). We may yet have to give up the God who we hope will at our convenience leave us strictly alone, and face the God who first has to shatter all our confidence.

But just there, and all at once, this quiet, central figure of the gospel takes on the stature of one in whom time and eternity meet. The lesson for the second Sunday in Advent (Luke 21:25-33) is like the ringing of a great bell in the turmoil of some huge catastrophe: "There shall be signs in the sun, and in the moon, and in the stars, and upon the earth distress of nations, with perplexity"—until he who once came in weakness should come again in power. As they huddled around him, the disciples took it to be the end of the world he was talking about; and without much question it was, at any rate in part. Why then should we here pay any attention to it at all? What could have less relevance, today and tomorrow? The Bible is too full of that kind of talk. Or should we turn a moment in our thinking from that final summing up of all things, and set our minds more soberly on the worlds that end now? The world that was yours on Monday, when suddenly all that was steady and firm gave way. Maybe it will be like that this coming Wednesday! Shall we pay no attention to it, as these signs of his coming slip down out of the future into the present? You remember Othello's stricken cry. He knew what it was for a man's world to come to an end.

> Perdition catch my soul,
> But I do love thee! and when I love thee not,
> Chaos is come again.

Then after a little,

> Farewell the tranquil mind; farewell content! . . .
> Farewell the plumed troop . . .
> Pride, pomp, and circumstance of war!
> . . . Othello's occupation's gone![23]

So it is, or would seem to be, with a good many in our generation. Here, wrote Stephen Spender shortly after World War II, is "the dilemma of the modern poet."[24] Unable any longer in himself to create "an order lacking in events," he either tries to make poetry out of "that which seems essentially unpoetic"—"the smell of steak in passageways. . . . The burnt-out ends of smoky days"—or he plunges up to the elbows into everything around him simply to fling it away, and with it all too often every heartening word that might yet be spoken to that human anguish which in the Old Testament found prophets to give it voice, and in the New Testament found One who is greater than the prophets; but now can find nothing for its comfort, nothing for its desire,

> Save that the sky grows darker yet
> And the sea rises higher.[25]

"Just you wait," says M. le Curé in Georges Bernanos' *The Diary of a Country Priest*. "Wait for the first quarter-of-an-hour's silence. Then the word will be heard of men—not the voice they rejected, which spoke so quietly; 'I am the Way, the Resurrection and the Life' "—but another voice, empty and hollow, "the voice from the depths: 'I am the door forever locked, the road which leads nowhere, the lie, the everlasting dark!'[26] (Cf. pp. 216-224.)

It is the tragedy at world's end. And is Jesus here in no sense addressing it? "Heaven and earth shall pass away: but my words shall not pass away." What if that were the point, and in such fashion as that nothing else is! He himself was to be the only sign of his kingly rule. Would you have believed him that day outside the walls of Jerusalem as the dark came on? When the whole huge panorama of life was folded up and laid aside in the archives of God, he would be there, and they should stand before him. They read it that way, anyhow, as the years passed. And they lived it that way. Irrelevant is it? Too confident to be true? Their world fell apart on Calvary, but never mind: he took it all up in his scarred hands, and it was whole again. Past and future, both were always in the present, and nothing ever had been or could be out of control. It was not the chaos that mattered: it was God. There could be no crisis anywhere without that word in the midst of it: "Steady on, lads!" "When these things begin to come to pass. . . ." What things? These things at world's end, your world, my world, anybody's world; in that loneliest spot on earth, what then? Shake your head?—as another has suggested. Shrug? Say nothing is of any use? "Look up!" Why should you? "Your redemption draweth nigh."

And with that we have come to the turning point. The season of Advent is half over. What God has done in Christ to bring us back home from our exile is all laid out in front of us: pressing in so quietly with his outrageous claims, standing so surely where everything that was nailed down has come loose. As the curtain rises now on the third act, we are introduced to the story of how life answers back. That "strongly agnostic note" which has been sounding beneath the surface all along gets itself put at last into words (Matt. 11:2-10). John the Baptist was in prison: and Jesus was not doing at all what he expected the Messiah to do. The situation fairly demanded thunder and lightning and tempest and the Holy Ghost; and here instead was someone who would not even break a bruised reed or put out a smoking candle: doing such obscure, compassionate things; stooping under the little doors of little men, because he was a king, and could afford to stoop; walking among the rich like a beggar, poorer than the foxes that had holes and the birds that had nests. So from prison John sent his messengers, and got the riddle of it clean out into the open: "Art thou he that should come, or do we look for another?" Nowhere in that will you come on the kind of false serenity into which so many bewildered minds try to settle back on Sunday morning at eleven. None of the confidence which in so many sermons struggles to make itself feel at home in the mystery. "Blessed assurance, Jesus is mine!" Or would it be far nearer the Christian gospel to sing, "Blessed disturbance, I am his"?

Will you then try to stuff John's question into your pocket? "Art thou he?" We cannot hide it behind the Creed, or sweep it under the Lord's Prayer. When the odds against such sleight of hand have piled up for a while, you will have to turn all your pockets wrong side out, and move the furniture, and look under the rug, and find out what is really there! No more tricks then, the game is up. And it may be simply because the question itself comes from God, for a man's salvation; so that nobody can shake it off, except to get away from one place where matters are bad to another where they are worse. It was Jesus' incredible manner of doing things that stirred the uneasiness in John's heart and brought it straight to his lips. There was no fan in that hand, no pitchfork, no shovel, to sweep the chaff into the blazing fire. Down there in prison a lonely soul had to come to grips with it. There was nothing but this clear face set unprotected against the storm. Was right to be forever on the scaffold, and wrong forever on the throne? What sense did it make? Said the disillusioned friend I mentioned a little while ago, "Don't ever talk to me again about your Kingdom of God. There is only the devil's kingdom, and I live in it!" But where do you suppose he ever got the notion of that unmeasured difference?

What if the questions that cry out against the prison house of our being here, shouting into the abyss, were God's questions, the only way he has of breaking through? Would a world without them, by any chance, be a world without God? Both the meaning and therefore the value of life lie from moment to moment in responding to the questions it asks and the tasks it sets.[27] A little girl looked up into her father's face. "Are there any churches," she said, "where Negroes are not welcome?" "And the Spirit of God moved upon the face of the waters" (Gen. 1:2). Camus gives this whole sorry business which we call human life just one glance, and dismisses God as the Death-bringer. But what is it that tears him apart and will not let him rest? And Sartre? Dragging them both so close to the Kingdom of God that you can only be staggered by their distance from it? They are as infinitely near as they are infinitely far away. Walt Whitman used to envy the cattle standing around knee-deep in clover. They never tossed about and beat the pillow at night because they had such a hard time to keep from feeling "rejected"; or because they were sure they were leading only "fragmented lives"; or were tormented with the thought that somehow they were strangers in a far country, not knowing quite how they got there. They were cattle, and nobody had told them. Walt Whitman was a poet, and there was a whisper in his soul. From what far-off land, and what sky? None of the answers that try to stand up to the questions men raise will ever serve us. God raises his questions. All the way from the first one, "Adam, . . . where art thou?" to the last one he will ever ask, "What wilt thou that I shall do unto thee?" (Gen. 3:9; Luke 18:41)

When the messengers went back, they took with them no plain spelling out of anything: they were simply to report what they had seen and heard. It was as if Jesus had said, "Tell John to read the prophets again, and this time to read all of what they wrote: not just the half about the fan and the fire, but that other half too with the dawn on its face, about the lame that walk, and the deaf that hear, and the lepers that are cleansed." Then he turned, and in one of the most touching scenes of the New Testament sprang to John's defense. I suppose the elders and the scribes were snickering in their beards. The herald was not making out so well with his heralding any more! He had been so sure. He had flayed them alive with his tongue. There seemed to be a few misgivings now, and a good thing it was! But Jesus would have none of it. He looked around the circle. Full in their teeth he flung it at them: "You think he was a reed shaken by the wind? Or a softling, like the fops who dawdle hours away in kings' houses? I tell you he was a prophet. No man was ever greater than he!" (Cf. pp. 195-304.)

Those gallant words keep ringing in our ears as the Advent season draws to a close. Moving on toward Christmas, the fourth of our lessons brings us back from the end of John's ministry to its beginning, with the voice of one crying in the wilderness (John 1:19-28). Here .at last is the modulation of discord into consonance, of every minor theme into the major harmonies of the Christian gospel: but only after all the straining, twisting, labored movement which has gone before. May it not be that our questions too, without finding answers, shall learn down the toilsome plodding of the years to resolve themselves into the peace which sang its way out of heaven across the fields of Bethlehem? We can see now as we look back that everything which there in prison seemed so wrong was really right, yonder on the hills of Palestine, and altogether as God had planned it. I think it must at last have seemed so to John himself, as he remembered the day he had stood by the river Jordan, a verse from the Old Testament flaming on his lips: "Make straight the way of the Lord." Was there now no shred of that confidence left? The wilderness around him, and the desert where he had preached, had been themselves symbols of humanity's desolation and loneliness: surely he came before he died to understand that the only God he had ever known, the only God Israel had ever known, was the God precisely of that wilderness and that desert. It was there always that God had been at home, to deliver his people. He had known his way out. Up from Egypt they had come, and back across the sands from Babylon. Their very birthright was a God many a weary day expected and many a weary day unknown. "There standeth one among you, whom you know not." John himself had said it of this Jesus, the world's perennial Stranger, its tragedy and its hope. Could it be that his own words would ever quit tugging at the dark, until for him too it grew light again, and the mystery, even there in the shadow of death, came its full round into faith?

In some such way as this, even when the promises of God are being most confidently pronounced, what the Spanish philosopher Unamuno calls in the title of his book "the tragic sense of life"[28] may never be allowed to fade from the picture. Of course Christianity is glad business. Every metaphor Jesus found for it was just another way of saying, "Be of good cheer!" Voices are raised; lamps are lighted; there is the sound of running feet; a farmer has found a treasure; some merchant gets his hands on a priceless pearl. But there is no froth about any of it. There is too much which is quite grim, and cannot be left out. There can be no Pollyanna view of human existence, like the grin of the Cheshire cat which stayed behind after the cat was gone. We are not under bond to set down something on every page of the sermon to be thankful for, especially toward the end. There has to be instead all the way along something that can speak to the "universal pain and tragedy" of the world. We are not asked to be somber. God forbid. Jesus never was. We call him the Man of Sorrows, and it has colored too much of our thinking. He lived out his few years in the very middle of life's sorrows; but if they had succeeded in setting on him the mark which the dying Middle Ages thought they had, it would never have made any sense for him to keep talking of his peace and promising to share it. What is asked of us is that we give a little decent evidence of knowing something of the shadows which steal across the sunlight: but always in this further knowledge, that the only pattern the sunlight can make is with the shadows it throws.

Remember Paul's paean of praise in the first chapter of Colossians: "Giving thanks unto the Father, which hath made us meet to be partakers of the inheritance of the saints in light: who hath delivered us from the power of darkness, and hath translated us into the kingdom of his dear Son. . . ." (vss. 12-13). How shall we understand that? Nobody in the average congregation feels very much like joining in. Neither do you, I dare say, when you announce it as your text. Then why not say so? Has the Christian faith become at last too tame even to tell the truth? Like the lion that prefers his cage, refusing to budge when you want him to leap out and strike down some monstrous evil. He just lies there, with his head between his paws, and looks up at you—"nice lion"! What chance does a tame Christianity have against the unrestrained thrust of a faith like Communism? Take your blood pressure once in a while, if for no other reason than to see how far below the New Testament level it is! Then look more closely into this thing that sent Paul's up to the danger point: "delivered us from the power of darkness." But is it so much lighter anywhere? "Translated us into the kingdom of his dear Son." Does the world look like that kind of place? Until by the simple device of making no effort to understand what he says we avoid what he means!

Have we lost sight of the gospel entirely? Have we never been told what it is supposed to accomplish? Or is it that we are afraid of expecting the wrong thing, and so have fallen into the way of not expecting anything? That is to be worse off than Hamlet was. Said he, "The time is out of joint." We agree with him there. But then he added, "O cursed spite, That ever I was born to set it right!"[29] He at least had an idea that perhaps he could. Many a Christian nowadays is not so sure. To say that we can do anything about anything sounds like a fairly "liberal" view of everything! Besides, Hamlet's effort to usher in the Kingdom of God can scarcely be said to have met with any great success. With Polonius dead, and Ophelia dead, and Laertes dead, and the king dead, and the queen dead, and Hamlet himself dead, just what was it precisely that he set right? But if you ask that question you have not understood life as Shakespeare understood it; and you have not understood tragedy at all. The very essence of tragedy is that you can bear to see the curtain go down on that final scene and know in your heart that this is no failure. Something is right now that was wrong before: something profound in the universe that was worth all the waste.

What we need to understand is how far more deeply and truly it was that way on Calvary. Ours is not a world where you can whistle a jaunty tune, as if every story were bound to have your kind of happy ending, and everything at last could be put away on a tidy shelf. It is a world, since Jesus of Nazareth died of it and rose again, where tragedy and triumph are so interwoven that nobody can ever disentangle them any more. Whoever does not realize that has to be told. We come on it in some of our hymns. "Before Jehovah's awful throne"—now see how altogether incongruous the next line sounds: "Ye nations, bow with sacred joy." The awful throne and the sacred joy, do they then belong together? And what of those stately verses, "Judge eternal, throned in splendor, Lord of lords and King of kings, with Thy living fire of judgment Purge this land of bitter things; Solace all its wide dominion With the healing of Thy wings." The fire and the solace, the purge and the healing! Who can separate them now? The goodness and the severity of God (Rom. 11:22), the beauty and the terror of life; this madness down here caught up and held fast by that majesty up there, and by the splendor of a love that "spares not itself or its object or any of the obstacles that stand in the way." "Who hath delivered us from the power of darkness, and hath translated us into the kingdom of his dear Son."

Paul got excited about things as they were, in the face of things as they looked. He got excited about the sheer effrontery of the gospel, and about how gallantly a man could lose who was on the winning side. Life hurled its defiance at him, as one day a rough, unyielding block of marble hurled its defiance at Michelangelo. Michelangelo carved out of it his David. Paul carved out of the present God's future by a power that was not his own. "Out of three sounds," says Browning, to "frame, not a fourth sound, but a star."[30] Or perhaps a host of angels, "eager eyed, with hair thrown back, and wings put crosswise on their breasts, choir above choir, face to face uplifted"![31] So did the song grow on the apostle's lips; and his is the only continuing song any man will ever sing. "O the depth of the riches both of the wisdom and knowledge of God! how unsearchable are his judgments, and his ways past finding out!" (Rom. 11:33) That joy was sired in pain. The ecstasy was like some sound of agony wrung from him. The triumph was over the tragedy, not out of it. He knew how deep and dark the shadows are; but he knew the Light that casts them! Such a gospel, with its ultimate affirmations, is strangely fitted to address the ultimate negations of our time.[32] It never suffers that diminution of power which inevitably comes of seeming altogether too confident to be true. Its kiss of peace is never the kiss of death.

But there still remains the third charge, that all too often the Christian gospel is both represented and understood as something far "too easy to be true." Lacking not only the "agnostic note" but "the note of austerity" as well, it seems at last to be anything but the scandal it is, a field of battle, the "good news" of a God who stands "against the needs of society and against the aspirations of the human heart."[33] Rather it seems, what of all things else it is not, an impertinence, which is to say an irrelevance, a field all over buttercups and daisies; and that in a world where realities are far too harsh to be dispelled by either Democrats or Republicans, liberals or conservatives, gathered for prayer: they have to be assailed, and by something much more radical and revolutionary than "religious ideas."[34] "The kingdom of God is at hand" (Mark 1:15). Whether or not the pulpit will "heed the rumble" of that "distant drum" is being set down now on the pages of history.

IV

Preaching as a
Radical Transaction

The sound of the trumpet. . . . II Samuel 6:15

To think of preaching as a radical transaction is to think of it in other than usual terms. It is not commonly assumed that the modern pulpit actually succeeds in getting at "the root of the matter." Preachers are under almost irresistible pressure from their congregations to become counselors, managers of an important community enterprise, administrators of a highly organized and going concern dedicated to the spiritual, social, and cultural improvement and welfare of mankind, both locally and nationally; while the magnitude of the demands made on them is matched only by the ludicrous inadequacy of what is provided by way of resource, in finance and personnel: so that the Sunday menu is likely to consist largely of half-hour homilies on handicaps and happiness. There is no time for anything else; and often enough to constitute a frightening conspiracy against the pulpit, there is comparatively little desire for anything else. The most vocal members of a congregation are likely to want that, or at any rate to think they do; they have been known to ask for it—otherwise sermons are much too hard to understand—and to complain when they fail to get it, citing the Reverend

Mr. So-and-So, whose church is crowded. At times it would seem that the most common charges being brought against the gospel are not at all that what is being said from the pulpit is "too small to be true," "too confident to be true," or "too easy to be true," but precisely the opposite: not small enough, not confident enough, not easy enough. And all this, be it said, in a day when propaganda, which is only another name for "preaching," has become the most effective of all weapons in the struggle for global supremacy!

Certain it is, nevertheless, that when preaching is understood to be what it properly is, it is bound to take on the character of a radical transaction; simply because in no other way can it represent the essentially radical nature of the Christian gospel. There can be no toning down of the lively Word of a living God, no softening of the "note of austerity," that note which is the very signature of all truth. For all truth is rigorous and demanding. It accords with unalterable reality, and will not willingly lend itself to compromise, or pass over lightly any inconsistency. It cannot be bent, or twisted, or fashioned to suit some whim. In the Biblical account of Israel's history, here precisely was to be found the difference between the worship of Baal and the worship of Yahweh: the nature gods were thought to be pliable; it was soon discovered that nature's God was not. It may well have been that Israel's desire for a king, to be like the nations around her, was to the mind of Samuel, if we may speak in such terms at all, the dreadful symbol of her desire for some kind of pliability at the center of her world. Truth is unyielding. It is not content with what appears to be the case; it is on the lookout for what actually is the case. Truth probes beyond the symptoms to the disease. It is radical in the sense that it gets to "the bottom of things"; and in the Bible "the bottom of things" is whatever is conformable to the will and purposes of God. That will is not difficult, as if a man by strenuous effort might do it: it is in its holiness impossible, beyond all effort. The purposes neither relent nor excuse: they require and exact. God never says "Please." Life never says it. There is very little of the "ought," or the "should," or "it would be a good thing if you would." There is only the indicative of what the world is as God made it, followed by the imperative that under penalty of death commands us away from what we have done *with* it to what *he* has done *about* it!

1. THE OFFENSE OF THE GOSPEL

To maintain therefore at New Testament levels the note of austerity in preaching, it is necessary first of all, and of absolute necessity, lest everything we say seem altogether "too easy to be true," to quit covering over the "offense" of the gospel in the effort to "do people good."[1] Nothing can do them good without disturbing them. And nothing will disturb them to any lasting effect unless it disturbs them deeply. It is therefore of less value than is commonly supposed week in and week out simply to address those needs which lie around on the surface of human life, needs of which everybody is conscious: how to keep from feeling lonely; what it takes to be brave; the way to bear up under disappointment; the secret of success. Jesus said astonishingly little about any of that. Instead, he addressed himself to those needs, so often *un*conscious, which lie at the root of a man's sense of bewilderment, alienation, and anxiety. He was forever getting farther in and deeper down; and that is never likely to be painless. The Pharisees had "religion," and he told them that they were without God. They looked down on the sinner and the outcast; and he said that the publicans and harlots would get into the Kingdom of God ahead of them. Precisely in the day when they were at long last becoming intensely missionary, he told them that they were only making others twofold more the children of hell than they were themselves. It was hard to take! His own followers wanted happiness and prosperity—who is it that wants anything else?—and he spoke to them of the meek and the merciful and the pure in heart. They had heard it said of old time, Thou shalt not kill, Thou shalt not commit adultery, Thou shalt love thy neighbor. It made sense. That needed to be said. But he talked to them also about not being angry, about never looking on a woman to lust after her, about loving their enemies. Forgiving seven times, then? He said seventy times seven. Had they no rightful claim on God's favor? Said he, God "maketh his sun to rise on the evil and on the good, and sendeth rain on the just and the unjust" (Matt. 5:45). All of it was deep enough down to offend, and far enough in to hurt: in where the quick is, and the needs that have to be stirred into consciousness before any need at all except the body's can be met, or life can issue out of death. Proximate answers to proximate concerns are altogether too often thoroughly fraudulent answers. There are no pre-fabricated substitutes for the disturbing gospel of a redeeming God.

And there are quite a few on the market, at the shopping centers. As we have seen, morals will not do. "What *will* they do?" is no doubt a question which needs to be opened up; but first it would be well to inquire how we can lay in a supply. Exhortation can never manage that, or advice, or pastoral counseling *en masse*—a recent, and to me a particularly unfortunate, definition of preaching. No amount of "thinking," however "positive," will ever suffice; nothing that offers itself as a solution of our difficulties or as an easing of our burdens: there is not much chance that any of it will outlast the next storm.

And we cannot even "make do," as the British say, with what many a time masquerades as Christian love—something that has to be spelled *l-o-o-v-e*, until it drips with sweetness. Most of us *l-o-o-v-e* to sing George Matheson's hymn, but we do not choose to come to it by way of George Matheson's experience. He was blind, and the woman he loved jilted him because of it. "O Love that wilt not let me go." It had sought him through pain, and he dared not close his eyes to it. It had to do with a flickering torch, and a cross that lifted up his head when life's glory was in the dust—because he had laid it there, not just because it was bound to come there in the end anyhow! So does the love of the New Testament come stalking in as "the lord of terrible aspect," in the phrase of C. S. Lewis: austere, like that gaunt symbol of death on a lonely hill; forbidding, in its own way, as it was to the psalmist who wrote, "There is forgiveness with thee, that thou mayest be feared" (Ps. 130:4). Whatever it is that God has shed abroad in our hearts (Rom. 5:5), it is by no means simply a gracious addition to life, to make living more tolerable. Without it life blows up, says St. Paul in the thirteenth chapter of First Corinthians. The tongues of men and of angels become as sounding brass and tinkling cymbals; prophecy and knowledge, faith and martyrdom, add up to nothing.

In short, life is a nettle, and when a man lays hold of it he has to take the sting and all, the peril with the promise. Here is the "offense" of the gospel: not its wonder stories, which many would dismiss, and so have done with the whole fantastic business; but its persistent upsetting of our religious applecarts. The real threat to human life lies in trying to have done with that. Mark Twain once said—whether or not he meant

it as we like to assume he did—that what troubled him about the Bible
was not what he failed to understand, but what he understood quite
clearly and could not stomach. It is not only with what we like that we
have to do; we have to do with what all too often we very flatly do not
like.

Partly for this reason, perhaps, apologetic sermons seem to me measurably suspect.[2] They set out to answer questions, and the Bible sets
out over and over again to provoke questions. Apologetic sermons assume
that the truth of God has to dig in somewhere and fight for its life, so
that some few people at least may accept it; the Bible assumes that
God's truth has a way of speaking for itself, in its own defense.
Apologetic sermons take it for granted that a sound rational approach
will help a man on toward faith; and life seems to honor the theory
more often in the breach than in the observance. Which is not of course
to say that faith is irrational: it is to say that strangely enough, and
frequently enough to be terrifying—Nazism and Communism have
borne their witness to it—the springs of action lie not only within
but beyond reason. It is to say that faith is what someone has called
meta-rational; because it has its being in the realm not just of the mind
but of persons.[3]

Yet there is no doubt at all that apologetic sermons have to be
preached: if for nothing else, then to undermine the false presuppositions
which condition not only the so-called modern mind against the gospel,
but often enough the so-called Christian mind as well. Efforts to prove
something are beside the point: nobody wants to lose an argument,
or see the preacher win one! Something has to happen—there is no
other goal for preaching: a meeting has to take place; the sermon has
no other aim, except that the underbrush may have to be cleared away
before there can be any meeting. And that—to mix my metaphor—
may ruffle somebody's fur; but it is always possible, it may even
be necessary, for such a one, like the proverbial cat that was being
stroked the wrong way, to turn around! Before the security, the insecurity; before the planting, the rooting out; before the building, the
shaking of the foundations!

"The preacher's task," writes Raymond Stamm,[4] "is not so much to
show man a way out of his predicament. It is rather to confront him
with the radical nature of his predicament. Man tends to appraise his

problem in terms of maladjustment to life," or in terms of health or personality difficulties or economic needs. "He is seeking peace, plenty, . . . happiness, and if he cannot find these elsewhere, he may turn to God as their source." "Why Not Try God?" was the title of a book written many years ago by Mary Pickford. In classic, devastating rebuttal Halford Luccock put the caustic question, "Why not try aspirin?" The God with whom the Bible brings us face to face, continues Dr. Stamm, "is not the source of rest, but the cause of unrest; not the simple purveyor" of life's goods. Instead, he is "the one who often invades our lives by smashing" life's goods; "not the kindly Father of our dreams who gently caresses our hands, but the God and Father of our Lord Jesus Christ whose only Son had to learn obedience by the things he suffered, and who often leads us on the same path toward sonship." Said the Lord to Ananias, sending him to the Saul who had been blinded by that blazing light on the Damascus road, ". . . he is a chosen vessel unto me, . . . and . . . I will shew him how great things he must suffer for my name's sake" (Acts 9:15-16).

It may well go without saying, and perhaps it should, that what the gospel always has in mind is "to comfort the distressed." What may not go so well without saying is that it never undertakes that role prematurely. It is equally concerned "to distress the comfortable," that our grief may "grieve on universal bones."[5] Jesus never occupied himself with the way out. One could think him intolerably cavalier about that. To him it was the way through that mattered. It was not as with us the problems of living that loomed so large; as Bonhoeffer somewhere points out, it was the problem of life with which he was primarily concerned. Novelists write about that, dramatists write about it, poets write about it.[6] Tennessee Williams has his *Cat on the Hot Tin Roof:* it wants to jump off, but where? Sartre hangs his *No Exit* sign over everything that once looked like a door. It is this ultimate bewilderment, this ultimate alienation, this ultimate anxiety that the gospel addresses; and the gospel addresses it by increasing it! Freud, with a distaste which almost amounted to nausea, called religion an "irrational delusion": man's assumption that he is invulnerable, immortal, backed up by the Almighty.[7] But where in the Bible is that? If he is backed up, he is backed up into a corner: to quote William Temple, "his finite self before the Infinite, the pollution of his life before the Holy, the creature in all its utter dependence before the Creator."[8] Who wants to face that? Who likes to look it squarely between the eyes? Does it seem to you, when you turn to God, that you are coming home to some dear shelter? Or does it seem that you are setting foot on the shores of an undiscovered land, perilous and untamed?

The fourteenth chapter of John is for many the favorite chapter of their favorite Gospel; that and the tenth, about the Good Shepherd who knows his sheep and calls them by name: favorites because they are so comforting, and induce such peace of mind. "Let not your heart be troubled": softly the words steal down the centuries from the quietness of an upper room, on the night before the crucifixion. But do we have the right to hear and appropriate them? The disciples had. They were troubled as few of us are: troubled by the gospel itself, its perils and its cost. The early Church had a right to hear and appropriate what Jesus had said about leading out his sheep and going before them: that little flock, scattered among wolves. What right have we to listen? Do we know anything at all which could possibly be worth such a promise, to justify it? Do we so bitterly look for a shepherd and a fold? Or can we manage pretty well on our own? Does Christ so trouble us that we indeed need to hear him say, "Let not your heart be troubled" (John 14:1)? A student once suggested in his sermon that we were in no imaginable way ready for that. The only start any of us could make would have to be like this: "Let your heart be troubled: ye believe in God!" That would be reason enough for being troubled. Paul thought so too. In the eleventh chapter of Second Corinthians he tells of his perils (vs. 26): "Perils of waters, perils of robbers, perils by mine own countrymen, perils by the heathen, perils in the city, perils in the wilderness, perils in the sea, perils among false brethren." It was a long list; but not complete. He had already told them of another peril. All along he had stood in it: "lest that by any means, when I have preached to others, I myself should be a castaway" (I Cor. 9:27). He was in peril of God! The only thing that shielded him was the coming of a child in a manger, and the death of a man on a hill! And that did not exactly ease the situation. There was a sense in which it made everything heartbreakingly more difficult.

In C. S. Lewis' novel *Perelandra,* a good and respectable man is one day confronted by a presence unknown and with the aura of holiness about it. "I felt sure," he said, "that the creature was what we call 'good,' but I wasn't sure whether I liked 'goodness' so much as I had supposed. This is a very terrible experience. As long as what you are afraid of is something evil, you may still hope that the good may come to your rescue. But suppose you struggle through to the good and find that it also is dreadful? How if food itself turns out to be the very thing you can't eat, and home the very place you can't live, and your very comforter the person who makes you uncomfortable? Then, indeed, there is no rescue possible: the last card has been played. For a second or two I was nearly in that condition. Here at last was a bit of that world from beyond the world, which I had always supposed that I loved and desired, breaking through and appearing to my senses: and I didn't like it, I wanted it to go away. I wanted every possible distance, gulf, curtain, blanket, and barrier to be placed between it and me."[9] It is quite possible that we never hear the gospel until we have been made uneasy by it: until we have ferreted out in every case not so much what it is that pleases us as what it is that offends us. After that, we may be ready for the pardon. The comfort may then have something to comfort, and the promise something to address—something ready to gird its loins, with a battle cry on its lips!

2. CONFLICT, DEMAND, CHALLENGE

But thus far we have done little more than break the ground. To maintain at New Testament levels this note of austerity we have not only to quit hiding out of sight the "offense" of the gospel in our effort to "do people good"; we have also to take serious account of the tumult which the gospel provokes, of the claims which it lays on us with an imperious hand, and of whatever possibilities there are on our part of creative response. It may seem at first glance that the only effect of all we have been saying, and of all which is still to be said, could well be to make the "good news" of God appear to be even less credible and more remote than it was before, and so of little immediate significance for these lives that we are living. But that risk has to be run. There is no other way of uncovering in its dimension of depth what the New Testament has to say about human life and human destiny.

Would it be safe to assert at once that the Christian pulpit in the

United States, because of our misconceptions of what the gospel is and what the gospel is for, has through the years been mightily busy cutting down the cost both of the Christian faith and of the Christian life? What God did cost him all he had; and one reads nowhere, from Matthew to the Revelation, that the price for us has been marked down to

> Little drops of water, little grains of sand

with the notion that after all they do indeed

> Make the mighty ocean, and the pleasant land!

Or to

> Little acts of kindness, little deeds of love

because they will no doubt help to

> Make this earth a heaven, like the heaven above!

In how many sermons does that seem to be what it comes to?—wrapping up a Care package, writing a letter to somebody, never pushing anybody around in the rush hour or kicking the dog; something we think is little, but God thinks is big; something that for all its loveliness is just a shade "too easy to be true." "So likewise ye, when ye shall have done all those things which are commanded you, say, We are unprofitable servants" (Luke 17:10). And you will be right!

If we are to be kept, then, from whittling down the imperatives of God, if preaching is to become for us what it fundamentally is, a thoroughly radical transaction, there are several major convictions which we shall need to formulate and hold fast. One is that the gospel comes to us not just as history, but as conflict. Another, that it comes to us not alone as succor, but as the succor which is inseparable from demand, and in such a way that in the demand itself is the succor. And still another, that therefore it comes to us not primarily as solace, an invitation to patient reliance upon God—faith is more than that!—but primarily as challenge, the summons to ceaseless participation in God's creative and redeeming act, as he shares with us his own dangerous life, moving day in and day out toward the accomplishment in us and through us of his eternal purpose. "We then, as workers together with him, . . ." (II Corinthians 6:1).

a. The Gospel as History and Conflict

First, the gospel not just as history but also as conflict. For a moment let me return to something which has already been said.[10] The preacher is not an equal sign between the past and the present. He is not pointing to something back there, so that his people may apply it up here. He is not a go-between, commissioned to move back and forth from B.C. to A.D. and thence to Q.E.D. The sermon begins by announcing that John in prison was bewildered, and so are we; it continues by pointing out that he took his trouble directly to Jesus, and so must we; and comes to its climax by reminding us that he got only an indirect answer, so do we. If anybody wants to listen, his mind has to swing from the first century to the twentieth and back again, like the heads of the spectators at a tennis match! The Bible is the preacher's book, not simply because it is the story of what happened once, but also because in it and through it and by way of it that very thing is happening now. Before we ever begin to write or to listen, we are to take our stand immovably in the present: "As it was in the beginning, is now, and ever shall be"![11] We are dealing with a vast kaleidoscope, events in history which transcend history. The Word of God addresses itself to particular people at particular times in particular situations; and we dare not lose sight of that particularity. But the historical particularity of the Word in any given case, even in the case of the resurrection of our Lord, lacks its profoundest significance when it becomes anything less than contemporaneous fact. "Buried with him by baptism into death . . . we shall also live with him" (Rom. 6:4,8). It is true that Paul was writing in Romans to a Jewish-Christian congregation during the early years of the second half of the first century; but it is also true that what he says is as timely in any century and in any congregation as a neighbor's gossip over the back fence. If the historical sense were the only sense, there would be little sense in anybody's turning to the Bible, and Paul's letter to the Romans would be a dead letter!

With our linear and horizontal minds, every time some Scripture is read in our hearing we find ourselves obsessed either with some distant future—like the end of the world, which we suppose is not due yet for quite a while, so why worry about it?—or with the distant past, which was a long time ago, and is pretty well finished now, so why worry about that? God never works in any such fashion any more. Could there be any surer way of laying down, as in many a Sunday-School class, a very hotbed for atheism? The chances are that even to the adult congregation very little seems to be happening where they are. If it is not somewhere in front, so that everybody can postpone coming to grips with God, it is somewhere behind, and everybody can work out a fairly peaceful coexistence with it. Whole paragraphs in the Bible begin with some such words as "And it came to pass in those days. . . ." —like a fairy story: "Once upon a time. . . ." And from that moment on there are very few who are likely to be upset. Because Christianity is rooted in history, people think they can bury it there. And preachers sometimes help! Countless matters that have to do with Bible and Church, matters which are proper for research, and more than proper, may have astonishingly little bearing when brought into the pulpit. Ronald Sleeth tells of a young Oxford graduate who at the high point of his sermon startled his congregation of charwomen and chambermaids with the rhetorical question, "Some of you are probably saying, 'So much for Cyril of Jerusalem, but what about Theodore of Mopsuestia?' "[12]

Scripture is the record of God's revelation; when it is nothing more, even in the house of its friends, it is as lifeless as the blackened stump of a Douglas fir.[13] The preacher himself may not indeed have such a backward-looking view of the gospel, yet actually convey it as he elaborates the ancient stories, and by so simple a thing as his persistent use of the past tense—prompted perhaps by his desire to speak from the authority of Scripture. I sometimes wonder to what extent this is responsible for the near-hypnosis which seems to spread over men and women in church, a kind of acquiescence with what is going on in their lives and in the world, contenting itself by shaking its head and noting with alarm. Is it because on the strength of what God once did, when he was really taking a hand in things, before he went back home and pulled down the shades, they have allowed themselves to be domesticated in this strange place, which seems so utterly deserted now and indifferent —when it takes time off, that is, from being viciously hostile. There is an Oriental parable about a flock of sheep owned by a magician. They all know that he is after their skin, and try to run away; but he persuades them at last that they are immortal: it will be good for them to lose their skin some time, but it will not happen soon, so that there is nothing to be disturbed about at the moment; besides, they are not really sheep at all, they are lions, they may even be magicians. With the result that they settle down once more to graze quietly in the meadow.[14] Like some Sunday morning congregation listening to a sermon! (See another context, p. 260.)

Observe, by way of contrast, how it is in the theater. Everything is alive and moving. Whatever else you find there, you will not find any bogging down in history. There is a play written by a German pastor, Günther Rutenborn, just after the last war, called *The Sign of Jonah*.[15] Nobody in the audience but plays his own part in it; and nobody can tell if the scene of the great trial that is being held is laid in Nineveh or in Berlin, in Rome, or Babylon, or Chicago, or New York. Jonah is someone you met in the subway, or in a submarine, or in the belly of a whale. Every man is that man of the street who is so sure he has done nothing wrong. Who could be responsible for all that has gone so terribly sour in the world? The merchant with his suitcase, the mother who has lost her children in the war, the Queen of the South? Or the government? Maybe that was it! Not once does it seem necessary to say in so many words how much everything here is like everything there. In one way or another, everybody here was also there: what was happening then is happening now. And so, since nobody is guilty of the horror of human history, the only thing left is to hold God responsible for it. Let him pay. Let him become man, a wanderer on the earth, homeless, hungry, thirsty; born of a woman, born a despised Jew, the misery of a tortured creation in his ears day and night. The judge looks around the court. Even the archangels that are present offer no protest. Gabriel will not speak for God. He will go instead to a virgin whose name is Mary, and tell her that she is to bear a child. Michael will order the hosts of heaven to leave him without protection, to strengthen him only from afar, that he might the longer suffer. Raphael will be there when he dies, and stand by his tomb. That was the verdict. The gavel fell, and the judge got down from the bench, because he had condemned God. Then he followed the archangels off the stage— because he *was* God!

So it is in *Macbeth, Hamlet, Othello, Lear.* You would not think of saying that they live across the street from you, or down the block, or around the corner: they live at your house, the whole motley crew of them. You are Macbeth, Hamlet, Othello, Lear: not historically—any numbskull knows better than that—but existentially, if I may use the blessed word! Shakespeare took that for granted. He began by taking it for granted. Why do we keep forgetting it? Christianity is a drama.[16] It is God's unrelenting assault on everything that sets its face against him. It is his ceaseless invasion of the world, with every man's name in the cast of characters.

And this is precisely to say that the moment it comes our length, it comes inevitably as conflict. Why on earth are there so few signs about that a battle is going on? Maybe a skirmish here and there. A little hostility in the ranks. But not the tramp of an army, or the shock of troops. Noise, perhaps. There was a great deal of noise once around a golden calf. Joshua thought that war had broken out in the camp. But Moses, on his way down from the mount of God, said, "It is not the voice of them that shout for mastery, neither is it the voice of them that cry for being overcome: but the noise of them that sing do I hear" (Exod. 32:18). The notion that the Christian gospel is at heart warfare takes too many of us by surprise, though we have had warning of it aplenty. Remember the Lord Jesus, how he said, "Think not that I am come to send peace on earth: I came not to send peace, but a sword . . . to set a man at variance against his father, . . . the daughter against her mother. . . . He that loveth father or mother more than me . . . and he that taketh not his cross, . . . is not worthy of me. . . ." After that he speaks of the finding of life which is losing—we shall have only what we forfeit; and of the losing of life which is finding—we shall save only what we squander! (Matt. 10:34-39)

And what he expected of others, Jesus himself endured. It began with the first act of his public ministry. On a Sabbath day, in the synagogue at Nazareth, he was asked to read the lesson. It was probably the appointed lesson; possibly he chose it himself. At any rate he found the place where a prophet centuries dead had spoken of Israel's restoration from the long and weary exile in Babylon. Luke uses the story as a frontispiece to his gospel (Luke 4:14-30). "The Spirit of the Lord is upon me," so the ancient verses ran; "because he hath annointed me. . . ." But clearly something was wrong. Neighbors began to glance at each other uneasily. Holy Scripture was coming alive, and Holy

Scripture had no right to do that! This carpenter's son was thinking of himself as he read. And it was strange language, that he should take it upon his lips. For a little while they "wondered at the gracious words which proceeded out of his mouth." But because it had never occurred to the poor among them that they were poor, and because the captives were quite sure they were free, he had to tell them things that filled them with wrath. He had to tell them that God could do nothing for their famine: so had it been in the days of Elijah, who had been sent not to any of the widows of Israel, but to a woman of Sidon. He had to tell them that God could do nothing for the leprosy which was eating its way into their flesh: so had it been in the days of Elisha, when only Naaman the Syrian was cleansed. And nobody can say that safely, not to people who have an idea that they are thoroughly at home with the Almighty, that they already know him in a book and already have him in a ritual. They "rose up, and thrust him out of the city." They were like well men, in one of Karl Barth's phrases, trying to get rid of poison or sick men fighting off medicine:[17] life was one way and death was the other. What to do, but lead him to "the brow of the hill whereon their city was built, that they might cast him headlong"?

I have read that in one of Von Schlegel's plays the curtain rises to show the inside of a theater where another audience is waiting for the curtain to rise. When it does, a second such scene is disclosed; then a third. By which time the original audience begins to grow uneasy and looks around to see if perhaps it too is on the stage. So it is always, both in the Old Testament and in the New. It is we who are in danger, not just the scribes and Pharisees. They were trying to live by their religion when they died of it! What shall we die of? "Maranatha!" "Even so, come, Lord Jesus!" (Rev. 22:20) Only a fool will say that if all he wants is to go on as he is. How will it be when a man finds out that this Bible is a constant knocking at the door which makes all his tinkering with life look silly? "Where are you?" it keeps asking; and if you are somewhere in the middle between right and wrong, it keeps needling you to take sides, even when you have to run the risk of mistaking the side: God can handle that, while he can only spue out of his mouth what is neither cold nor hot (Rev. 3:16). In the morning when you get up, it wants to know what you will be straining at today, in what prison. At noon, "Tell me your name, bruised as you are!" It has to find out if it can! And at night, "How is it with you now? Poor and blind?" People will fight it all right, when you let it speak. It makes trouble for every one of us, out of bounds as it usually is, with something to say about our attitude to Russia, which is none of its business; or maybe down in the shops, instead of up in the office where it belongs; or over there putting in its word for somebody whose skin is not at all like God's!—or does God have any skin?

It makes trouble even at Christmas time. Matthew says, "When Herod the king had heard these things, he was troubled, and all Jerusalem with him" (Matt. 2:3). I wonder if it should bother us more than it does? The candlelight service is so lovely. The carols, we say, are "out of this world." They are; perhaps too far out! Berlioz, the French composer, heard the tumult, and gave it over to nervous wood winds and deep bass viols: the lonely night, sleepless, or all disturbed with dreams; the tramp of armed guards on the bare, hard earth; the cries of women and children. Brueghel shows you on his canvas the sheer terror of it, as if it were all out yonder on the streets of his own little Flemish town, among the neighbors: the cruel, grinning faces of the soldiers; doors being battered in; running, stumbling figures, in the very midst of that slaughter of the innocents. How ever can we get it out of its wrappings, and the tinsel, so that it may come alive? Not part of it, all of it! God would have no trouble with Christmas at all if we had more!

In Mr. Auden's *Christmas Oratorio*[18] Herod sits on his throne bewildered, trying to figure it out. He has tidied up his bit of a kingdom, and it looks quite safe at last. You could get a decent lunch in the drugstore at reasonable prices. Truck drivers could go without their guns now. There was a heavy tax on playing cards and ouija boards, and all such. But the common people refused, in spite of everything, to come to their senses. Day after day they wanted God to leave his heaven and come down to earth: to be their uncle, forsooth, or play chess with Grandfather, baby-sit perhaps, help Willy with his algebra, see to it that Muriel should have a handsome naval officer as her partner at the dance! It was all nonsense. If God did come, what a trick that would be to play on everybody! Then a man would have to kick Poetry downstairs, and be a long sight better than any man could be! O dear, what had he done to deserve this? He was a Democrat. He had never meant to hurt anybody. He brushed his teeth twice a day. Why did this troublesome infant have to be born around here? Why not somewhere else?

And it begins to dawn on you that you cannot call Herod by his own name any longer! This wretched child has come to disturb all of us. He wants to send us out on this most disappointing of all the quests in which humanity has ever been engaged—and the most exhilarating! He shows me that self of mine, until I can hardly stand to live with it; and when I am willing at last to get out and away toward the star, he talks to me about peace—the peace of sin forgiven, and I still sin! About joy, the joy of being forever uneasy, because he has taught me to care, and nothing anywhere is as he would like it to be! And about hope, enough of it anyhow to throw up my head, no matter what happens, and try to sing with St. Francis some Canticle of the Sun:

> All creatures of our God and King
> Lift up your voice and with us sing
> Alleluia![19]

Yeats has a poem about a rough beast somewhere in the desert, with its slow thighs, and its blank and pitiless stare—slouching toward Bethlehem to be born![20]

b. The Gospel as Succor and Demand

So does the gospel come to us not just as history but as conflict. That is one of the major convictions which we have to formulate and hold fast if preaching is to be a radical transaction and the gospel is to be kept from seeming "cheap," far "too easy to be true." Another is this, closely related, yet different enough to call for separate, if briefer treatment: We are to understand that the gospel comes to us not just as succor, but as the succor which is inseparable from demand, rescue and requirement at once, each indeed implying and presupposing the other. The odds are against my being able to put it bluntly enough. Perhaps I should come right out and say that even in our thinking the demand which *is* the succor has to be given priority. Partly because the emphasis is so commonly the other way around, and partly because all through the Bible and human experience there are such obvious limitations on the help God can give a man.

Once more take the Christmas gospel. There is no need yet to leave it. Go out where the shepherds are and listen: "Unto you is born this day in the city of David a Saviour, which is Christ the Lord" (Luke 2:11). A Savior is someone who, when you are quite beyond helping yourself, snatches you from the jaws of death, or of whatever it is that threatens your life. And the New Testament makes a great deal of our being unable to help ourselves. It tries to be true to the facts. But nowhere does it suggest that there is any magic about what God does, that a man is not called on himself to do anything at all. Apparently God will not save him *without* his help. The help given him when he is helpless is the help that helps him to help himself. In the very word "Savior" which the angels used, there is an insistent moral connotation, coming down through the turbulent history of Israel, as over and over again God her Savior, though never without her own agony and obedience, delivered her out of the hands of her enemies. It may even be, as B. S. Easton suggests,[21] that the use of the title "Savior" as applied to Christ came more fully into its own as "a protest against the abuse of the word as an honorific epithet in the emperor-cult": not Caesar, with the power no man could share, but Christ was the Savior, and the power a man had from him to struggle through, at whatever cost, out of the bondage of sin into freedom. The succor was itself demand.

The real "scandal" of the gospel, therefore, lies not in the realm of the miraculous but in the realm of the moral.[22] The tension is not so much between what is "within history" and what is "beyond history," between the "this worldly image" and the "otherworldly truth"; the tension is between the will of God, which is both within history and beyond, and the will of man, which is solidly enough within history to continue doing a great deal of damage! The angels, the carols, the shepherds, the wise men; the inn, the mother, and the little child—how much of it is prose and how much of it is poetry? Believing never will be simply dependent on knowing the answer to that question. What is going on here in Bethlehem is for the most part well beyond the reach of evidence. And we should be content to have it so. The one thing with which we may not be content is the sheer beauty of it. It is a beauty that demands something of us! As far as we are concerned, the whole thing may just as well be legend, "myth" sure enough, and in the pejorative sense of the word, a child's book of verse illustrated —unless it lays its imperious claim on us. That happens precisely at the point of God's choice to become man, his preference for the commonplace and the humble, his self-manifestation, in a love that comes not as Lord but as servant, and so condemns me. If Jesus had come as Lord, the Jews might well have received him; they rejected him because he came as a servant. And that irks me too. I know what such a God would have of me, what he requires of this self that struggles to usurp his place. I want to draw the line at uncouth peasants and smelly stables. I'd rather take it all out in distant and nostalgic moods: "Silent night, holy night!" Until one day this incredible thing confronts me and actually tries to turn my world upside down. Then I have to do some crucifying on my own—or else! Or else? God pity us, do we have even any desire to be like him? I have read of Virginia, the martyr of Carthage, and how with great hooks they tore her flesh from the bones; and I remember the song I used to sing, without the foggiest notion of what it meant, "I want to be more like Jesus!"—that One who is still the great revealer of all the facts about us, of the good, which is so much worse than we thought, and of the evil, which is so much more desperate than we dreamed! Rudolf Bultmann knows where it hurts, and calls Jesus "God's conflict with us": he asks too much!

Or take Easter. What is Easter for? To comfort us all, and make of death, that "last enemy" of which Paul speaks, a friend? It is the life-denying religions that think of death as a friend. Christianity is a life-affirming faith, as Judaism was, and knows death to be the enemy of life. Every effort to represent it in any other role is not only sub-Christian, it is anti-Christian: covering it over with flowers to make it look pretty—partly in tenderness, and partly no doubt in the effort to get away from the ugly facts—keeping all our funeral processions on side streets when we can, and having the chimes ring out, as in Evelyn Waugh's *The Loved One*, when the cars enter the massive gates of the cemetery, "The Indian Love Song"![23] It is not the function of Easter to underscore the notion that we are immortal. We are not. No use trying to marshal the arguments which would seem to support it. In the Biblical faith, when we are dead, we are dead all over. It is God who raises us to life again, by his own mighty act, even as he raised Jesus from the dead. There was an illustration once, in an otherwise excellent sermon, which pictured death as a kind of swinging door at the end of life's corridor, and by so much seemed to me something less than Christian. Illustrations often are. A little girl, who always came from school through a graveyard, even on dark winter evenings, was asked why, and if she was never afraid. "Oh no," she answered, "Never! It's just the shortest way home—that's all!"

Easter means rather that God is the God of life and death. It is the affirmation of true life, at the expense of what we call life, which is itself too often a denial of life. The Resurrection sets me in a world which is not self-contained, but open, and draughty, with the winds of eternity blowing through it: a world far too small for my loyalties, where I am not to be left comfortably alone, to find in shoving its furniture about and running its errands the reason for my being here. Now I have to pick up all the stuff from life's counters, take its goods away from the glare of artificial lights, and look at them in front of an empty tomb with an angel at the door: instead of just holding fast to my bargains without ever seeing how shoddy so many of them are. Mark says that the women "went out quickly, and fled from the sepulchre; . . . for they were afraid" (Mark 16:8). One can understand very simply why he wrote that. You would have been afraid too. But I keep asking myself, "Afraid of what? Afraid of death, or afraid of life?"

Of course there is much about Easter that we like. Elaborate that. Everybody needs to hear it. But never forget what there is about it that we do not like. It opens up vistas that make our world too small, and make us bigger than we seem—no end bigger than most of us would choose to be. To turn from a world that has dwindled and be forced to face a self grown dizzy at being a sudden giant calls for courage.[24] There are still those who talk endlessly of the "inferiority complex." Sermons are preached about it now and then, and about how to be rid of it. The question that keeps intruding itself is whether or not we wish to be rid of it, and to what extent. At times it is most convenient. Why go to church? Nobody will miss you. Why stand out against the evil, there in the office where you work? You are only one in a hundred. Or in the community where you live? You are only one in ten thousand. Or in the state at the polls? You are only one in ten million. As the fraction grows smaller, it grows more comfortable. I have never been able to worry overmuch about a man's fear of being too small. What worries me is our fear of being too great. Is it greatness we want, and everything that goes with it? To live as big as we are, without all these distinctions of color and class? To go the second mile and maybe the third! To forgive seventy times seven? The Easter gospel is a costly gospel because it refuses to let us flee from that, and under the vast Colossus of our civilization be satisfied to find for ourselves the peace of some little grave. The Resurrection gives to life dimensions which we have to either accept or reject: and there will be a kind of suicide either way. Which kind will you choose?

c. The Gospel as Summons and Response

But there is still another major conviction which needs to be made explicit. If the gospel comes to us not just as history but also as conflict, not only as succor but as demand too, then it comes as well not primarily as an invitation to patient reliance upon God, but as a summons to ceaseless participation in his eternal and redemptive purpose. In his second letter to that quarreling little congregation at Corinth, Paul writes, "We then, as workers together with him, beseech you also that ye receive not the grace of God in vain" (6:1). Of all men else the apostle understood that the religion which Jesus had taught and then become was essentially creative. Reinhold Niebuhr once said that the phrase "called to be saints," which Paul so often applied to these scattered groups of Christian men and women, meant that at least they were to be as decent as other people! That, and more than that: they were to know themselves as those who were not simply repairing some breach in the wall, or shoring up the foundations a bit, or patching the roof where the rain came in. Under God they had got their hands on the very substance of things hoped for; they were themselves the evidence of things not seen.

There was no objection, no earthly objection, to anybody's using the Christian faith as a refuge. No apologies had to be offered for it on that score. There are hours when you need shelter, just as there are hours when you need a roof: shelter from the mind's fear and the heart's anguish, from the utter futility and the ultimate despair of a godless world. But there is no hope for the man who goes on supposing that refuge is enough. No nation can stand still, no army can, no soul can, and be safe by fighting off attack. The secret of physical health will scarcely be found in spraying oneself with disinfectants or in the liberal use of germicides. Unless we can get out from behind the defenses we have built, we are done. Christianity is not first and foremost a shelter.

Neither does it shape up very well as a race, though many a hymn calls it that, and the New Testament sometimes speaks of it so. We are not just taking out after heaven, or saintliness of one sort or another: panting along in the wake of some duty we have to discharge, all out of breath chasing down some privilege we are supposed to enjoy, clutching and stumbling every Sunday morning at eleven—and at eight o'clock in the evening too, if we are desperate—after some power that may help us to adjust our lives to certain situations. The Christian religion is not a life-adjustment technique, which assumes that both the questions and the answers are to be found in the situation itself. It is not a situation-overcoming technique, which assumes that the questions posed by the situation are resolved in the answers provided by the Christian faith. It is not a correlating technique which assumes that for any given situation, with the questions it puts, the primary significance of the faith consists in its answering quality.[25] Christianity is not a technique at all. The situation becomes for faith the occasion for both question and answer—the questions which are God's questions, and the answers which lie in the indicatives of his gospel and in the imperatives of his will for our lives. On no other terms can it be profoundly understood that Christianity is intended to create situations which were not there before. It will not play second fiddle to any problem. It is not even the concertmeister. It is the conductor; or better yet, it is the composer and writes the score!

Instead then of extending an invitation to patient reliance upon God, the gospel is designed to provide an outlet for the deepest urge of human life, the urge to make things. Artists have it, and you stand spellbound before those frescoes by Fra Angelico on the walls of his cell in San Marco. Authors have it, novelists have it, poets have it, playwrights have it. God has it. In this of all things else we are most Godlike. It is this that Christianity was intended to serve. It was the very savor of being to the men who wrote the New Testament. The joy that sings its way along through their pages did not come of resisting temptation. "O the depth of the riches both of the wisdom and knowledge of God!" (Rom. 11:33)—this week I picked fewer pockets than I picked last week! Nor did it come of being good. "Blessed be the God and Father of our Lord Jesus Christ" (I Peter 1:3)—I told the truth yesterday morning, and forgave an enemy in the afternoon. I visited a sick friend in the evening, and wrapped up a Care package before bedtime. One rarely sings about any of that. The song springs from a man's heart, and breaks through the barrier of his lips, when he stands with God against some darkness or some void, and watches the light come: when he is having a go where he is at shaping, by God's grace, whatever he can of what God wills, as a potter shapes a vase.

"We then, . . . workers together with him. . . ." With such an incomparably great thing as the grace of God involved, Paul could not settle for anything less. The grace of God would not suffer itself to be set only meager tasks that men might reap from it only scanty harvests. To receive that grace in vain would be to harness the tides and turn nothing but a flutter-mill. It would be to garner the driving energies of all creation, that hold the sun and the moon in space, that push up out of the hard earth the green of spring, like an army with banners—to garner them one by one, only to be stopped by some silly thing that keeps standing in the road with arms akimbo, grinning at us, making lewd gestures, holding us cowed. "The grace of God"—the breadth of his compassion, the length of his patience, the depth of his mercy, the height of his justice—all the gallantry of his saving love in action: to no point, and no effect! The apostle was not afraid that God would waste anything; he was afraid that people would waste God.

I like the story of the little girl at the weekend party whom Burne-Jones found one morning in such deep distress, and asked her what was the matter. "Somebody," she moaned, pointing to the bushes that lined the garden path, and brushing the tears from her eyes, "Somebody has gone and set traps out there for the birds." "And what have you done about it?" asked the artist. "I have prayed about it," she answered. "I have prayed that none of the birds would go near the traps!" Then a long pause, and a sob. "And I have prayed that if any did, the traps would not work!" Another long pause, and another sob, though not so bitter now. "And just a few minutes ago," she went on, looking up at him through her tears and smiling, "I went out there and kicked the traps to pieces!" To preach is to raise the question, not so much of what there is about us that calls for God's mercy, as of what there is about us, and the lives we are leading, that calls for God's power. Biblical faith assumes that there is a grace in God which makes it impossible that his will for us should be defeated, except by our own will to have it so. And his will for us is life to the full, all the way up! Not hereafter. Now. We desperately need to say that. I have an idea that partly at least because the Church had quit saying it, the people of Sweden turned to the welfare state, only to find that there was something still wrong in Paradise, with alcoholism, juvenile delinquency, and the suicide rate mounting to unprecedented heights.[26]

There is a tortured mural on the wall of the Library at Dartmouth College: a colossal figure of Christ leaning on an axe. All around are broken temples, shattered stones, everything at sixes and sevens; and one knows how it happened, because at his feet is a cross too, which he has just cut from where it stood on a hill. Perhaps by this time we have to read history itself that way. I am told that in the Pyrenees the dawn comes with a kind of tumult, as if there were an earthquake, with a mighty wind rushing. How is it with us? Do we think God should be doing something? But he is not a God who will be relied on, as if we knew what it is that he is about; or waited for, as if some day he would come, and we could enter upon him and possess him. He will manifest his hidden power as he will—with nobody to say what the signs are that things are getting better or getting worse. One sure sign we have: he is looking for the scars in your hands and mine, left there because we have tried to take hold of human life as he did!

He is like the sea, writes Macneile Dixon. "Men are said to love flattery. The sea never flatters. They are said to love ease. She offers toil." Yet every time they come home to some poor shelter, and swear never to embark again, with an "aching heart" they hear her call, and long for her "bitter and incomparable society."[27]

"Therefore," St. Paul would add, "my beloved brethren, be ye stedfast, unmoveable, always abounding in the work of the Lord, forasmuch as ye know that your labour is not in vain in the Lord" (I Cor. 15:58).

We are in the company of One who never denies a man peace except to give him glory.[28]

Notes

PREFACE

1. The Lutheran Church of the Holy Trinity, New York City, 1920-45.

2. Associate Professor of Homiletics, Union Theological Seminary, New York City, 1945-46; Brown Professor of Homiletics, 1946-60. Visiting Professor of Homiletics: Union Theological Seminary, Richmond, Va.; Lutheran Theological Seminary, Mt. Airy, Philadelphia, Penna.; Princeton Theological Seminary, Princeton, N. J., 1961-63; Francis Landey Patton Visiting Professor, 1963- .

3. New York: Oxford University Press, 1951.

4. I should like to borrow for my purpose here the words of Reinhold Niebuhr: "There is of course a strong element of presumption in the effort to make such judgments which will seem intolerable to those who disagree . . . ; and which can be tolerable even to those who find them validated . . . only if it is recognized that they are made in 'fear and trembling.' " *The Nature and Destiny of Man* (New York: Charles Scribner's Sons, 1943), Vol. II, p. 205.

I. A GREAT GULF FIXED

1. "The Reader Writes," Charles Crane in *The New Yorker*, July 8, 1939.

2. Theodore Wedel, *The Religion of Main Street* (New York: The Macmillan Co., 1950), pp. 1-55, 65 f., 78, 108. It should not be necessary to say that the whole educational enterprise of the Church is deeply involved, as well as the pulpit. There have been Sunday Schools that served as veritable hotbeds for atheism! Happily there have been many exceptions in both areas, and at the moment the number seems to be on the increase.

3. Sabapathy Kulandran, *The Message and Silence of the American Pulpit* (Boston: Pilgrim Press, 1949).

4. Curricula recently adopted in certain theological institutions reveal a striking tendency to reduce the time given to homiletics, making most of the courses elective, and unmindful of the fact that the whole discipline belongs to the learning process in every department, confining it as nearly as may be to a semester or two, perhaps even in the senior year—as if it had to do chiefly with skills, and little if anything to do with the Bible or theology or Christian ethics! The result is that the sermon is far too often no more than tenuously related to anything that otherwise occupies the

student's time! We seem to have lost faith in the spoken word precisely at
the time when governments have learned to rely on it heavily, calling it
propaganda; when all of the seven devils, as David H. C. Read puts it, "are
talking themselves into the vacuum of the human soul." *The Communication
of the Gospel* (London: S.C.M. Press, 1952), p. 82. Would it not be good
strategy to throw in reinforcements where the line is weakest? Retreat there
is the entering wedge of disaster.

5. Herman Melville, *Moby Dick* (New York: Modern Library, 1926).
"The pulpit is ever this earth's foremost part; all the rest comes in its rear;
the pulpit leads the world. From thence it is the storm of God's quick wrath
is first described, and the bow must bear the earliest brunt. From thence it
is the God of breezes fair or foul is first invoked for favorable winds. . . .
The world's a ship on its passage out, and not a voyage complete, and the
pulpit is its prow" (p. 38).

6. Anthony Trollope, *Barchester Towers* (New York: Modern Library,
1950), pp. 252 f.

7. Helmut Thielicke, *Nihilism* (New York: Harper & Brothers, 1961), p.
36. For a humanist's view see Charles Frankel, *The Case for Modern Man*
(New York: Harper & Brothers, 1956). He would not have us attempt to
"restore sobriety and humility by the remarkable technique of fixing men's
minds on transcendent and unattainable ideals" (p. 25), which I dare say he
supposes to be the function of the Christian gospel. Naïvely enough he reminds
us that "the vision behind liberalism is the vision of a world progressively
redeemed by human power from its classic ailments of poverty, disease, and
ignorance" (p. 29). All our hardheaded doctrines of sin are to him "contrived
nonsense" (pp. 99 f.). "The triumphs of Science," he goes on, "may not have
affected history yet, but they will!" (p. 159) When the world was on the brink
of nuclear war, that sounded dangerously like a threat. For the humanist's rebuttal, see Joseph Wood Krutch, *Human Nature and the Human Condition*
(New York: Random House, 1959), pp. 197-211. *Quo Urania ducit.* "Wherever wisdom leads," was the wise motto of the ancients; we may not, he insists,
safely substitute for it *Quo Uranium ducit!*

8. Martin E. Marty, *The New Shape of American Religion* (New York:
Harper & Brothers, 1959), pp. 1-89. Its sequel, *A Second Chance for American
Protestants*, appeared in 1963. Peter Berger, *The Noise of Solemn Assemblies*
(Garden City, N.Y.: Doubleday & Co., 1961), describes "the revolutionary
forces which are storming across the American scene" (p. 29), fashioning a
"religion of democracy" as "the most important common possession of all the
denominations" (p. 69), and "an essential element of . . . the O.K. World"
(p. 93). Samuel Laeuchli tells of how the language of the post-Apostolic period
was "threatened by cheap popularity conquered by the desires of a Christian
mob, which wanted to be spoon fed or entertained with the fantastic"; and so
degenerated into empty phrases, was stored away "in the closet of liturgical
formulas," and became quite painless. *The Language of Faith* (New York and

Nashville: Abingdon Press, 1962), p. 162. Hendrik Kraemer regards all this as "one of the aspects of purification, contained in secularization . . . one of the ironic ways of God to call the Church back to its true nature." *The Communication of the Christian Faith* (Philadelphia: Westminster Press, 1956), p. 87. Certainly it is the outstanding form of that "dialogue" into which the preacher and his congregation have to enter, each with the other, and both with the world. Reuel Howe provides an extended discussion of it in *The Miracle of Dialogue* (New York: Seabury Press, 1963).

9. Will Herberg, *Protestant, Catholic, and Jew* (Garden City, N.Y.: Doubleday & Co., 1955), p. 97.

10. J. A. T. Robinson, Bishop of Woolwich, thinks that not much of it is there any more; with all that has happened in the world of science and philosophy, how can there be? *Honest to God* (Philadelphia: Westminster Press, 1963). Nathan Scott comments on "the gap between modern secular experience and traditional religious forms." He insists that it is not of a kind that any "true artist can bridge by mere assertion . . . the attempt . . . can only lead to . . . rhetoric and abstraction." *Rehearsals of Discomposure* (New York: King's Crown Press, 1952), p. 220.

11. D. H. Lawrence speaks of "the ghastly sentimentalism that came like a leprosy over religion." "If the salt hath lost its savor, wherewith shall it be salted?" "With sugar!" suggested Paul Claudel. Quoted by Amos N. Wilder, *Theology and Modern Literature* (Cambridge, Mass.: Harvard University Press, 1958), p. 21. See chap. IV, n. 2.

12. Eugene O'Neill, *The Iceman Cometh* (New York: Random House, 1946).

13. *Op. cit.*, (above n. 4), pp. 24-28.

14. So did Dr. John Baillie remark, in another connection, to a group of reporters at the meeting of the World Council of Churches in Evanston, Ill., 1954.

15. Stephen Spender, in an article on the "Dilemma of the Modern Poet in a Modern World," *The New York Times Book Review*, Jan. 4, 1948.

16. The schizophrenic symptoms resulting from this "loss of center," this "sickness unto death," are strikingly set forth in a chapter by Helmut Thielicke on "Nihilism as a Psychiatric Phenomenon" (*op. cit.*, pp. 41-54). Paul Tillich too, in his Earl Lectures, *The Irrelevance and the Relevance of the Christian Message,* stresses that same loss of center, except that this time it is rather the removal of the earth from the center of the universe, and therefore the removal of the cosmic significance of Christ, all symbolized by our obsession with space exploration, which tends to render "the Christian message" irrelevant. Can we then no longer find it possible to think of time as instinct with eternity, or of the particular as instinct with the universal? In the Bible, the arena of God's activity is rather in the fourth dimension of time than in the three dimensions of space! It is the course of history which justifies the dynamic and refutes the optimistic interpretations of "religion" and culture.

The faith induced by creative despair makes sense out of a life "which would otherwise remain senseless." Reinhold Niebuhr, *op. cit.*, Vol. II, pp. 205 f. See n. 15 of the next chapter.

17. *Op. cit.*, pp. 11, 15, 18, 20, 80 ff. See n. 8.

18. "For the garden is the only place there is, but you will not find it Until you have looked for it everywhere and found nowhere that is not a desert."

W. H. Auden, "For the Time Being," *The Collected Poetry* (New York: Random House, 1945), p. 412.

19. New York: Vintage Books, 1955.

20. "Religion is picture thinking, which means that it is thinking of supersensible reality in terms of sensible things, and of the invisible in terms of the visible." So writes John Baillie in his Gifford Lectures, *The Sense of the Presence of God* (New York: Charles Scribner's Sons, 1962), p. 102.

For further reading: Jules Lawrence Moreau, *Language and Religious Language* (Philadelphia: Westminster Press, 1961), especially what he has to say on the subject of translation; as for example, "The translator is no longer free to render word for word a literature that is distinctly religious and in part theological into a language that will alter the semantic structure of that literature beyond recognition" (p. 143). John Dillenberger contends that the "Darwinian impact . . . marked the culmination of a period in which no adequate symbols were left for expressing and thinking about the classical Christian heritage. . . . The late nineteenth and early twentieth centuries may have been one of those rare periods in history in which theology was virtually impossible, when the crisis of language and imagination excluded the essential depth of both God and man." *Protestant Thought and Natural Science* (New York: Doubleday & Co., 1960), p. 251.

Frederick Ferré's *Language, Logic and God* (New York: Harper & Brothers, 1961) is an extraordinarily useful book. On the "verification principle," A. J. Ayer, *Language, Truth, and Logic* (London: Victor Gollancz, 1936). On its relevance to the language of religion, Antony Flew's introduction to "Theology and Falsification" in *New Essays in Philosophical Theology,* Antony Flew and Alasdair MacIntyre, eds. (London: S. C. M. Press, 1955), John Baillie's critique, *op. cit.*, pp. 63-87. See also Amos Wilder, *op. cit.*, p. 83, with his reference to Fr. Martin Jarrett-Kerr's studies in *Literature and Belief* (London: Rockliff, 1954), where form and style are seen to be conditioned by the author's world view. Cf. Erich Auerbach's treatment in *Mimesis* (Garden City, N.Y.: Doubleday & Co., 1959) of "the continuing revolution effected in the literature of the West by the Hebraic-Christian influence" (Wilder, *op. cit.*, p. 67). The reader may also wish to consult notes 14-19 of the following chapter.

21. "Theological language . . . acts as a communicative bridge between the *religious* ethos and a *secular* environment. . . . Seizing wherever he can upon categories that are useful, the theologian tries to create that situation in the secular thought world which will make the church's religious affirmation understandable. . . . Therefore, *theological* language is always a function of

two factors: (1) the semantic structure of the church's religious affirmation as it is most responsibly understood and (2) the semantic structure of the world addressed by the church." Moreau, *op. cit.*, pp. 181, 185. Laeuchli (*op. cit.*, pp. 19, 169, 220) speaks of the transformation and transmutation in the Hellenistic of Greek concepts into Biblical concepts. This process is totally unlike liberalism's effort to adapt the Christian faith to the modern world. Richard Luecke has a recent book, *New Meanings for New Beings* (Philadelphia: Fortress Press, 1964), in which he proposes the kind of open-ended, dialogic discourse for Christian communities that undertakes in vital areas actually to speak with fresh understanding out of the encounter between the "language of the world" and that other language of Christianity.

22. The legend appeared in a book for children by Ernest von Houwald (1820), and is now repeated to "forlorn and . . . bewildered tourists" in many forms by the guides in the Pitti gallery, Florence. E. H. Gombrich, *Raphael's Madonna Della Sedia* (London: Oxford University Press, 1956), p. 6.

23. "The Catacombs and the Spirit of Early Christianity," *Union Quarterly Review*, Vol. 12, No. 1 (Nov. 1956).

II. THE NATURE OF REVELATION

1. "Revelation means the moment in our history through which we know ourselves to be known from beginning to end, in which we are apprehended by the knower; it means the self-disclosing of that eternal knower. Revelation means the moment in which we are surprised by the knowledge of someone there in the darkness . . . the moment in which we find our judging selves to be judged. . . . When . . . the great riches of God reduce our wealth to poverty, that is revelation. When we find out that we are no longer thinking him, but that he first thought us, that is revelation. . . . Revelation means that in our common history the fate which lowers over us as persons in our communities reveals itself to be a person in community with us." Richard Niebuhr, *The Meaning of Revelation* (New York: The Macmillan Co., 1941), pp. 152 f.

2. Francis Thompson, "The Hound of Heaven," *British Poetry and Prose*, Vol. II (rev. ed.; Boston: Houghton Mifflin Co., 1938), p. 928. Also published separately, with an introduction by G. K. Chesterton (Boston: Bruce Humphries, 1936).

3. These paradoxes of the faith are manifold and inevitable, since the encounter is not logical but existential. Only the knowing which is meeting can bring us knowledge of the mercy which is judgment, and the judgment which is mercy; of the strength which is weakness, and the weakness which is strength (I Cor. 1:25). "Whenever . . . we attempt to extend our knowledge to the realm of supersensible realities, . . . we are forced to say two apparently contradictory things about them. Yet these are not really contradictory . . . , for of two contradictory propositions one must be false and the other true. They are rather *dialectical* opposites, both of which are false." Baillie, *op. cit.*, p. 107.

4. As the Latin Fathers of the Church put it, *Deus comprehensus non est*

deus. A few blocks down the street from my church in New York was the Ethical Culture Society. There were times when I took an evil delight in carrying on a controversy with their announced topics. When one week on their bulletin board the subject appeared, "A Rational Religion," I had posted on mine the sentence "If we understood God we should do well to doubt him." It's a point we should be making more frequently in our sermons. God is the subject, not the object; the knower, not the known. See chap. III, n. 7 and 20. The Jews were accused of all kinds of idolatry because they refused to name their God, calling him only *Adonai.* Karl Barth, on Rom. 1:16-17, quotes Kierkegaard: "If Christ be very God, He must be unknown, for to be known directly is the characteristic mark of an idol."

5. George Ernest Wright, *God Who Acts* (London: S. C. M. Press, 1952). "Primarily and essentially *revelation is deed* . . . The word itself is to the Israelite a deed" (p. 39).

6. *As You Like It,* Act II, Sc. i.

7. George Ernest Wright, *The Old Testament Against Its Environment* (London: S. C. M. Press, 1950). Perhaps the statement calls for some modification. Professor James Barr has provided an extraordinarily incisive essay on "Revelation Through History in the Old Testament and in Modern Theology," *Princeton Seminary Bulletin,* Vol. LVI, No. 3 (May 1963), showing with great persuasiveness how necessary it is to re-examine the thesis that revelation takes place centrally and primarily in and through "history." Yet with all the difficulties involved, it is still possible to think of history as God's workshop, "the great drama played for the salvation of the world," in which "God 'makes himself known.' " S. Sigmund Mowinckel, *The Old Testament as Word of God,* R. B. Bjornard, trans. (New York and Nashville: Abingdon Press, 1959), pp. 35, 45. It is this "that more than anything else distinguishes the religion of Israel from the neighboring religions" (p. 38).

Beyond all question, however, a difference in climate has overtaken us. We may no longer draw too simply the contrast between the Hebrew and the Greek, building all too many of our theological superstructures on what Dr. Barr has called a "grossly misused etymologizing method." *The Semantics of Biblical Thought* (London: Oxford University Press, 1961), pp. 10 ff., 138. Yet cf., for a nineteenth-century statement, *The Influence of Greek Ideas on Christianity,* by Edwin Hatch (New York. Harper & Brothers, 1957). See also C. H. Dodd, *The Bible and the Greeks* (London: Hodder & Stoughton, 1954., and more recently Thorleif Bowman's *Hebrew Thought Compared with Greek* (Philadelphia: Westminster Press, 1960)—Professor Barr in rebuttal! Gerhard Eberling nevertheless points out correctly I believe that because of the hybrid character of the language in which the New Testament is written, Hebrew stems with Greek grafted on them, the hermeneutic has to be "treated as a special kind." See his chapter, "Word of God and Hermeneutic," James M. Robinson and John B. Cobb, eds., *The New Hermeneutic* (New York: Harper & Row, 1964), p. 91.

8. "All the work of God. . . , even when he judges and punishes, in reality is part of his plan and work of salvation. . . . History . . . is his most authentic and direct revelation. Because there . . . he gives himself." Mowinckel, *op. cit.* (above n. 7), pp. 40 f.

9. Victor E. Frankl, *From Death-Camp to Existentialism* (Boston: Beacon Press, 1959), has set up a "third Viennese School of Psychotherapy"; for its basic concept, not the will-to-pleasure (Freud) nor the will-to-power (Adler), but the will-to-meaning (p. 97).

10. C. H. Dodd, writing of "the historical problem of our time," reminds us of the difference Hitler made by persuading a whole generation of German youth, "despairing and cynical," that they were "living in the crucial moment of the historic destiny of the German people," and by "linking their . . . action to its agelong movement . . . convinced [them] that they were making history." *The Bible To-day* (New York: The Macmillan Co., 1947), pp. 122 f. See Eric C. Rust, *Towards a Theological Understanding of History* (New York: Oxford University Press, 1963).

11. Cf. Calvin's *Institutes*, Bk I, chap. III.

12. James M. Robinson, *A New Quest of the Historical Jesus* (Naperville, Ill.: Alec R. Allenson, 1959). pp. 35 ff., 73 ff.

13. The thesis developed by John Knox in *Christ the Lord* (Chicago and New York: Willett, Clark & Co., 1945) and in *The Church and the Reality of Christ* (New York: Harper & Row, 1962).

14. John Baillie, *op. cit.*, pp. 1-13, 19-40, *et passim*, distinguishes between the certitude which we may have and the certainty which is quite unattainable. Instead of "claiming certainty or finality for our particular thoughts about God and the unseen world," we must content ourselves with "claiming that certainty 'pulsates through all our thinking' or that our experience in this realm is everywhere 'transfused with certainty' " (p. 12). "The objects of faith are all apprehended by us in a mode of knowing which, though it may be accompanied by full conviction, nevertheless falls short of full comprehension. Our thought can reach *up to* them, but we cannot, as it were, get our thought *round* them" (p. 161). He insists that it would be as difficult to discredit all our "primary apprehensions" of God as it would be to distrust our "sense of perception as a whole" (p. 72). "Musical theory is . . . drawn from musical experience and from nothing else, and can be verified in no other way than by appeal to such experience" (p. 63). John Hick, however, in *Faith and Knowledge* (Ithaca, N.Y.: Cornell University Press, 1957), holds that "*within* our experience there is no such distinction" between certainty and certitude (p. 15). "All our actual certainties are perforce psychological certainties. . . . Human knowledge can never rise above the status of subjective certainty" (pp. 15-17). "Divine existence . . . must be known . . . through human experience," with religious faith as "the interpretative element within that experience" (p. 22). "The reasoning by which we arrive at many, perhaps most, of the certainties by which we live, does not consist in acquiring . . . perfectly cogent chains"

of logical proof, "but rather in appreciating the drift of a miscellaneous mass of evidence" (p. 95). This is the role that interpretation has to play. "There is in cognition of every kind an unresolved mystery. . . . We cannot explain . . . how we are conscious of sensory phenomena as constituting an objective physical environment; we just find ourselves interpreting the data of our experience that way. . . . The same is true of the apprehension of God. The theistic believer cannot explain *how* he knows the divine presence to be mediated through his human experience. He finds himself interpreting his experience in this way. He lives in the presence of God, though he is unable to prove by any dialectical process that God exists" (p. 132).

15. "Here are two brief formulations of this challenge from the pens of two different contributors to the same volume of essays:

"What would have to occur or to have occurred to constitute for you a disproof of the love of, or of the existence of, God?

"If, then, religious 'statements' are compatible with anything and everything, how can they be statements? How can the honest enquirer find out what they mean, if nobody will tell him what they are compatible with?" John Baillie, *op. cit.*, p. 69; quoting from *New Essays in Philosophical Theology, supra,* chap. I, n. 20.

"This basic scientific attitude and method which regard the fragmentary, discontinuous data of the world as the only facts available to scientific knowledge we call positivism. It is therefore always combined with a nihilistic view of the world. . . . The positivist sees the individual elements, but not the fact that in this form they are only the remains of a terrible destruction, that . . . they represent a catastrophe. . . . [He] agrees with the Christian on one point, namely, the conclusion that God . . . cannot be found in the world itself. . . . God is beyond our power of perception, not because he is unreal, but because he is himself the upholder of reality. . . . He . . . is not to be found within the world, because he is the lord of the world. . . ." The "loss of God is [not therefore] an emancipation." It is "the cause of . . . disintegration and discontinuity." Helmut Thielicke, *op. cit.,* pp. 63-65. It is for these reasons that the preacher must have about him what R. E. C. Browne calls an "untidiness of mind." *The Ministry of the Word* (Naperville, Ill.: Alec R. Allenson, 1958). See n. 14 above, and pp. 55 ff.

16. See above. It cannot therefore be asked of us that we verify the assertions of faith on the level of the natural sciences. They are verifiable only " 'on their own level.' " Baillie, *op. cit.,* p. 63. To the Hebrew, God was "not . . . an inferred entity." He was "an experienced reality." John H. Hick, "Necessary Being," *Scottish Journal of Theology,* Vol. XIV, 4 (December, 1961), pp. 353-69. See also Professor Hick's treatment of revelation and faith, of the problems of religious language and of verification: *Philosophy of Religion,* "Foundations of Philosophy Series" (Englewood Cliffs, N.J.: Prentice-Hall, 1963).

17. I draw here on my notes taken down as he spoke. Cf. *The Idea of*

Revelation in Recent Thought (New York: Columbia University Press, 1960), especially pp. 49-56, 62-70, 83-100, 140.

18. Bultmann's demythologizing undertakes to " 'eliminate' the inadequate mythical conceptualization for the sake of stating more adequately the myth's meaning." James M. Robinson, in Robinson and Cobb, *The New Hermeneutic, supra cit.,* p. 34. In the process, however, what takes place is exchange and not elimination (pp. 36-39). And the modern myth beside the ancient so often seems shallow! See chap. 1, n. 21.

Writes Amos N. Wilder: "The mythological representation of the course of the world in the New Testament is to be seen . . . as a new wisdom about man and God, based on Israel's experience, . . . but corrected by that primordial re-creation of man to be identified with the crucifixion of Israel's truest representative. . . . These pictorial vehicles . . . convey to us a revealed understanding of such things as the life of men and nations in time, the relation of Israel to other peoples and the Church, the historical significance of Jesus of Nazareth, the way in which God works in the world through situations and events, the destiny of the individual and all creatures. . . . The myth-making powers of the Christian movement . . . meant the portrayal of the real nature of things and of the course of existence so far as human speech could encompass such mysteries." *The Language of the Gospel* (New York: Harper & Row, 1964), pp. 134 f.

Prof. Wilder sees Bultmann's work as "a heroic effort to surmount the rigidities of centuries as well as of first-century mythology. . . . [It] represents an extreme recourse to overcome the dead hand of the past. . . . It is a way of salvaging confession as faith without confession as doctrine, the word as address but not as meaning—for meaning has become hopelessly identified with outworn associations." *The New Hermeneutic, supra cit.,* p. 204.

19. Jules Lawrence Moreau, *op. cit.,* pp. 137-39.

20. See Kittel's *Bible Key Words* (New York: Harper & Brothers, 1961), Vol III, p. 62 ff.

21. Quoted by E. G. Homrighausen, *The Interpreter's Bible* (New York and Nashville: Abingdon Press, 1957), Vol. XII, II Peter 1:1b, p. 169.

22. "It is God himself, as he comes to meet us in Christ, of whom the Christian is indefeasibly certain, and not such statements as he can make about God." Baillie, *op. cit.,* p. 91. Cf. the "parable of a telephone conversation," p. 138.

23. "Because the Christian affirmation is fundamentally one of relationship, Christian faith has no built-in metaphysics. . . . Philosophy and theology are occupied with the same subject matter . . . the difference between them is one of stance" with regard to it. Moreau, *op. cit.,* p. 169. See n. 14 above.

24. William Newton Ewer (1885-?), published in *The Week-End Book* (London: Nonesuch Press, 1924), p. 117. So Joseph L. Baron, ed., *A Treasury of Jewish Quotations.* Used by permission of the publisher.

25. Thornton Wilder, *The Bridge of San Luis Rey* (New York: Albert and

Charles Boni, 1928). The bridge, "woven of osier by the Incas," was under the protection of St. Louis of France. When it broke and "precipitated five travellers into the gulf below," Brother Juniper, in what the author called "the flower of a perfect skepticism," devoutly undertook to explain the providence of God historically and mathematically. What other proper issue could there be but that he should "lean upon a flame" and die? See n. 4 above.

26. See pp. 72 f., on "apologetic sermons."

27. Victor E. Frankl, *op. cit.* We need to "stop asking about the meaning of life, and instead to think of ourselves as those who (are) being questioned by life. . . . Questions about the meaning of life can never be answered by sweeping statements. 'Life' does not mean something vague, but something very real and concrete, just as life's tasks are also very real and concrete. They form man's destiny, which is different and unique for each individual" (p. 17). On p. 103 he quotes Nietzsche: "He who has a why to live for can bear almost any how." In its patristic form it ran, "He who hears God's word can bear his silences."

28. "Herein lies a uniqueness that characterizes New Testament heralding: while it proclaims, it brings to pass the proclamation. The proclamation of liberty at the same time frees. The preaching of sight opens blind eyes." Robert H. Mounce, *The Essential Nature of New Testament Preaching* (Grand Rapids, Mich.: Eerdmans Publishing Co., 1960), p. 18. On p. 183 he quotes John Knox, *The Integrity of Preaching* (New York and Nashville: Abingdon Press, 1957), p. 92: "Preaching does more than recount and explain the ancient event. The Spirit makes the ancient event in a very real sense an event even now transpiring, and the preaching is a medium of the Spirit's action in doing so. In the preaching, when it is truly itself, the event is continuing or is recurring. God's revealing action in Christ is, still or again, actually taking place."

29. T. S. Eliot, "Little Gidding," in *Four Quartets, The Complete Poems and Plays* (New York: Harcourt, Brace & Co., 1952), pp. 144 f. Used by permission of the publisher.

> ". . . while the light fails
> On a winter's afternoon, in a secluded chapel
> History is now and England."

Whenever you read the Bible, says Kierkegaard, "remember to say to yourself incessantly: 'It's talking to me; I am the one it is speaking about.'" *For Self-Examination* (Minneapolis: Augsburg Publishing House, 1959), p. 39.

30. Friedrich Baumgärtel, in "The Hermeneutical Problem of the Old Testament," calls the Old Testament the "Word outside the gospel"; yet "it is a witness which . . . meets us in our existence together and as one with the evangelical witness." Quoted from *Essays on Old Testament Hermeneutics*, Claus Westermann, ed., and James Luther Mays, ed. of Eng. trans. (Richmond, Va.: John Knox Press, 1963), p. 152. Cf. Von Rad, "Typological Interpreta-

tion of the Old Testament," *ibid.*, pp. 35-39: "The same God who revealed himself in Christ has also left his footprints in the history of the Old Testament covenant people" (p. 36). Mowinckel asks, "How then can the Old Testament be Divine revelation. . . . .?" And answers, "The *presupposition* for the existence of the problem and for the possibility of its solution is that we start from a *positive Christian standpoint*" (*Op. cit.*, pp. 21 f.).

31. Writes Martin Noth in the "Re-presentation of the Old Testament in Proclamation," with regard to Deuteronomy 5:3, "The author simply 'forgets his past' and for a moment drops the projection of the Deuteronomic law back into Moses' time to think of the later generations of Israel who, when the law was proclaimed, were expected to listen . . . as if they themselves—and not their ancestors—were standing at Mount Horeb . . . ." (*Essays on Old Testament Hermeneutics, supra*, p. 82).

So with the "three great annual festivals of pilgrimage," in which "the situation of the Exodus from Egypt was again and again contemporized" (*ibid.*, pp. 80 f.). Cf. also Von Rad, "Typological Interpretation of the Old Testament" (*ibid.*, p. 19), on the "return of paradise" (Isa. 11:6-8; Amos 9: 13), of David (Amos 9:11), of the wilderness experience (Isa. 52:11 f.; Hos. 2:16-20). Especially useful is Von Rad's article on "Ancient Word and Living Word" in *Interpretation* (published by John Knox Press, Richmond, Va.) Vol. XV, No. 1 (1961): the amazing freedom with which the book of Deuteronomy "has spoken the traditional word of God" to more than one changing present. See also chap. IV, n. 13. "In the *cultus of the feasts* ancient Israel experiences not only the presence of God and his coming, his re-creation of nature and life, but also a real repetition of his mighty work in history, of the deliverance from Egypt and the wonder at the . . . Red Sea." The Word is "primarily and essentially *revelation in deed*." Mowinckel, *op. cit.*, pp. 37, 39.

32. Hans Walter Wolff, in *Essays on Old Testament Hermeneutics*, p. 160. Read pp. 189-99, on "The Carrying Out of Typological Interpretation," as "the Old Testament Word continues to speak in the community of Jesus" (p. 198).

It has often seemed to me that the New Testament, pointing to Christ with one hand, so to speak, includes with a gesture of the other the whole sweep of the Old, saying what Peter said on Pentecost, "*This*—is *that*" (Acts 2:16), *all* of that! Mowinckel's comment (*op. cit.*, p. 135), "The proposition that the Old Testament says *what* Christ is, the New Testament *who* he is, simply is not correct," is based on the assumption that such a view demands "an arbitrary interpretation that reads the whole New Testament into the Old." I should say that quite obviously it demands nothing of the kind.

33. As witness the "sermons" reported in Acts, and the whole argument of the Epistle to the Hebrews; to say nothing of what is to us Paul's generally unconvincing use of the Old Testament. These matters are of course subjects for detailed study, and all such indictments as this are open to correction.

34. Lawrence E. Toombs' *The Old Testament in Christian Preaching* (Phila-

delphia: Westminster Press, 1961) has many helpful suggestions. See also T. Vriezen, *An Outline of Old Testament Theology* (Oxford: Basil Blackwell, 1958), pp. 97-115.

35. Contrast chap. 11:1-9 with chap. 12:1-7 of Genesis.

36. Consult Walter Zimmerli on "Promise and Fulfillment" in *Essays on Old Testament Hermeneutics, supra*, pp. 89-122: "The prophetic promise proclaims at its deepest level not a coming *something*, after the manner of the fortune-teller," but Someone who is coming, and "who remains Lord over the way in which his will is to be realized" (pp. 105 f.). . . . Only Yahweh himself can legitimately interpret his promise through his fulfillment, and the interpretation can be full of surprises even for the prophet himself (p. 107). . . . [The] fulfillments of which the Old Testament speaks . . . are always the will of God which has become event. Thus the question concerning further fulfillment always involves the more pressing question of the still further, the ultimate will of Yahweh. But because this is so, every Old Testament event receives increasingly the character of a fulfillment which in turn presses the question of deeper fulfillment. All Old Testament history, insofar as it is history guided and given by Yahweh's word, receives the character of fulfillment; but in the fulfillment it receives a new character as promise (p. 112). . . . In Jesus Christ the Apostles attest the Word of God which has become wholly event, and the event that is the Word of God, wholly and completely (p. 113). . . . "Now every effort to run toward the goal and to lay hold of it becomes a running toward him who has already laid hold of the believer, before all of his running. Every cry for redemption is a cry from the mouth of one who knows that he is redeemed" (pp. 114 f.).

37. Hans Walter Wolff, "The Hermeneutical Problem of the Old Testament," *ibid.:* "The proposition that the Old Testament can be properly understood only in the light of the New . . . stands in need of its converse: The New Testament Christ-event can be fully understood only in the light of the Old Testament." We do not superimpose on "the historical meaning of the Old Testament text a second meaning. . . . Rather we . . . listen to how the historical meaning of the text continues to speak in the New Testament situation" (pp. 187-89). Then, toward the end, this "sharp sentence from Bonhoeffer: "He who too quickly and too directly would be and feel in accordance with the New Testament is, in my opinion, no Christian" (p. 199). Cf. Tom Driver, *The Sense of History in Greek and Shakespearean Drama* (New York: Columbia University Press, 1960). Also *God's Unfolding Purpose,* by Suzanne de Dietrich, Robert McAfee Brown, trans. (Philadelphia: Westminster Press, 1961), pp. 152 f., 196. Bultmann, as is well known, stresses the "newness" of the gospel, and is impressed by the discontinuity between the Old Testament and the New. See the theological discussion of the problem in *The Old Testament and Christian Faith,* Bernhard W. Anderson, ed. (New York: Harper & Row, 1963).

38. *The Church and the Reality of Christ* (New York: Harper & Row,

1962), p. 30. See also p. 107, n. 11.

39. John Knox, *The Integrity of Preaching*.

40. "The Christian understands all he reads in the law and the prophets through the illumination which has come to him from the things that long afterwards transpired in Galilee and Jerusalem. Indeed the same is true of everything that the Christian reads anywhere. He reads it with Christian eyes, for he has no other." John Baillie, *op. cit.*, p. 135. Writing of "Lev. 14:1-7 and 16:1-22 as 'prophecies of Jesus Christ, pictures and stories which have in him their meaning and fulfillment,' Barth argues that the 'meaning' of these passages can be 'understood' only when we are 'aware' that God is here speaking to us about the nature and purpose of his election. And since we Christians know God's election as fulfilled in Jesus Christ, we must read these passages as speaking of him . . . because the mystery of election was the actual topic and meaning that the original authors had in mind. Otherwise . . . we would have to conclude that the subject of the Old Testament witness is an unknown quantity, or even worse, that there is no subject at all." So Arnold B. Come, *An Introduction to Barth's "Dogmatics" for Preachers* (Philadelphia: Westminster Press, 1963), pp. 196 f.

41. Douglas John Hall, in "The Suffering of the Church" (unpublished Ph.D. dissertation, Union Theological Seminary, 1963), has this interesting observation about the way in which the denouement of a mystery story sheds light on everything that precedes: ". . . events which had appeared to mean such-and-such . . . actually meant something quite different, and people who had appeared to be thus-and-so . . . were cast in other roles entirely."

42. I have set some words and phrases here in quotation marks because I have an uneasy feeling that they are not my own, but do not know whose they are!

43. See pp. xi, 75 ff. of these lectures. "The Word has already made itself relevant to the world: He did so when He created this world and reconciled it to Himself. . . . It is absurd for us to worry as we do about 'making the Bible relevant.' The Word of God is far more relevant than we could ever be, and if we will be obedient to the Bible, really obedient, then we shall find ourselves far more deeply involved in the lives of our people and in the 'situation' than we ever were when we were anxious to be 'relevant.' God's Word is devastatingly relevant when it is truly preached and truly heard." Paul M. van Buren, "The Word and God in the Church," *Anglican Theological Review* (October 1957), pp. 348, 354. Quoted by Dietrich Ritschl in *A Theology of Proclamation* (Richmond, Va.: John Knox Press, 1960), p. 50.

44. P. T. Forsyth, *Positive Preaching and the Modern Mind* (London: Independent Press, 1949), p. 10.

III. The Credibility and Relevance of the Gospel

1. Herbert H. Farmer, *The Healing Cross* (London: Nisbet, 1938), Introduction.

2. December, 1951.

3. See reference in n. 4 below. Paul Tillich sets down the Biblical, credal, liturgical language we use as the first in a series of six indications that the Church in the "post-Christian world" has become irrelevant; that is, no longer speaks intelligibly to man's existential concerns: Who am I? Why am I here? What is the purpose of life? What is its meaning? How can I hope, and for what? (*The Relevance and Irrelevance of the Christian Message,* The Earl Lectures, February, 1963.) It is for this reason that the preacher and teacher are under obligation to spell out the inner content of the words they use until the elemental language of the Christian faith once more has meaning for those who hear it. See the Index, under Definition, Gospel, etc. Such spelling out is what Jules Lawrence Moreau (chap. I, n. 20 and 21) calls "the operational definition," which "springs from a dynamic concept of reality and releases much of our thinking from the tyranny of words. . . . [It] brings the hearer into closer relation to the objects of his own experience . . . so that whatever is being defined may be experimentally participated in" (*op. cit.,* p. 94). See chap. IV, n. 6 and 11. See also index under Faith, Hope, etc.

4. See pp. 5, 15 f., 19, 26, 31, 47, and 93, n. 10. John Baillie, *op. cit.,* pp. 196 ff., has an extended "operational definition" of the word *salvation.*

5. See chap. II, in these lectures, no. 23. *The Divine-Human Encounter* (Philadelphia: The Westminster Press, 1943), p. 85.

6. R. Gregor Smith, *Theology* (April 1955).

7. See chap. II, n. 4 and n. 20 following. Cf. John Dillenberger, *God Hidden and Revealed* (Philadelphia: Muhlenberg Press, 1953), an interpretation of Luther's doctrine of "the hidden God."

8. Cf. Jaroslav Pelikan, *Fools for Christ* (Philadelphia: Muhlenberg Press, 1953).

9. I say "in some sense"; see chap. II, n. 7. With us "the true" is generally conceived as a proposition. In the Christian religion we are concerned not primarily with the "knowledge of propositions," but with the "knowledge of being . . . knowledge by acquaintance." John Baillie, *op. cit.,* p. 88.

10. Gilbert K. Chesterton, *Heretics* (New York: John Lane Co., 1909), p. 15. See pp. 285-305.

11. John Macquarrie, "Feeling and Understanding," *Theology* (May 1955), p. 182.

12. John Baillie, *op. cit.,* pp. 140 f.

13. Jaroslav Pelikan, *op. cit.* Also his *Human Culture and the Holy* (London: S. C. M., 1959).

14. John Baillie, *What is Christian Civilization?* (New York: Charles Scribner's Sons, 1945), pp. 43-59.

15. Kenneth J. Forman, *Identification: Human and Divine* (Richmond, Va.: John Knox Press, 1963), p. 117. "The gospel goes forth in the form of commandment, but . . . the commandment must never be anything else than the communication of the gospel. . . . If gospel and law do not really coincide, are not entirely identical, the one can only annul and destroy the other."

Eduard Thurneysen, *A Theology of Pastoral Care* (Richmond, Va.: John Knox Press, 1962), pp. 255, 257.

16. See above, n. 3. Also the Index, under *Language*. Also n. 3 above.

17. The dialogue between "the spiritual man within me" and "the natural man within me . . . is carried on, not in certainty and security, but in *Anfechtung*, in faith assailed and tempted by doubt and despair." Helmut Thielicke, *Man in God's World* (New York: Harper & Row, 1963), p. 218. Cf. John Baillie, *op. cit.*, p. 161: ". . . conceptions of super-sensible reality . . . are not of such a kind as to allow us to rest speculative conclusions upon them, making them the foundations of a metaphysical scheme." See chap. II, no. 14 and n. 23.

18. Westermann, *op. cit.*, 105 f. See chap. II, n. 36.

19. A hymn for Whitsuntide by the Rev. William H. Draper (1855-1933); a metrical version of St. Francis's "Canticle of the Sun."

20. See n. 7 above. Also chap. II, n. 4, 14, and 25. In the Bible God is *deus nudus, deus absconditus*, of so terrible a majesty, both hidden and revealed in Christ, as to be beyond our knowing; how much more beyond our describing!

21. I follow here the Lutheran Order, and am of course not assuming that the pattern I suggest was consciously designed; only that it may now be discerned with some measure of justification, and so may provide the preacher with rich material for the whole season.

22. See Karl Barth, *The Epistle to the Romans* (6th ed.; Oxford: Universitly Press, 1933), pp. 42-54. I am sure that elsewhere he uses these very words, but cannot now cite the exact reference.

23. Act III, Sc. 3.

24. *Loc. cit.* (cf. chap. I, n. 15).

25. From *The Ballad of the White Horse* by G. K. Chesterton (London: Methuen & Co., 1911). Used by permission of Miss D. E. Collins, Dodd Mead & Co. Inc., and Methuen & Co., Ltd.

26. *The Diary of a Country Priest* (New York: The Macmillan Co., 1938), pp. 20-21.

27. See chap. II, n. 9 and 27, and chap. IV, n. 2.

28. See chap. IV, n. 28.

29. Act I, Sc. 5.

30. "Abt Vogler," stanza 7.

31. I am unable to trace this quotation.

32. Joseph Sittler, *The Ecology of Faith* (Philadelphia: Muhlenberg Press, 1961), p. 69.

33. Peter Berger, *op. cit.* (cf. chap. I, n. 8), p. 123.

34. See pp. 68 ff.

IV. Preaching as a Radical Transaction

1. Hugh T. Kerr reminds us of the frequent "verbal play on the word for 'gospel' " in the Old Testament. It can be good news or bad news, or just

indifferent news. He cites particularly II Samuel 18:19-31, the passage in which Absalom's death is reported to David. "What is *good* news for some is *bad* news for others." So in the New Testament the good news includes the cross—and exacts it! "To speak of the gospel as good news is definitely *not* to indulge in superficial, romantic optimism. This important reminder is foreshadowed by those perverse, sardonic Old Testament passages where the good news is often very bad news indeed." From *Theology Today,* Princeton Theological Seminary. See in the index under the *offense* of the gospel.

2. "The second characteristic of apologetics is that it proposes to give Christian answers to human questions. . . . I have tried to show *in extenso* that Christ is actually the one who prompts the real questions, and that by no means does he accept as binding upon him the questions men put to him and then proceed to answer them. I hope that the readers of these chapters will sense something of the fact that the faith of Christianity is not simply the solution of human questions about life and its meaning, but that rather, on the contrary, it attacks the world with *its* questions and forces it to face them." Helmut Thielicke, *Man in God's World* (New York: Harper & Row, 1963), p. 217. Paul Tillich thinks of the kerygma itself as the best apologetic. *Systematic Theology* (Chicago: University of Chicago Press, 1951), Vol. I, p. 31. See pp. xi and 72 f. of these lectures.

3. See p. 85.

4. *Interpretation* (October 1956).

5. From William Faulkner's Nobel Prize speech at Stockholm, December 10, 1950; *The New York Times,* December 11.

6. I should like to refer at this point to Amos N. Wilder's *Theology and Modern Literature; op. cit.,* and to Nathan A. Scott's *Rehearsals of Discomposure, op. cit.,* where he deals with the portrayals of cosmic exile (Kafka), isolation from community (Silone), isolation of the self from other selves (D. H. Lawrence), and estrangement in "all its various aspects" (T. S. Eliot). Cf. too his book on *The Tragic Vision and the Christian Faith* (New York: Association Press, 1957), and his *Modern Literature and the Religious Frontier* (New York: Harper & Brothers, 1958). There, in the chapter on "Man in Recent Literature," he enumerates what he sees as the most pervasive myths currently employed to describe the human situation: the myth of the Isolato, of Hell, of the Voyage, and of Sanctity. Prof. Wilder (*op. cit.*) adds Paradise, the Flood, Sodom and Gomorrah, Belshazzar's feast, the end of the world, Adam innocent and fallen, Joseph in Egypt, and Judas, pointing out that "the unbelief of today is more affirmative than the shallow skepticism of yesterday. The poignant atheism of today is more poignant than the dogmatic rationalism of yesterday" (p. 35). "The modern agnostic writer is often unconsciously appealing to a living religious tradition against one that is moribund" (p. 115). Joseph Sittler (*op. cit.,* p. 69) comments on "the addressability" of our present day's ultimate negations." See especially his two chapters on "The Role of the Imagination in Preaching" (pp. 45-75).

Such studies are of inestimable value to the preacher. Literature has done a better job than the pulpit of laying bare the deep and underlying causes of man's alienation from both God and his fellows; with here and there profound suggestions of at least the direction in which some measurable reconciliation may take place. John Killinger, with all this in mind, points out, however, *The Failure of Theology in Modern Literature* (New York and Nashville: Abingdon Press, 1963).

7. Will Herberg, "Biblical Faith and Natural Religion," *Theology Today*, Vol. XI, No. 4 (January 1955).

8. I have not been able to find the exact reference. As I remember it, the words were used in an article he once wrote on the purpose and aim of Christian worship: to enlighten the mind, warm the heart, and sharpen the conscience! With that I found myself in violent disagreement—as if we were intended in some way to whet our lives on the Almighty!

9. New York: The Macmillan Co., 1962, p. 19.

10. See p. 38 of these lectures.

11. "The later event is conceived as present in some sense with the earlier and the interpreter who views them both becomes contemporaneous with both." Paul Minear, *Horizons of Christian Community* (St. Louis: Bethany Press, 1959), p. 67. See chap. II, n. 31. Quoted by James Smart in *The Interpretation of Scripture* (Philadelphia: Westminster Press, 1961), p. 67. "What Minear does, then [in *Eyes of Faith*, 1946], is to take us through the words into the inside of the Biblical faith, that we may understand it from within" (p. 287). James M. Robinson, in his chapter on "Hermeneutic Since Barth" (*The New Hermeneutic, supra cit.;* chap. II, n. 7 of these lectures), cites Mezger's word of caution: " 'The short cut of putting myself in the skin of Moses or Paul is popular but no good, for my name is neither Moses nor Paul.' Thus hermeneutic as translation stands in contrast to the Schleiermacher-Dilthey hermeneutic of becoming 'contemporary' with the author—reliving his experience. Mezger's "Guidance for Preaching" includes and tests the whole path of translation over the cleft of the historical distance into our life. Since it sees to it that what was once said is not simply repeated but is to be said anew, it must show what understanding means and make clear how what is understood comes to expression. . . .' "

Dietrich Ritschl (*op. cit.*, see chap. II, n. 43 of these lectures) makes the same point, and I am by no means happy with it. Historically I am neither Abraham nor Moses nor Paul; yet God calls me to a land that he shall tell me of, he sets me on the road with his people out of my own Egypt and theirs, sending me word of how many things a man may well have to suffer for his sake! The old and the new: "What God hath joined together, . . ."

12. Ronald Eugene Sleeth, *Persuasive Preaching* (New York: Harper & Brothers, 1956), p. 11.

13. *Traditum* is no synonym for *praeteritum*. Under the influence of existentialist thought, the kerygma has come to be understood in many quarters

as the proclamation of the past event in such a manner that it becomes a living present chap. II, n. 31). It follows that both as witness to past event and as experience of present event, "the kerygma is central in primitive Christian and contemporary theology." ". . . The communication of the past does not have the meaning of a historical report, but rather is a call, in which the past is contemporized." So James M. Robinson in *A New Quest of the Historical Jesus, supra, cit.*, p. 42, n. 43. Samuel L. Terrien writes: "An exclusively historical approach to Scripture tends to produce paradoxically two opposite and mutually exclusive results. On the one hand, it places us in the position of witnesses, observing a resurrected past with a hitherto unsuspected realism. On the other hand, it tends precisely to confine the Bible to that remote past, thereby removing us from the Presence that created it, isolating us from the People who wrote it, and silencing in effect the Word that brought it forth." *The Bible and the Church* (Philadelphia: Westminster Press, 1962), p. 70.

14. Colin Wilson, *The Outsider* (London: Victor Gollancz, 1956), p. 268; quoted from George Gurdjieff.

15. Günther Rutenborn, *The Sign of Jonah*, George White, trans. (New York: Nelson, 1960).

16. One may perhaps quarrel with Tillich's *Courage To Be* (New Haven: Yale University Press, 1952) on this score. Reinhold Niebuhr's *The Self and the Drama of History* (New York: Charles Scribner's Sons, 1955) would almost seem to have been written in reply, with its emphasis on the dramatic aspect of the Christian faith.

17. The figures, I believe, are Karl Barth's, though I cannot now track them down.

18. W. H. Auden, "For the Time Being." in *The Collected Poetry* (New York: Random House, 1945), pp. 454 ff.

19. See chap. III, n. 19.

20. William Butler Yeats, "The Second Cming," from *Collected Poems* (New York: The Macmillan Company, 1924). Copyright 1952 by Bertha Georgia Yeats. Used by permission of the publishers.

21. Alan Richardson, *A Theological Word Book of the Bible* (New York: The Macmillan Co., 1950), s. v. *Saviour*, p. 220.

22. See pp. 169 ff.

23. Evelyn Waugh, *The Loved One* (Boston: Little, Brown, & Co., 1948). Jessica Mitford's *The American Way of Death* (New York: Simon & Schuster, 1963) has not only satirized but documents our cluttering of what she calls "the narrow passageway to the unknown" (p. 287).

24. See Eugene O'Neill's *Lazarus Laughed (Nine Plays* [New York: Random House, 1932]). I was interested and somewhat puzzled by the fact that Mr. O'Neill, one of the most significant American dramatists of our time, seems to have gone unmentioned by either Amos Wilder or Nathan Scott in the books to which I have referred (n. 6 above).

25. It was Carl Michalson of Drew, somewhere in one of his articles, who

pointed out for me and carried much further this analysis of the relation of Christianity to the situations it faces.

26. So at least it was reported in a television program on many of our stations. Helmut Thielicke's *Nihilism, op. cit.* (chap. I, n. 7) is an extended comment on the purposelessness of modern existence once it loses its creative center in God.

27. *The Human Situation* (New York: Longmans, Green, & Co., 1937), pp. 88 f.

28. Miguel de Unamuno, *The Tragic Sense of Life* (London: Macmillan & Co., 1921), p. 330.

PART II
The Word in Search of Words

The voice said, Cry, And he said, What shall I cry?
—ISAIAH 40:6

Dark and cold we may be, but this
Is no winter now. The frozen misery
Of centuries breaks, cracks, begins to move,
The thunder is the thunder of the floes,
The thaw, the flood, the upstart Spring.
Thank God our time is now when wrong
Comes up to face us everywhere,
Never to leave us till we take
The longest stride of soul men ever took.
Affairs are now soul size.
The enterprise
Is exploration into God.
CHRISTOPHER FRY, *A Sleep of Prisoners**

* Copyright 1951 by Christopher Fry. Reprinted by permission of Oxford University Press, Inc.

THE THUNDER OF THE FLOES

Through a Glass Darkly

The eye that is blind, O God, touch Thou into sight, and the deaf ear into hearing: that seeing Thee we may love Thee, and attending to Thy word do it; finding there fullness of life, and the peace which is in Christ Jesus. Amen.

LUKE 14:1-11; 18:9-14.

I have borrowed my subject from Paul's great hymn to love: "For now we see through a glass, darkly"—that is to say dimly, as in a mirror; "but then face to face." You must know that these Corinthians to whom he is writing prided themselves very highly on their mirrors, made of burnished metal. They saw nevertheless—one couldn't help it— how indistinct the images often were when compared with the object itself. The outlines were nothing like as sharp; sometimes actually blurred, perhaps even broken and distorted. It was an experience you ran into every day, and it suited Paul's hand. He was saying to them that we see everything in this life of ours like that. It's all pretty much of an enigma, and that's the very word he uses, by the way. The King James Version translates it "darkly." All of our being here seems little other than a riddle for the most part, like the murky fragment of a shadow, as if there were a film over our eyes. That's the best we can do now, says the apostle. It's how we see; reflections at best, and none too clearly.

But let's not think about the how, let's think about the why of it. And much of that you will find in the short passages of St. Luke that I have taken as my text. There are three scenes enacted in that brief compass, and from them we are to understand what it is that on one level after another twists the whole world out of shape for us, until we can scarcely make heads or tails out of anything.

The first scene is at the beginning of the fourteenth chapter, verses one through six. It is laid in "the house of one of the chief Pharisees," and provides the lowest level on which the distortions begin to take place. Here a dinner is in progress to which Jesus has been invited. Now whenever you have the stage set like that, whenever there's a feast of any kind, you can be sure you're going to hear something about the Kingdom of God. The chances are it will be something about those of us who have an idea we are in it—and aren't! Every time Jesus sat down at table, his mind seemed to run off in that direction. A feast was such a happy sort of affair that he couldn't help thinking of God's bounty in relation to it; and it was such a desolate business to be left out that he could never quite keep still about it. I suppose you've never been hungry and lonely and cold. You've never known what it was to find yourself one evening standing outside of a lighted window, your nose flattened against the glass, looking in on a gala party with the white linen and the china and the crystal and the great platters of food. Well, can't you at any rate imagine it? Because that's how Jesus saw these men learned in the Law of Israel, and so careful to do it. They weren't inside at all, and they were sure they were. They were outside, and they were his own people, God's people. And only God knew how far outside they were!

How do they seem to you?—watching him as if he were a prisoner and they were there to stand guard: waiting to find out what he would do on the Sabbath day with the man who had the dropsy. They may even have smuggled the poor fellow in just to lay a trap. "And Jesus answering"—they hadn't said anything, they had just looked their question at him. And he answered them: "Is it lawful to heal on the sabbath day?" Still they said nothing. He'd get no justification from them. So he took the man, and healed him, and let him go. Then he answered them again: "Which of you shall have an ass or an ox fallen into a pit, and will not straightway pull him out on the sabbath day?" The Greek is not altogether clear as to precisely what it was that had taken such a tumble. Maybe we should read "Which of you shall have a son or an ox. . . . ." It might even be a pig or an ox! Certainly "the Pharisee and his pig," as someone has remarked, would be a sweet touch! But whether the manuscripts are clear or not, the point is: here they were, insistent on doing only what God permitted them to do. But just let some concern of theirs, something they had and wanted to hold on to, get in the way of their obedience, and they would think nothing of stepping out of line for as long as it might take to do what they themselves thought had to be done. Without a moment's hesitation they would break even the law of the Sabbath. The fact is, their rabbis allowed them that much latitude. They could look out for an ass or an ox. But there were a good many other p's and q's and Jesus would better mind them!

One is inclined to think that perhaps Paul understated the whole thing: "We see through a glass, darkly." It's hard to see at all when a little real estate or a bit of personal property gets in your eye! A new car can transform a perfectly harmless pedestrian into a very demon at the wheel, with only one thing between him and disaster: the radio warning he heard last night, "The life you save may be your own." That might very well be a great pity! Or take the Negro family that moved in only last week, four houses down the block from where you have lived ever since you were married; what's going to happen to your investment now? Two little words, "your own," and they can turn good breeding into bad manners, a fintailed model with the forward look into mayhem, conviction into bigotry, freedom into license. To say nothing of making cowardice out of prudence and nonsense out of religion. Indeed, most of our riddles, what we think of so often as religious problems, have their origin somewhere in that first person singular possessive pronoun. Job's did, and ours do. The first person singular so often becomes exceedingly singular. There was a very great lady once who at ninety-five told me that her two sons who had recently died, both of them over seventy, had rarely if ever had a sick day, and she couldn't for the life of her understand why God had taken them from her now! Do you think Jesus wouldn't have seen the bitter pathos of that?

But we have to do with more than pathos at the moment. You'll notice that in this none-too-gentle company, gathered as we should say for Sunday dinner, a Pharisee's pig, or whatever it was, had maneuvered a human being clean out of the reckoning. That's what's so startling; and it's why I think "son" could scarcely be the correct reading. A beast had fallen due—and I have seen this happen—for a spot of compassion so far ahead of a man that the man wasn't even in the running any longer. Mark says that on another occasion very much like this Jesus swept the whole circle with a glance, and there was anger in his eyes, because he was "grieved for the hardness of their hearts." That day in the Pharisee's house it was a sick man—every bit as much a child of God as any of them, and a good deal worse off than anybody or anything in a pit. No wonder you could cut the silence with a knife. Would any of you like to brazen it out with them?

Some fine morning you should try measuring the extent to which, for all our humanitarian pretensions, things still keep coming in while persons keep going out—which of course is the essence of what we call secularism; and we are ready and willing to take up the cudgels and belabor that at the drop of a hat. We say it's dreadful, then help to shape it; living by our codes, acting on principle, being as impersonal as we can about everything; listening to sermons which direct us seriously to ponder a universe governed by natural law, and a society that would better not lose sight of moral law; in the afternoon perhaps, because it's Sunday, talking thoughtfully about Man with a capital M, and how he ought to behave at the eighteenth hole—though if you have no objection we'd just as soon not find it necessary to go over and make his acquaintance!

The plain truth is that what with our scientific procedures and the economic order, our international relations and the proletariat, technics and the State, the man we are talking about so thoughtfully is rapidly approaching the vanishing point! He's an average, or a statistic, or somebody on the street craning his neck to watch an airplane spell out the name of a cigarette. He's the chap who launders your shirt, reads your column, invests in your business, buys a ticket at your window, feeds the computer in your office, and in the rush hour crowds into the subway ahead of you. He's the voter, he's the landlord, he's the tenant, he's the customer who is always right. You hardly see him really. Dives didn't see Lazarus.

And many a time the trouble is we are just too busy to look—busy if you please on his behalf, with community chests and hospital drives, housing conditions and the birth rate: laying ourselves out for his sake, getting together all the facts about him we can find—while he disappears in the middle of them. It's a strange thing, this obsession with facts. Facts, we say, are the measure of truth. What is truth? Give us the facts! An advertisement in *The New Yorker* put it this way: "How much is a fact worth? By itself, nothing. But in relation to other facts, it becomes a priceless part of truth." Does it? One zero isn't worth anything, and that's what a fact is—"by itself." But in relation to other facts, each by itself a zero, it becomes priceless? Besides, when you talk about a priceless part of truth what do you mean? Facts don't constitute truth. Let's hold words to their meaning! A little hydrogen and a little sulphur and a little oxygen can sit together on a shelf from now to eternity and never constitute any truth about sulphuric acid. That takes people. One and one are two, if they are apples; if they are atoms, the answer may be a bomb. To suppose that facts impose some truth, which is a necessity, on God, is to have God disappear. To suppose that they impose some necessity on us—catch your breath now, it's touch and go!—is to be ourselves on the point of disappearing.

It is here that this story of the Pharisee, his back turned on a man who had the dropsy, his heels dug into the ground, pulling on a rope tied to an ox, all in the stillness of the Sabbath day, brings our civilization under such radical judgment, and the Biblical situation becomes our own. For four hundred years and more we have been talking about the worth of the individual, the dignity of the human soul, the age of the common man; and all of it is good doctrine, Christian doctrine, Renaissance doctrine, Reformation doctrine. Generations have taken it at face value, plunging into one revolution after another in order to heave up the under crust and put it on top. With what results? Today we have nations enslaved, without the possibility of any revolt that's likely to succeed: that's one good big part of the result. Whole races are bartered back and forth in the struggle for power. One lonely little man with the dropsy is picayune: we operate in the grand manner. A native Formosan was remarking not long ago on how very busy, for many years now, Japan and Communist China and the United States had been about Formosa: so busy that eight million Formosans had been pretty much lost in the shuffle! We disavow war as an instrument of national policy; but what else is there to do in Vietnam, Cyprus, Santo Domingo? We may even have to go in and clean up things in Cuba. Our interests are at stake. Then there's segregation, the public schools, civil rights, riots in Harlem, crime, and delinquency, juvenile and adult. Plenty of facts, for what they are worth; and who knows what to do about any of them? Meanwhile, for God's sake, what's a man worth? I put it to you: How many of us, anywhere on this sad earth, ever undertake with any seriousness at all, with any, even the most fleeting sense of gratitude, to love God; not in his majesty—as Luther once said, and rightly so, you can't do that—but in his creatures? And the dreadful account keeps piling up! "There was a certain man before him which had the dropsy. . . . And he took him, and healed him, and let him go; and answered them, saying, Which of you. . . .?" He still wants to know. The chapter from beginning to end is disturbing. You should read it. What else could it be, with such a story as a frontispiece?

But we must leave that now and get on. There are two other levels on which our vision may be distorted, and the world we live in, with the life that's in it, turned into a crazy quilt. In the silence that followed the healing of the sick man, dinner was announced; and suddenly with a clatter of tongues, and no end of pushing and shoving, every man was elbowing his way to as good a place at the table as he could get to before anybody else took it. It's the second of our scenes, a swift and fitting sequel to the first. I suggest that we take the third in connection with it, about a Pharisee who was trying to do exactly the same thing, except that he was in the house of God. That's over in the eighteenth chapter of Luke. He had gone up to the temple to pray. And there he stood, making no bones about it: he simply wasn't like other men, and there was no reason, as far as he could see, why God shouldn't be informed about it, admit it, and accord him some priority. Luke may possibly have felt that these two sharply etched medallions really belonged together, in memory at any rate: he associates them with the same pronouncement. It may be that Jesus himself labeled them with it. "Whosoever exalteth himself shall be abased; and he that humbleth himself shall be exalted." They are almost like two pictures carrying the same inscription. The subject is still warped vision, the film over our eyes, the riddle life seems, why we can't see straight. But now it isn't things that get in our way. We do. We do it with our elbows, as at the dinner party; or we do it with our virtues, as in the temple.

It's interesting, and I think significant, that this "parable," as Luke calls it, about the impolite guests just doesn't make sense if you come at it with a literal and pedestrian mind, as if it were a lecture on how to act when you're invited out. You can see at a glance how much there is that's wrong with it. Remember, Jesus himself was a guest, like these others: have you ever been puzzled by his company manners? Whatever the century or the culture, he was hardly within hailing distance of what would normally be regarded as genteel behavior. He took everybody to task, all around the table; you couldn't very well miss the irony, even if it was kindly. Whereupon he delivered himself of a bit of "worldly wisdom"—he didn't often do that—on the matter at issue, about not trying to push oneself forward; making use of a handy proverb, how after all it was better to be called up than to be called down. Maybe he himself had been called up higher on this very occasion—one can't tell. After which he came right out and said that if you were actually interested in getting ahead and having everybody admire you, you should take pains to start back there at the foot of the line.

How about that? What do you say? You'd still be looking out for number one, wouldn't you? And by feigning a humility you didn't have —turning your pride wrong side out, and wearing it that way to attract attention. In any case you'd be running a considerable risk that the host wouldn't take any notice; or if he did, wouldn't do anything about it, would simply let you stay where you were. I have read that the early Christians used to quote this precept to their most ambitious and troublesome bishops: "He that exalteth himself shall be abased." But maxims like that don't always work with bishops. They don't always work, period. It's altogether too difficult to become somebody by shrinking modestly out of sight!

You've got to have more imagination to catch what Jesus was driving at. Surely he wasn't seriously trying to tell us how to "have worship in the presence of them that sit at meat" with us. Any more than he was trying to tell his disciples how to calculate their way into greatness by devising some means of being a servant to all. He didn't wash their feet that last night of his life in order to win their esteem, or commend the practice to them so that they could win ours. He wanted these people squarely to face what they were, that's all. And he thought he might succeed if only he could show them how it would have been with them if they had really been as important as they were trying to seem. It would never have occurred to them then to jostle their way to the front like that. They wouldn't have had to depend on such strategy. They would have gone in and not given a thought to being "near the salt," or far and away down the board from it. If you're a genuine McGregor, then "wherever McGregor sits, there is the head of the table!"

And perhaps he did all of it—who knows?—with a touch of the humor that's never far from tears; because being as great as they were, they were so little about it. They were nowhere within sight of their true stature, these people of God, and never would be. If you listen beyond the words, you can almost hear the yearning in his heart, the same yearning that broke through at last there on the Mount of Olives, as he gazed out over the city: "O Jerusalem, Jerusalem, thou that killest the prophets," how often—how often would I, and ye would not! Possibly there were times like this when he could cover it up with the ghost of a smile he couldn't help. This that they were doing, children of the Most High, you could come across almost anywhere in the barnyard if you looked. Getting ahead with your elbows—and God there watching!

All right then, if elbows won't do, try your virtues. Why not spread them out before God, as the Pharisee was doing in the temple? "I thank thee that I am not as other men are, extortioners, unjust, adulterers, or even as this publican. I fast twice in the week. I give tithes of all that I possess." Tell him how well you've done, much more than you needed to do, and so be somebody where it really counts. Do you have to be shown how ridiculous that is—as if, though unable to impress anybody else, you could cut quite a figure in that Presence? Who in the world ever dropped his knitting and took to reciting the Apostles'

Creed because he had caught sight of any one of us here? Yet I hazard the guess that every time we read about these people in the Pharisee's house we say to ourselves, "Maybe I'm a little like them, but not a great deal, thank God! Certainly not much like that good man in the temple, of whom Jesus simply said that he wasn't good at all!" It must have occurred to you now and then what a small fraction of the New Testament gets home to us, not because of sin, as we think of it, but because what so frequently passes for virtue straddles the road and stands in the way. With God looking on!

I remember visiting the Hermitage, down near Nashville, the home of President Andrew Jackson, and reading there on the wall the letter he wrote when he was seventy-eight years old, just a little while before his death in 1845. He had been offered by a Commodore of the United States navy an ancient sarcophagus, thought to have been used for the burial of the Roman Emperor Septimius Severus back in the third century: on the condition that at his death his body be placed in it and there lie in state. Jackson declined the offer. "I cannot consent," he wrote, "that my mortal body shall be laid in a repository prepared for an emperor or king. My republican feelings and principles forbid it; the simplicity of our system of government forbids it. Every monument erected to perpetuate the memory of our heroes and statesmen ought to bear evidence of the economy and simplicity of our republican institutions and of the plainness of our republican citizens, who are the sovereigns of our glorious union, and whose virtue it is to perpetuate it." I wonder if, as I did, you feel like grinning at the way humility can strut —sitting down! I almost laughed out loud. "Thank God," I started to say, and, suddenly thought of the Pharisee here, so didn't just know what I wanted to thank God for!

It isn't very surprising, is it, that Paul called life, without the love that transforms it, an enigma? "We see through a glass, darkly." What else can it be but a riddle, when what we have and mean to hold gets so persistently in our way; or if that doesn't, we do, moving out on stage, front and center, by hook or by crook, by elbow or by virtue: to the end that in all things, in God as well as in our neighbor, we may serve ourselves! In wealth and in poverty, in giving as in getting, alone and in a crowd! Said Jesus of the Pharisee, he "stood and prayed thus with himself"—not out loud, silently, over there away from the others.

And there is no escape from it by any of the exits that are so commonly and widely publicized in our time. That we know very well what the problem is, seems clear from the phrases you so often hear on our lips: getting away from myself, forgetting myself, losing myself. It's all right to keep talking about it, but just try it. Try getting away from yourself down by the shore, or up in the mountains; and see how promptly that self of yours catches up with you. It's the same with forgetting: the minute you set your mind to forgetting the self you start remembering it. Do you think you can ever really lose it then in something bigger than it is? That's what they write about in books. So you espouse a cause; and before you know it the cause becomes a means of enhancing the self. You take on an interest, and the interest becomes a dividend. What a squirrel cage it all is!

Until the day you come face to face with something that has broken its way into this world on purpose to wrench our lives free from that insanity of forever turning in and curving back: face to face, not with truth, not even with the truth about yourself, but with God. That's what had happened to the publican. He could only beat on his breast. And it's what happened to Paul, on the road to Damascus; though there was a cross in the picture now, a gaunt thing, on a lonely hill. And Paul, trembling, asked the only question anybody can ask at the foot of it: "Lord, what wilt thou have me to do?"

Have you ever set yourself to find out why it is that on Calvary you can come nearer getting rid of the incubus which the self always turns out to be—nearer than you can come by way of any devotion to anything else, even to friend or loved one? On my walk one day I deliberately tried to work out the *abc* of it. This, I think, is the *a*: God never *ups* your rating, as a friend is likely to do, a husband, or wife, or child; he always lowers it, and to considerably less than zero, before he accepts you, and then accepts you anyhow! The chances are you will not stride into that with your boots on. The publican didn't even lift his eyes to heaven. He just smote his breast, and said, "God be merciful to me a sinner." When you meet that God on Calvary—and this was *b*, the second item—concern for the self becomes a good deal more distasteful than at any other spot on earth. Before the crucifixion the disciples were quarreling about who was going to be greatest in the Kingdom of God; they weren't doing that afterward, huddled there in the evening of the first day in the week, behind locked doors. So came item *c* in my reckoning: from then on it was not only love that made them reckless, it was this love; and reckless, not for any ends that were in sight, not for any ends that were theirs—for God's ends. What became of them didn't matter. They weren't even seeking their own salvation now, discounting self-interest because it wouldn't work. They were in Christ's great company, and didn't have to think that way any longer.

Only on such terms can you understand the unerring wisdom that turned the broken body of their Lord, and the blood he had shed, into what they called the Eucharist. Eucharist meant thanksgiving. They thanked God for the death of a man! And you? May I only say that the fullest, deepest breath you'll ever take, you'll take when in the love you bear him for all he has done you come to understand at last that you are rid of more of the burden you have been to yourself than you had ever dreamed was possible. Rid of it enough to rely now upon God's healing mercies in the very hurt life does you for his sake. Getting away from yourself—in the grace of our Lord Jesus Christ. Forgetting yourself—in the love of God. And losing yourself—in the fellowship and communion of the Holy Ghost.

God, our Father, we thank Thee for this love-haunted world! Not unto us, O Lord, not unto us, but unto Thy name give glory, for Thy mercy, and for Thy truth's sake. Amen.

Take That Thine Is

Be present to us, O God, even in this thought we have of Thee; and touch all our thinking and willing with the radiance of Thy thought and will for us; through Jesus Christ, our Lord. Amen.

MATTHEW 20:14 (part)—Take that thine is, and go thy way.

Which is the dignified and stately language of the King James Version, such as God might well be expected to use. Moffatt translates it, Take what belongs to you and be off.

You may think that if there is any parable at all in the New Testament which doesn't fit any of us here, it's this one. That bit about having labored in the vineyard from morning to night, and "having borne the burden and the heat of the day"—that's all right. You can say that again. But not all this about quarreling over the way God treats us. We aren't going to do that, not in church anyhow, not right out in the open, as this fellow did. And we hope we aren't going to be resentful either, as he was, and the whole twelve-hour shift with him, if somebody else who hasn't done as much as we've done still gets what we get, relatively a good deal more, if you want to count it up. We are trying our best not to be like that. It's wrong, and we know it's wrong. No argument.

But you see that isn't the point. The quarreling and the resentment are quite incidental. At its core this parable is precisely about us, because it raises the question we are always raising in one way or another. "Take what belongs to you. . . ." It raises the question of what does belong to us because we are religious people. What claim have we—to put it crudely—what claim have we on high heaven for having said some kind of Yes to God, and for having worked at it ever since? Peter wanted to know, in the chapter immediately preceding: "We have forsaken all, and followed thee; what shall we have therefore?" Let's see if we can arrive at anything that even looks like an answer.

Part of it, when you undertake to spell it out, has to be this: not how remarkably like the world's business God's business is, but how utterly and incredibly unlike! "What you are looking for," Jesus seems to be saying, "is a kind of day-laborer's wage: you, a son in your Father's house, and you are behaving like a servant! You are out on the highways of God, and you talk like a hireling!" He may have been aiming his shaft directly at Peter. He was certainly aiming it at the Pharisees. And they of course were the religious people of his day, as we are of ours. We shouldn't be forever looking down the nose at them. They just didn't like it that nonreligious people were being given priority over them. They had done their duty for the most part, and had indeed derived no little satisfaction from it. It was only right that they should. But Jesus was brushing it all aside, as if it didn't rate very much in God's book. Tax collectors and harlots were getting into the Kingdom ahead of them. He was flinging the gates wide open to the scum of the earth. Where was the justice in that? Or even decency? If "good" people had no edge at all for the good they'd done, what in God's name was the use? And it's a good question!

Jesus met it head on. He said in effect, "Well now, everybody thinks very highly of you. Isn't that a fact? So—there's your penny; what's the matter with it? You bargained for it, didn't you? It's what you wanted. As for these others, is God not allowed to do as he likes with what belongs to him? Can't he give them what he wants to? You take this that belongs to you and be off!" And it sounds a bit too much like the crack of doom for any of us to shrug and dismiss it. I think of that last sentence in the story of the scatterbrained girls who hadn't brought any oil in their lamps, and while they were running down to the store for some, the bridegroom came, "and the door was shut." Or of what Jesus said one day about the pious who wanted their piety to show; so they did their alms, and prayed, and fasted to be seen of men. "Verily I say unto you,"—it was his only comment—"they have their reward." "Already," I suppose we could add. Those whisperings in the crowd about how holy they were, the pointing fingers, the solemn reverence, the bowed head—God pity them, it was all they'd ever have. It was what they had billed heaven for, and heaven was sending the goods, cash on delivery. "You have your peace of mind. You have your standing in the community. You have the knowledge that you are not as other men are. You told your beads and sent a Care package to Europe. Whatever it was you were using God for, take it and go away!" Debit nothing, credit nothing, balance nothing. Account closed.

That's how it is when what we want of God is what matters most as far as we are concerned. I'm not saying we shouldn't want anything of him. Every time we get down on our knees or come to church we want something of him. And we should. It's absolute nonsense even to suggest that we shouldn't. You can't love God "for himself alone"— and there's no earthly use trying to exercise your muscles in any such direction. To say you love your wife for herself alone is to say you have no need for her. To say you love God that way would be blasphemy. It would mean that you could get along very well without him, thank you. The moment which perverts all religion and distorts it, the moment—and it's quite inseparable from our humanity—which can make of Christianity itself what has been called "the loftiest summit in the land of sin," is not the moment when we ask God for what we want, but the moment when we think he ought to give it to us, it's our due; the moment when we only half believe yet do not wholly doubt that we deserve some consideration for pity's sake: some of the ordinary goods of life, some share of health and happiness, some acre or two of the safe ground on which Democracy may rest!

And that's the kind of religion which the Bible keeps challenging from cover to cover. It should have been buried as far back as Genesis. When it survived Genesis, they should have buried it in Exodus. Open the Bible anywhere, and they should have buried it there. But nobody did. The religion of Israel was like that from start to finish. From start to finish the prophets kept saying so, and from start to finish God kept trying to knock the props out from under it. But people went on counting their pennies. The Old Testament was a strange place for it. The New is even stranger. "Blessed is the man that walketh not in the counsel of the ungodly," says the first Psalm; "he shall be like a tree planted by the rivers of water." How about a tree, asks the New Testament, planted outside the walls of Jerusalem with Jesus on it? What if the only blessedness you can count on is the kind with which the Hebrew word itself brings you to grips: the blessedness of a man who steadfastly sets his face, as Jesus did, to blaze some sort of trail with his life, and with everything he has to give?

It may be that Scripture finds its unity in the fact that religion can never be turned into a pay-as-you-go proposition! That would be to enter on a cash-and-carry relationship with God, which would make of him not the God of the Bible at all, but a god we have fashioned in our own image. Look at the cross. What else does it mean? It's God's way of canceling all wages! Desire them, extol them, labor for them, and you run into his blunt dismissal: "Take what belongs to you and be off!" You won't like what you've got. You'll think it should have been more. But away with you! The cross is the frontier between this world, with all that it's after, and the Kingdom of heaven. And there on the frontier the sentry cries "Halt!" And the sentry is God.

The first thing the parable says, then, is that what you're likely to be after is not likely to amount to very much. The poorest wage paid that day was the wage that was bargained for. All the best God has to give moves in along other lines. So the parable goes on to say, doesn't it, that only when you claim nothing do you have something! In the foreground of it is not God's debt to you, but his debt to himself, if you like; because he's the kind of God he is. That's what you have: something in him that keeps saying "I will give unto this last, even as unto thee. Is thine eye evil, because I am good?" And that goodness isn't just a quality which he keeps to himself through all eternity. It's what the New Testament calls "the grace of our Lord Jesus Christ," and says of it that it doesn't go in for accounting. Which of us would be here if it did? It doesn't obey the law we'd like to lay down for it. If any employer should act as this one did, he'd get into bad trouble, and the quicker the better: it would serve him right. But this isn't a lesson in economics. We are here, and God is there, and that means we have come clean away from all our human

lore

Of nicely-calculated less or more!

We're in his country now, and his reasons may very well be our unreason! That's why Christ seems so irrelevant at times—in the Christmas carol service, now and then even on Good Friday. Have you never felt it? It's because, says Charles Williams in one of his plays, everything is "grab" with us, and we can understand that; while everything is "grace" with him, and that puzzles us: almost terrible grace, as whimsical sometimes —so Williams represents it—as harum-scarum a bit of prodigality, as you would care to see. The Middle Ages thought of it like that. I suppose they got the idea from the way God flings his rain around, and the winds, and the snow, and the dark and the dawn, and the riot of daisies and buttercups and cherry blossoms in the spring. In his novel, *War in Heaven*, Williams wants us to see that that too is what the book of Job means. "I always understood," remarked Mornington to the Archdeacon, "that where Job scored over the three friends was in feeling natural curiosity why all these unfortunate things happened to him. They simply put up with it, but he, so to speak, asked God what He thought He was doing." "He was told he couldn't understand," put in the Vicar. "He was taunted with not being able to understand— which isn't quite the same thing," Mornington answered. "As a mere argument," he went on, "there's something lacking perhaps in saying to a man who's lost his money and his house and his family, and is sitting on the dustbin, all over boils, 'Look at the hippopotamus!'" Quite so. The grace of God in all of his creation seems so whimsical at times as to be irrelevant. The author of the book of Job, I think, designed that irrelevance: because in some strange way he knew that to "look at the hippopotamus" may well be in wonder to become again the child of "your Father which is in heaven," and "maketh his sun to rise on the evil and on the good, . . . sendeth rain on the just and on the unjust." Whoever wrote Ecclesiastes thought it spelled indifference. To Jesus it spelled God's lavish generosity.

But that's exactly what shatters all our fancied security! Religion at its best "compels the perception that God isn't to be found in it"! How do you "find" a God when you can't—what shall I say?—pin him down, put your finger on him, and on the way he will act? When his dealing with you is by way of a grace which turns and twists into this world far more ingeniously even than the snake in Eden? It's there at your elbow when there's something you're sure you can't do—is there any such thing on our roster at the moment?—and when there's something you're equally sure you can do. It's there not to bestow on you, but to snatch away from you, that "dreadful assurance" which is so likely to mummify your faith; because you have what you want, and no longer seek as you once sought—some inner serenity, and you rest on it now; some sense of belonging which has already rewarded your love; some confidence that all things will work together for good, you have felt like that about life for a long time! Kafka writes of the man who wondered at how easily he went the eternal way, until he discovered that he was rushing backward along it.

> Just when we're safest, there's a sunset touch
> A fancy from a flower-bell, some one's death,
> A chorus-ending from Euripides, . . .

How else can God surprise and outflank all our lines of defense?

> And that's enough for fifty hopes and fears
> As old and new at once as nature's self,
> To rap and knock and enter in our soul.

Somebody once said there were really three thieves on Calvary, and the greatest of them all was the one men called Jesus: "breaking and entering" the storehouse of your life and mine, and making off with all the treasures we have laid up on earth, so that maybe some day there would be a few laid up in heaven for us, where moth and rust do not corrupt, and thieves cannot break through and steal!

"Take what belongs to you." If you try asserting any claim, you'll find that what belongs to you will not seem to be a great deal. Is that what the parable means? If you've never given a thought to asserting any claim, knowing very well you have none, what belongs to you will be "the grace of our Lord Jesus Christ," and all that follows it in the New Testament, without even a breath between, "the love of God, and the communion of the Holy Ghost." The Church, for all these centuries, has called that a benediction—and it isn't at all, unless you will quit hugging your penny and crying, "No, no! I want this!" If that's what you're bent on, the grace and the love and the communion add up to the most devasting prospect on earth; because they speak of a God who doesn't care about your penny, but will have nothing less than the future to be yours, knowing what that will cost!

And so he sets about it by holding out to you his pardon, when pardon is the last thing you deserve. That's why it's never cheap. You're not at any bargain counter now. That day up by the lake, after the Resurrection, Peter would never even have dreamed of asking his question, "We have forsaken all, and followed thee; what shall we have therefore?" He was beginning to think less of what he had left for Christ's sake, and more of what Christ had left for his sake. If such a reversal ever happens to you, you'll hardly know what you can do to keep your life from seeming a paltry, indecent thing. You'll try to turn your face away, as Peter wanted to do, hoping to get off somewhere into a corner to be alone with the little you that's left, begging God to turn his face away from all the days you have lived! But you will not be done with him. Forgiveness can't be earned, but it can't just be picked up for nothing. Three times over Jesus kept asking "Lovest thou me?"—once for every denial back there among the shadows by the fire in the court of the high priest's palace. How did it feel to be dealt with that way? Christ will take good care, says Kierkegaard, "to be heard when all about [you] is still, when the stillness makes [you] lonely." And if you ask him, "Do I then love thee, Lord?" he will answer as if to disclaim all knowledge, telling you only of how the case stands: "Lovest thou me?" "He adds not one syllable more, he takes not one syllable away, he alters not his voice, . . . ; unchangeable as a dead man, calm as eternity, he repeats it: 'Lovest thou me?'" Peter could scarcely bear it—as who can?—and kept blurting out, "Lord, thou knowest that I love thee." I wish I could say that nothing else mattered to him any more, but I can't. At the first hint that the future wasn't going to be a bed of roses, he wanted to know how John would get along. Everybody knew that Jesus loved John: how would

John do? The answer he got was the only thing this God of the broken heart could say, the only thing left for him to say: he would take Peter even on those terms. "What is that to thee? Follow thou me."

You may have whenever you will the grace that means pardon, though pardon is the last thing you deserve: but you can't settle down in it, because he has taught you to care; and there is so very much everywhere that is not as he wants it to be! So the grace has to mean power too, except that you can't build any castles in Spain with it; because it means more even than that: it means the very giving of God's own dangerous life to you in Christ. That's what you have! A God who never has been safe in our world! Run along a few verses in Matthew, here where the parable is, and you'll see. Jesus had barely finished speaking when the mother of James and John came bustling up, wanting to know if they couldn't please sit in his kingdom, one on his right hand, the other on his left: two such ominous phrases, used at last of the malefactors crucified with him, one on the right hand, the other on the left. You almost wonder, as someone has suggested, if they weren't intentional; if Matthew and Mark and Luke weren't hinting that it was James and John who rightfully belonged at his side on Calvary that bitter day. At any rate Jesus asked if they could drink of his cup, and they said they could. Poor lads! With true hospitality he held it out to them when the tally of their years was made up, and they drank of it. It was death. That was his cup.

The Gospels say that people were astonished at Jesus' teaching: amazed, struck dumb—that's the word they use—quite beside themselves. Might one suppose it could ever happen in church? What if it should come to us that we cannot have the God we want: a God who never moves the furniture around or upsets anything; just sees to it every day, with his feather duster, that what we are already is in apple-pie order? What if it should come to us that the God we have will never keep house like that? I have read that there was a man once "who looked . . . back on his way to hell." God said to him, "You've read the black scroll of your misdeeds. What did you expect? Why do you tarry?" And he answered, "I had great hope of Thy loving-kindness," So God turned to another who had labored long and said, "I will give unto this last even as unto thee."

Show us, O God, as much of Thy purpose, because we have it, as shall steady us. We do not ask that the way be made smooth, or even that Thou wouldst bestow upon us now the strength which Thou hast promised. We ask only for the grace to use what Thou hast already provided in Christ Jesus. Amen.

The Kingdom of God
Keeps Coming

We have come, O God, at Thy bidding. Unless we are willing to be healed, Thou canst not heal the world's hurt. Grant us now in the power of Thy Spirit to hear the Word which maketh whole the sick, and all things new that were old; through Jesus Christ, our Lord. Amen.

MATTHEW 22:4— . . . everything is ready; come to the . . . feast.

I am told that in one of Von Schlegel's plays the curtain rises to show the inside of a theater where people are waiting for the curtain to rise. When it does, another such scene is disclosed, with still another curtain. Then a third. Whereupon the original audience grows uneasy, looking around to see if perhaps it too is on the stage. So it is in the Gospels. Here is this Kingdom of God which Jesus is continually trying to describe, never saying what it is, only saying what it's like. And there's the invitation which keeps coming, as if a great banquet were ready; and the men who go on turning their backs with a shrug— so that the love and the mercy and the goodness have to go somewhere else, to some place where they're wanted. You watch the unfolding and the movement, generation after generation down through history, drama inside of drama, one beginning before the other is over, like the boxes children play with that slide into each other: until you too take to wondering who it is really that's out there in front of the foot-lights. Is this somebody else, or is it you?

Take the invitation to begin with. Who are these people that were invited to the wedding? They had been invited a long time ago—don't overlook that; and now the summons came—that's how it was done in the East—when the oxen and the fatted calves had been killed, and everything was ready but the guests. When was it the word reached you? And mind this: from the faces we wear sometimes, I am not always sure how you and I think of it. Jesus thought of the Kingdom of God every time as a feast or a wedding or some other glad thing. It moved in to the sound of opening doors and running feet, with voices calling, and lamps being lighted in the dark. One lively metaphor would trip on the heels of another. It was somebody on a spring morning sowing good seed; then after a while the full corn in the ear. It was a woman putting leaven into meal. Story after story reads that way. It was a farmer who had found one day in some neighboring field a buried treasure, and made off to buy it; a merchant coming home with a pearl of great price, a net cast into the sea and drawn full to the shore. The figures are taut and breathless: things new and old brought from their hiding place; a king moved with compassion for a servant who owed far more than he could ever pay; a householder who had left all his goods in trust, getting back after a long journey when none of his agents was looking for him; a landlord hiring laborers into his vineyard, with something for everybody to do, early and late. Flags flying in the wind, multitudes of them, overtures of God, carillons tumbling their wild changes over the countryside. Forever there is a process that's been going on unnoticed; when suddenly, at some zero hour, all of it comes to a head unexpectedly, perhaps disconcertingly, and people have to make up their minds about it and decide what to do. It isn't a kind of Utopia that's on the way, never think that; it's life, abundant life, life as God intended it, with "music and dancing" and "harvest home."

Listen to God's unfailing word for it: "All my preparations are made. I've finished now, and I'm waiting." What do you suppose was in Jesus' mind when he said that? Could it have been anything as far back as the first chapters of Genesis, when the earth took shape, and the heavens were spread out? And God saw that it was good! There are times when we stare with unblinking eyes at this creation of his, which every once in a while turns so sour, and can't see why on earth he ever did it. And the only hint the Bible gives is that the yearning in his heart just came out that way, in the light, and the darkness, and the stars, and the green valleys, and—man! All of it somehow good up to that point. Then it went wrong. A devilish kind of self-will set itself against God's will, and began cropping up everywhere. But if there was ever to be anybody to love him freely, that was the risk he had to run. So he kept at it, and got Abraham up out of Ur of the Chaldees, and the children of Israel up out of Egypt, and on a day after that out of Babylon. The weary epic is like a lump in your throat if you read it with any imagination at all: kings and psalmists, priests and prophets; a star over Bethlehem, and this Someone at the center of it who is always trying; a child in a manger, a man weeping over Jerusalem, a tired Galilean only thirty years old on a cross!

Did you ever see a housewife getting ready for a dinner she was giving, the hurrying in and out, the sounds in the kitchen, the bit of linen with which at last, as she smiles, she wipes the sweat from her forehead, and says, "It's all done now, I'm through"? Jesus takes the slow, aching misery of the centuries and folds it under, until the only thing you see of the heart of God is like that image of a weary woman, glad and happy about her work. Think of the naked pity of it. He takes the whole vast plan of the Eternal, with the love for his people in it, and the suffering in it, and presses it down to the tiny compass of a feast, so that you can understand what it means, and holds it out to you. "There's not a thing unthought of" he says, "just come." Says it up and down the roads of Galilee and Judaea, across the Jordan; to Mary of Magdala, and Mary of Bethany, and Peter the fisherman, and Zacchaeus the publican, and to how many of us? While the little band of disciples around him watch the multitude go away, and huddle close to each other against the storm; and men leave off their muttering, and clench their fists, and begin to shout. When did it happen? This morning? I don't know!

So, almost without realizing it, we are brought on nearly every page to move over under the ominous possibility which always lies at the heart of the gospel. On this side a glad and undiscouragable business is going on: "Tell them which are bidden, . . . all things are ready"; and on this side the fellows who St. Luke says were all of one mind: they made light of it and went their ways, one to his farm, another to his merchandise. Please hear more than the bare words. Hear beneath them the thing that whispered its sneer in Eden, like a snake slithering along the branches of a tree, only to change into a wild beast that roared out its madness on Calvary. It has come to my generation in the spitting fire of long guns, and the hiss of flamethrowers; in the blinding, searing heat of the bomb. You think that's worse than this simple record, "They made light of it"? I don't. Nothing is worse than to treat all you know of God and what he wants as if it were a matter of no moment at all: before Good Friday or after it, who cares?

But, you say, you aren't that sort of person. Granted, the story is picturesque: the man with the piece of ground he had bought; he just had to see what it was like—and the other, with the five yoke of oxen to be gone over, chest and shoulders and legs. "I pray you," they both said, the first somewhat more graciously than the second, "I pray you have me excused." Because the only reason they had was no more than an excuse, and they knew it, they tried to turn it back into a reason again by tipping their hats and being reasonably polite about it. But you can't do that. Be as polite as you like—so what? No is still No. The third did have a reason which might well have passed muster: only a few days ago, or a few weeks, or a few months, he had been married; even the law allowed him a full year to get over that, and, I quote, to "cheer up his wife" without being bothered by any such engagements as this. No doubt when the invitation first came he could have foreseen how it was going to be with him, and so declined in good time. At any rate he didn't have to be so rude about it. There was no hat-tipping now. All he said was, "I can't come." And that was very definitely that.

Picturesque, you agree; but not a little remote. I wonder if we can't do something about it. As I read these two accounts again, Matthew's and Luke's, with all the surrounding text, two kinds of refusal seemed to emerge, both of them dealt with in these chapters. One kind is overt, forthright, frank, and not too polite: three men—would it help any to dress them in gray flannel, and have them worried about real estate or the stock market or some domestic crisis? Never mind the piece of ground, the oxen, the wife. Let's just swap them for whatever it is that keeps so many of us from having anything vital to do with God, even when we come to church and say our prayers: things that get between him and us, and block the road, and detour all the traffic; the treasures we've cached away somewhere, the commitments we have from day to day, the cake we'd like to eat, or the plain bread we try to earn.

Scarcely to be distinguished from that is the other kind of refusal—the kind that isn't out in the open and forthright and frank, but none the less efficacious: all the more so because we don't fully understand what we are doing, are not fully aware of the substitutions we are making, the sleight of hand that turns piety into idolatry, and makes a No out of what everybody takes to be a most praiseworthy Yes.

Take for example the man in the story who came without a wedding garment. Have you ever been puzzled by what happened? I'm not sure I'd be too sorry for him if I were you, gnashing his teeth there in the outer darkness: sorry perhaps, but not so sorry that you miss the point. You may take it pretty well for granted that if he could have laid any claim at all to any one of the excuses which people have tried to make for him, he would have done it. He was given the chance, by one who called him friend and asked him why: and he was speechless. He was the kind that gets in, but doesn't belong in. He wasn't dressed—that's how Jesus puts it—as he should have been.

Interesting, don't you think, that Freud used to say no Christian ever is! He was nearer the truth than a good many who lashed out at him. He said we were all wrapped up in illusions: about the sense of security we can have in our faith, how completely confident and assured we can be, how immortal and therefore invulnerable we are, with God at our right hand. Will Herberg writes of a well-meaning psychiatrist who recently set out to show that psychiatry, like religion, has as its real business not the destruction of these natural and necessary defenses, but their strengthening. While the Bible, strangely enough, sets out to demolish every one of them! It tells us to strip off our devotions and all our pious practices long enough to see what it is we are really after; so often not God at all, but these selves of ours: how we can save them, seeing that we so much dread to lose them; save them and make the most of them—kneeling in front of our little altars, tugging at the sleeve of our little God, whose undertaking we think it is to listen and make everything come out all right. Said Luther, "Man serves himself in everything"; then added, "even in God!" Praying the Lord's Prayer backward, as he saw it: starting with "Deliver us from evil," from all the misfortune and the suffering we'd like to get out of; and only after that coming along to where we should have started, to forgiveness, and a will that has to be done, and a Kingdom, and a Holy Name to be kept unsullied!

But that isn't the only form idolatry takes among those who wouldn't think of refusing the invitation, but accept it and come. Did you notice that St. Luke introduces the parable by telling of a pious soul at table with Jesus that Sabbath day in the house of one of the chief Pharisees, who suddenly clasped his hands at all the wonderful things he had heard, and looked up, way up, and sighed, and said, "Blessed is he that shall eat bread in the kingdom of God!" It's King James English for "What a marvellous place heaven is going to be!" He had an acute case of what a friend of mine once called "premature sanctification." To launch out right off, as Jesus did, on the story of the marriage feast was almost to say, "Wait a minute, my friend! Hold on a bit! Are you sure you're going to make it?" That man's name among us is Legion! Men and women who come, sometimes come in droves; sit in church Sunday morning misty-eyed. They know what they want. They want now some of the upholstering they're sure they're scheduled for after a while. You must not annoy them with any of your negative thoughts about positive thinking. You have no right to do that. They have come, haven't they? They are there, aren't they? Doesn't that amount to anything? So throw the accent where it will rest most comfortably. Don't talk about the enormity inside of us, underneath our routine, compensating observances, our extenuating obsessions with right and wrong. Maybe that's partly why our literature of late has run off into "romantic diabolism": if the pulpit won't dig in, the poet will, and the novelist, and the dramatist; only, when he gets through, he has no place to go.

With all that Isaiah says about a God who hides his face, and all that Paul says about his wrath, how can any of us be so busy being righteous as not to hear either of them? I remember a cartoon in the *New Yorker* about a man who had just passed a sign reading PREPARE TO MEET THY GOD. So he stopped in front of a mirror to take off his hat and smooth his hair and straighten his tie! It was an etching with acid, a sardonic comment on the shallow, cosmetic make-do which likes to strut around in heaven's face, hoping to collect a little credit. There are sober treatises that pooh-pooh the naïve passages in the New Testament which mention the wrath of God. Nothing much was made of it in Herman Melville's day either; which may in a measure account for *Moby Dick*. But all the prophets of Israel were on Melville's side, with his dark sense of some remorseless evil on the voyage out, just under the surface of life. Mr. Emerson's chatty optimism was never their cup of tea. They were forever talking about something, as Jesus did, which you could well be afraid of, and the terrible left hand of God that was raised against it. Hair lotions indeed! And who said comfort? There's a soft word that gets harsh treatment in the gospel. We insist on being told that God is near; that it wouldn't occur to him even to go away. But what if the God we have is farthest off when we think he's nearest, and nearest when we think he's farthest off? Is that what Luther meant— again I am reminded of him—when he said in his violent fashion, "Nobody is in this life nearer God than those who hate and blaspheme him. He has no more dear children than they." At least they realize that the God they have is not the God they want!

In Luke, over against all our trifling preoccupations with beauty and peace, with sweetness and light, even with right and wrong, the pious soul with his deep sigh who introduces the parable is balanced at its end with these outlandish words: "If any man come to me"—then that gesture which brushes aside father and mother, wife and children; and afterwards talks of bearing a cross, and counting the cost before you build a tower or fight a battle! Jesus knew only too well how easily sentiment can turn into idolatry—the same Greek word serves for both! —at the drop of a tear.

So through all the gospel runs a deep undertone—"The king came in to see the guests." It's like the far-off roar of breakers dashing against some rock-bound coast, like the roll of distant thunder. But the music is never drowned in it! On every page of the Old Testament as well as of the New it's always high time for that, and the music is always there. Scarcely any dramatist or novelist of our day seems able to hear it. They want only to persuade us of our peril. This parable does that too. G. K. Chesterton does it in his *Ballad of the White Horse*.

> I tell you naught for your comfort,
> Yea, naught for your desire,
> Save that the sky grows darker yet
> And the sea rises higher.

Perhaps because our skin is so thick. Said John Donne, "I have a grave of sin. . . . Where Lazarus had been four days, I have been for fifty years. Why dost Thou not call me, as Thou didst him? I need Thy thunder, O my God; Thy music will not serve me."

Yet it's there. It's always there. Matthew very aptly sets this story down in the midst of a storm, with the sound of the wind blowing. He wants us to read it after the cleansing of the temple, which was so hard for everybody to take. Who on earth gave Jesus such authority? Then you turn the page, and the Herodians are baiting their trap, with their question about the taxes, whether or not it was lawful to pay tribute to Caesar. After that the Sadducees try to make him look ridiculous with their trumped-up business about a woman who had had seven husbands and didn't know which one she was supposed to live with in heaven! When they fail, the Pharisees have a go at catching him up in his theology: what other purpose could they have had in asking him what he thought was the Great Commandment? They weren't exactly looking for information, that's sure! And we are supposed to remember, against all that noise and turmoil, that the invitation to the feast still stands. It stands even when it's turned down. The summons, as Jesus tells it, goes on repeating itself. It veers away only when there's nothing else for it to do. When people won't come even for the food's sake, how will you manage? How can anybody manage? It veers away at last to the city's poor. You despised these outcasts if you were a Pharisee. It wasn't at all like God to look them up. He'd never do such a thing! Both "bad" and "good" says Matthew; "the maimed, . . . the halt, and the blind," says Luke: out on the street corners, in the parks, down the dark alleys; there by the hedgerows, in the open country, where the tramps are, along the highways. It's the music! It's the sound of the trumpets which Satan in the old legend missed so much every morning after he had fallen from his high estate, missed them more than anything else in heaven: so piercing loud sometimes when we hear them on earth that we almost want to stop our ears. They have to be loud if they are to cover up our surly refusals, and the threat that in the gospel keeps running at our heels!

Luke alone of all the evangelists tells us, in the chapter which follows directly, Jesus' stories of the lost sheep and the lost coin and the lost son. It's the music still, and any man can hear it at any time! Said C. S. Lewis, writing of those years when he himself had been "surprised by joy," "The Prodigal at least walked home on his own feet. But who can duly adore that Love which will open the high gates to a prodigal who is brought in kicking, struggling, resentful, darting his eyes in every direction for a chance to escape? The words, . . . compel them to come in, have been so abused by wicked men that we shudder at them; . . . properly understood, they plumb the depths of the Divine mercy. The hardness of God is kinder than the softness of men; . . . His compulsion is our liberation"—throwing wide its arms even there where the elder brother sulks in the yard and will not go in; saying to him, "Son, thou art ever with me." Could it be God who was saying that to these muttering scribes and Pharisees? "Thou art ever with me, and all that I have is thine."

May we here, then, still speak of the peace of God? Jeremiah couldn't stand the thought of the false prophets who went around crying "Peace, peace; when there is no peace." And indeed there is none, except that dangerous, disturbing peace which Christ has left all of us as a heritage. "Everything is ready," says the New Testament. Everything but the guests. It is told of George Sand, that all too vital and therefore weary and turbulent spirit, that one day she threw the book at the head of her tutor in philosophy, shouting at him, "All this is killing me, great man! It's far too long-winded, and I'm in a hurry to love God!" "All that I have is thine." Perhaps we should leave it there, where the gospel leaves it: and muse for a while on the mystery of the Kingdom that keeps coming!

If the dark come upon us, O God, our God, let it be Thy darkness. And if our hope is for the wrong thing, let us wait in that dark while the hope fails, and without peace, until Thou canst make us ready for what Thou hast promised, and for the peace which is in Christ Jesus.
Amen.

THE UPSTART SPRING

Let God Be God

O Thou who art eternally both merciful and just, be Thou our God: and that not in our way but in Thine; through Jesus Christ, our Lord. Amen.

MATTHEW 4:1-11.

My subject has nothing to do with permissive counseling. It doesn't mean that we should really allow God to be God. I dare say he will be in any case. Carlyle is said to have remarked of Margaret Fuller, I believe, when he was told that she had accepted the universe at last, "Egad, she'd better!" "Let God be God" is the battle cry of a man who has drawn his sword and is reaching for the sky with its point! That's how it was with Jesus in Matthew's weird story of the Temptation, which in the calendar of the Christian Church has long been associated with the beginning of Lent. No doubt it seemed almost unintelligibly remote when it was read to you—those two shadowy figures weaving in and out like gigantic silhouettes against the dawn. What on earth could it have to do with us? That there should be anything contemporaneous about it is a notion which scarcely ever occurs to anybody.

"If you are actually God's Messiah," Satan said, "why not give some indication of it? You are hungry, and a great many people in this world are hungry. Why not a little bread perhaps—from these stones? You can do it.——That doesn't appeal to you? Well then, better still, some more spectacular sign. And not for your sake, for theirs. Show that crowd milling about down there in the temple court that you are indeed what you think you are, and what they hope you are: leap from this pinnacle, and appear among them heaven-sent and unhurt. Childish as they are, they rather expect that sort of thing, and you very well know it. You won't even bruise your foot. God will see to that.——No? You're being unreasonably difficult. There's something else though. Come with me a moment. Look yonder, from this mountaintop. You can see all the kingdoms of the world and the glory of them. How much simpler it would be all around if I'd just bow out and let you have them! I'll do it at the snap of a finger—if you'll just acknowledge that for all practical purposes they are mine and not yours. If you'll admit that they belong to me"—that's what he's getting at. "Men out there do what I say, not what God says." He's being realistic. "Why not accept as fact what is fact? If it weren't for my control over them, you'd have an easy time of it. They would make you a king. No cross that way, only a crown!"

But now let me get into this picture and ask you something! Can you honestly think that Jesus told his disciples of this vast and dark encounter simply to encourage them, under like circumstances, to do as he had done? Of itself, that would have been almost too obvious to be true. And the Bible is never obvious. It's forever probing into how things are, not on the surface, to be read at a glance, but underneath. What if this were the symbol of that age-old controversy which God keeps waging with his people? There he is, with his love and his power; and here we are with our need, plucking at his sleeve: why does he just stand there? Why doesn't he do something? Could it be that the Bible has found out who it is that does the tempting? From generation to generation, through the Old Testament and through the New, it keeps gazing steadily at us!

I'm afraid we shall have to begin with that. One of my students put the case in a sermon of his. There wasn't enough compassion in it, but it was startlingly vivid. He said that all too often when we pray we are like some technician on a platform, leaning into a microphone and lifting up his eyes to heaven with nothing much to say but "Testing—one, two, three. Testing—one, two, three." It would be an appallingly shameless sort of relationship to have with God, but it's an ancient one. It runs back to the saga of two little people named Adam and Eve, daring God in a garden to let them take life up in their own hands and do as they pleased with it. It runs back to the children of Israel, that nondescript horde of slaves trudging through the wilderness on their way out of Egypt, "tempting God"—these are the very words set down in the record—by asking meat for their lust. "Can he furnish a table in the wilderness," they'd like to know, there in the seventy-eighth Psalm. It's the theme that runs through every one of the gospel lessons for Lent. In Matthew and Mark and Luke it breaks out all around like a rash when they tell their story about the feeding of the multitude, and the bread he gave the hungry, and the crown they offered, as John recalls it: on to the piteous question Jesus asked when men were baiting him, "Why tempt ye me?" And so finally the taunt hurled at him as he was being crucified: "If thou be the Son of God, . . ." Where have you heard that before?

"Is the Lord among us, or is he not?" the people said to Moses. In its crudest form it's the demand that somehow the covenant God has made with us should pay off. Come now, let's have a little "what's-it" —manna in Hebrew; that's what the word means. How about a little of this stuff we're after, the results we're looking for? There were thirteen possible subjects for sermons listed some time ago in a newspaper supplement, and readers were asked to choose the one they would most like to have their minister preach on. Seven thousand picked "How Can I Make Prayer More Effective?" Maybe it's wrong to guess what they had in mind: how to get what they wanted when they prayed. But who can help guessing, when by far the fewest takers of all were for the titles that had to do with the Christian approach to the chaos of our time? Opening up such matters, inquiring about them, suggesting ways and means of exploring them—it's all beside the point if what we are actually trying to do is to be God by using him! "We have forsaken all and followed thee." Well, not quite all. And at some little distance no doubt. But we haven't just stood stock-still. We've executed a number of maneuvers in the right direction. "What shall we have therefore?" No what-you-may-call-it, no manna? In the book of Job Satan shrugs his shoulders, puts his tongue in his cheek and his thumbs in his armholes, kicks up the star dust, and gives it out as his opinion that no man will serve God for nothing. And of course no man has to. H. G. Wells used to say that he didn't care for Christianity precisely because it held out too much of a bribe, in the way of golden streets and pearly gates. If he was to be good, he preferred to be good for nothing! You do have that option! But you can't be good —for nothing; not in God's world. Neither, be it said, can you be good —for something. Virtue still has its rewards, but you'd do well not to take out after them. And friendship has its benefits. But don't try to cultivate any if that's all you have in mind.

All right, you say; I'll go along with that. But if there isn't to be any "what's-it" then let this God prove that he is what he says he is by giving us just one sign, for heaven's sake! What's wrong with that? Anything but this dreadful silence. This two-faced world he makes us live in, where you can read him in or read him out as you like! I remember hearing Herbert Farmer tell of what happened to him on a quiet spring morning in an English apple orchard when the trees were in blossom. The daffodils, the soft, heavily scented air, the blue sky, the tender light—everything spoke of God. When suddenly there hopped from behind a bush the thrush that had been singing its heart out just a moment before; followed stealthily by a cat that pounced on it so quickly that he could do nothing at all, and bit off its head at his feet. On the instant the Yes he had been saying to God in his heart came face to face with a No, and the No got to his lips first. It isn't any stunt we want. A pinnacle, a few passes in the air, presto! That's child's play. But when the child is my child and quits playing and dies—what then? No sign? A friend of mine this very day would like to know. Will anybody tell him? Or will anybody blame him?

After all, it's for God's sake, not just for our own, that we'd like to see him take some hand in his world. The prophets used to call on him to vindicate his honor against the enemies of his people; and he allowed his people to be driven away captive into Babylon. The psalmists called on him, and the Greeks came. It was no way to act! And after them the Romans. Tide after tide. Then that strange man from Nazareth, who seemed bent on doing nothing that mattered, just giving himself over into the hands of the crowd that hated him. What a plan of campaign that was, marching out against all the kingdoms of the world and the glory of them! When he told his disciples how he must go up to Jerusalem, and suffer many things, and be put to death, Peter rebuked him; and Jesus flashed back, "Get thee behind me, Satan!" Have you heard that before? He had to do it. It was the old offer again, of easier terms than God's! The only way to win was by losing; by the wisdom of this folly, the strength of this weakness: the cross, the nails, the crown of thorns; and the gibe written over it all, "Jesus of Nazareth, His Majesty from Nowhere, King of the Jews"! God can't be God except on his terms. Sometimes I wonder why we try to keep him from it!

So he resists us. That follows, and I suggest we come to it next. It ought to go without saying that we aren't always tempting him. Nobody would want to say such a thing. We are to ask him for what we want as a child would ask. Why try to hide it from him? Neither is he always having to resist us. But we do have to be ready for it when he does; when for reasons that are not our reasons he has to meet us with his silence. Do you remember that poignant little sentence, after all the turbulent years in the book of Judges, when the glory was about to depart from Israel, and Samuel was only a child in the house of Eli? "And the word of the Lord"—so it runs—"was precious in those days." But the meaning is not as it sounds. I wish it were. "The word of the Lord was rare in those days"—that's the sad fact of it; rare, like a jewel, and men longed for it, because they had heard nothing from him, they had seen nothing to remind them of him. Again it happened, in the time of Amos: "Behold . . . saith the Lord . . . I will send a famine"—not of bread, nor water, but of hearing. "And they shall wander from sea to sea . . . they shall run to and fro to seek the word of the Lord, and shall not find it." Once more, on a day while it was yet dark, before the dawn. Caiaphas, the high priest, stood up and said, "Answerest thou nothing?" But Jesus held his peace. Herod too questioned him in many words; but the silence was unbroken. And Pilate, at the last. It's the hour that may come to any man, when he shall put his hand on his lips; for "there is no answer of God."

Just don't think of it as if it were some strange phenomenon, a perplexity of the faith, one of the problems of religion. We are in too big a hurry to locate it over among the inscrutable ways of Providence, as if God alone were to blame. It may just not be God who is the puzzle! The mystery is not always, and it's never altogether, somewhere in the heavens, on the other side of the sky. "From the crafts and assaults of the devil," runs the ancient Litany, "Good Lord, deliver us." And to-morrow and tomorrow and tomorrow—is no better than today. We simply can't make him out. "From war and bloodshed, from sudden and evil death"—and you read the story of the last fifty years for comment. "Give to all nations peace and concord"—and Berlin still hovers like a cloud in the East, and religion doesn't get back into Russia, and the cold war goes on. Maybe it means that God isn't as pliable as we should like to have him. Not a thing is ever to be gained by trying to keep that a secret, in Sunday School or in church!

But neither is anything to be gained by taking our frustrations as proof positive that nothing but a jaundiced view of life makes any sense. There is another possibility. There may be a different reading. Some years ago Sean O'Casey wrote an article in *The New York Times* about the "great galaxy of darkened stars," as he called them, that dull the spirit of our age. He quoted from one of them: "Everybody's hedged in; nobody can move; nobody counts." From another, "Rules, Laws, Promises, Traditions; into the pot with the whole bloody lot of them!" These men are not rebels against any stupidity, said he, or any in-justice; they are merely runners away from life, who think that "the rhythm of the universe" starts from them, and the ticking of time's clock "goes with their heart's dead beat."

It may all mean something else entirely: disappointment, defeat, frus-tration, loneliness. It may mean that if God intends to go on being God —and I have a kind of notion that he does!—he has to hold out against us just at the point where importunity starts sliding over into exploita-tion. That's the hard lesson that has to be learned; and many a time God has only the most sinewy of means for teaching it. To say nothing of the fact that what we ask of him may not be at all in his line, so to speak. It isn't for him to gather up the feathers after we've made them fly, and put them back neatly in place, smooth and unruffled. It isn't for him to undergird the American way of life—give all of us some little sense of global stability; strengthen the Church where she is weak, unite her where she is divided. Instead of wondering right away if there is a God, or if there is anything at all in religion, or if prayer is really worth the candle, why don't we put it to ourselves quite soberly, before we get down on our knees or open our mouths: Whose business is this that I'm spreading out before him? Those "crafts and assaults of the devil," the "war and bloodshed," the "sudden and evil death"—is that his business? And how much of it that isn't his is ours? Down that road we could quite conceivably stumble on more honesty than we have ever dreamed of.

Who is to say that history itself isn't in large part God's way of resisting temptation: never forcing anybody, never being cajoled into anything, never abdicating; so fearfully steady that even when the foundations are shaken, you can go ahead and build on that steadiness: fixed as the law of gravity is fixed—so that all that happens when you fool with it is that you prove it? That may be what *foolproof* means! Willing himself to fail by a cross, willing that we should, without ever once letting that cross turn into a forlorn hope: holding it there with tense muscles against the changing years, so that everybody can see it and nobody can budge it—the only hope of a world forlorn! Do you get the feel of it? It isn't soft. It's love, that's what it is, outrageous, violent love, that knows what it has to do when we tempt it!

After that, there is only one more step, and any one of us here can take it; just one short step to the place where the victory he's bound to win over us becomes the victory he wins for us, and so our victory. That's what happens when we make up our minds to let him be God not in our way but in his; and that not by allowing him, but by wanting it that way. Wanting it because it's there, and only there, that he can hold out to us, both hands full, the gift of his own life—which is all he ever has hoped people would take with ultimate and utmost seriousness; while ironically enough it has been the one thing they have rarely had the stomach to ask for. One day he did give them bread to eat, out of his compassion for them; and when the talk came round to the bread from heaven, they said that was what they longed for: "Lord, evermore give us this bread." But when he opened his arms to them and told them it was theirs for the taking, "I am the bread of life," they muttered to each other, "Why this man is nobody but Jesus, the carpenter's son!" And when he went on to assure them that the life he would give them was eternal life, that was too much even for many who had believed on him, and they turned back, and walked no more with him.

That's why at odd times he has to give us up, as Paul puts it in Romans, before we can understand what he means by giving himself up! I listened in one Sunday afternoon to an interview on television, as college students sat around in their fraternity houses, girls in their dormitories, trying to figure out for some reporter what life was all about, and not making a great deal of it. Some of them, when they were asked what they were looking forward to, said they wanted to be married and have a family; others were thinking more of a career in law or medicine or business: everybody wanted to succeed, everybody wanted to live in a split-level house. If they were lost, they preferred to be comfortably lost. Then the lens shifted to some downtown resort, where still others lolled about, heads drooping or on each other's shoulders, eyes and faces blank, while someone read verses that were equally blank, to the insane, stupefying beat of bongo drums and the strumming of a bass viol. From nothing that was said could you get the slightest hint that God had ever done anything about the stupid mess, or made possible any horizons beyond their own. If there was a God—and the question wasn't even raised—he had quite obviously let them down.

There was a time in Paul's life when he too thought that God had let him down. He had something he wanted to get rid of, called it his thorn, and prayed about it, but nothing happened. Again he prayed, and with the same result. A third time, and nothing came of it except that God's grace would have to do. Sometimes I think we assume too much when we take it for granted that a voice spoke which anybody could hear. There may have been nothing but the dreadful silence where for us there is no sound at all. Whatever it was, it was for his ears alone; and he said Yes to it, knowing that to say Yes, as Antigone cried out when she stood before Creon, was to "plunge both hands into life up to the elbows"!

In the library at Westfield, Massachusetts, there is the journal of a circuit rider, from pre-Revolutionary days, recording his fear that after one of his sermons during a camp meeting the young people might have found occasion for a frolic. It came to me what a sober spot in heaven he must occupy now, there among the rows upon rows of saints who are about the solemn business of being saints—and how far away from Paul, over where the cherubim and seraphim, after the Bach is over, are dancing to the music of Mozart! Karl Barth once said he saw it that way.

"Giving thanks unto the Father . . . who hath delivered us from the power of darkness"—and you would like very much to know where on earth the light is!—"and translated us into the kingdom of his dear Son." What is there anywhere that looks like a kingdom? "Thanks be to God who giveth us the victory"—when Paul's life was one long story of frustration! But he called it fulfillment, said it was a very pageant, setting down all his assets as liabilities, and all his liabilities as assets! He was forever so busy going somewhere that he couldn't wait for the bookkeeping. The perils were on the road to the promise; defeat was a way station, a flag stop with the signal set to go straight through head on. "O the depth of the riches both of the wisdom and knowledge of God"—and he threw down his pen, because he was unable to make anything at all of what was going on, and sang a doxology. That's the place for it! "How unsearchable are his judgments, and his ways past finding out!"

All he knew was that in his own life and in the life of his people, as in the Bible from beginning to end, from the garden of Eden to the garden of Gethsemane, when the love of God holds out against us, it's never idle. And it's never as silent as we think. It's weaving its own quiet pattern even in the human bewilderment which seems to us so utterly sterile. Over and over again our love looks around among its treasures and chooses for you something that's all wrong. God's love looks around and lays hold on the best he has. And we stare at it as if it were a cup far too bitter to drink. Jesus did too—until the moment came again which marks the turning point of every life, where importunate pleading stops short, and doesn't even want God to be God in any other way than his. "Nevertheless not my will, but thine, be done."

Is that a dead end, a blind alley, a pitiful surrender, a grave for all your bright hopes, with the heavy earth falling? It's God's way of winning! It's the victory over us that's for us. It's God bringing the issue as near the level of his love as his power can lift it! Satan whispered, and the crowd shouted, "If you are the Son of God, don't just stand there, do something!" Maybe we should turn it wrong side out! "If you are the Son of God, don't just do something! Stand there, in my sorrow and loneliness, in all my frustration and defeat, where the shadows are—until the day breaks, as thou wilt have it break, and thy grace makes my weakness strength!

Against all that sets itself in the way of Thy will, O God, even against us, be Thyself, to redeem us by such means as shall please Thee, out of our darkness into Thy light; through Jesus Christ, our Lord. Amen.

God's Great Nevertheless

For all that we know of Thee in Christ, O God, we give Thee thanks; and for all that Thou art in him, which is beyond our knowing. Amen.

LUKE 21:28—When these things begin to come to pass, then look up, and lift up your heads.

There you have the studied and settled effrontery of the whole New Testament. The gospel sets down its account of every situation with its eyes wide open. "There shall be signs in the sun, and in the moon, and in the stars"—only to throw all our careful deliberations to the winds: "When these things begin to come to pass, then look up." It takes a pencil and a piece of paper and reckons in every human resource, like a man getting ready for battle: lists the terrible odds over there on that side, piles them up high enough to suit anybody's taste; then blithely wrecks the whole business with something over here about lifting up your heads, or something about being filled with all joy and peace in believing. Say it's nonsense, but don't say it isn't intentional nonsense. It is. If we really are what the Bible would have us know we are, then nothing else but a sort of nonsense could possibly make God's kind of sense. For those who think the world is right side up, he has to talk upside down on purpose.

Take first the state of affairs in this excited, topsy-turvy panorama of monstrous evil. Everything seems to be just enough out of focus to keep us from bothering a great deal about it. On the earth "distress of nations with perplexity." That's all right. Even after two world wars, there is still this seething unrest. But we do have some hope of managing now without having a nuclear holocaust. "The sea and the waves roaring"—that would mean to the Jew primeval chaos; but there is now in the world at least some semblance of order; what with the United Nations and our own preponderance of power, we can no doubt take a deep breath every once in a while. Possibly, we say, Jesus was thinking about the destruction of Jerusalem, if that doesn't mean attributing even to him a little more foresight than he may have had! But, we add, the destruction of Jerusalem was a good long time ago. Why worry at this late date? Perhaps, with his Oriental, kaleidoscopic imagery, he was also looking beyond every one of these things to the end; which, we observe, promises to be a good long time off. Nothing there of any immediate concern. Suppose we change the subject.

But these strangely urgent words have no intention of allowing you to do any such thing. They don't let go so easily. There is a certain stubbornness about them which keeps clamoring at the mind. Because, you see—if you will read the whole chapter you may be surprised to see—the core of all this was neither the wars nor the rumors of war; neither the destruction of Jerusalem nor what was going to happen when time had run out. Dig down to rock bottom, and it will begin to dawn on you that in everything Jesus said he was actually thinking all along of something else, on the other side of the words, in a still vaster context. Indeed, to be somewhat bolder, we may lay it down bluntly that nothing you can put your finger on, no what or how or when, nothing in any of the circumstances of life, ever cut a very large figure with him. Perversely enough, he simply didn't locate the real crisis of human existence anywhere in this "contaminated world." Not even at the end of it.

When he says, for example, "Take heed to yourselves, lest that day come upon you unawares," he doesn't mean that every time we get all stirred up about things in general, and the going gets rough, we'd better start packing our bags for a return to religion, so as to be as far over on the safe side of God Almighty as we can—just in case. Besides, nobody seems to be exactly clear at present about what religion we should be returning to. Could the one that's most often recommended in revivals and in magazine articles be no more than another *ism* in what has been called this "gigantic parade of idols" that look so very "comical from behind"? There are any number of racial, cultural, economic, nationalistic *isms* putting themselves forward as substitutes; and certainly God hates every one of them. He hates our belief in things— money, status, power, institutionalism; and he hates no less much of what goes by the name of piety, charity, and orthodoxy. The Old Testament says so, and the New Testament says so too. All through the Bible he is setting his face squarely against everything that has run off at a tangent, and therefore fundamentally misreads the nature of this that we are up against.

It isn't any kind of trouble, here or hereafter, from which we may hope to be delivered by a bit of maneuvering, whether by means of our atomic stock-pile, or by way of adding a dash of religious education or group therapy here and there, and going back to church again. Jesus was almost intolerably cavalier about all manner of trouble! Not that he was lacking in compassion. He was crucified for having too much. Simply that getting through was what mattered to him, not getting out. He talks in this particular passage about being accounted worthy to escape. What we fail to realize is that it was escape right down the middle, not around the edge; so that you could stand, not have to cringe, or budge an inch, even before the Son of man: because by his grace you had succeeded in being bigger than things. And that was a large order as Jesus put it, over against all this that was happening to the sun and the moon and the stars!

It is not so much that we are up against trouble. Maybe quite the opposite. What seems to be implied by the "hearts overcharged with surfeiting, . . . and cares of this life," is that Jesus is far more concerned about us when the days and the weeks and the months are all ironed out flat and going as we'd like them to go. He tells us so elsewhere, at any rate, over and over again. He never says anything like "Look up!" then. He says, "Look out." You may well be able to handle

the "quick repulse," or face even the "slow defeat." Robert Louis
Stevenson was stuck in both of them up to his neck when he wrote

> Lord, if this were enough—
>   With the half of a broken hope for a pillow at night,
> To know that somehow the right is the right,
>   And the smooth shall bloom from the rough.

What we've got to dread is the "complete success," lest we perish
by finding what we seek. In the parables, none of the bad men goes
bankrupt, or loses his wife, or forfeits the respect of the community.
Nothing happens to them in this world that ought to happen. You are
in fine fettle when you brush by the beggar at the door without even
seeing him. You get away with your plan to win friends and influence
people by cheating the lord of the manor. Your barns are filled with
wheat when one night God whispers, "You fool!" There is very little in
what Jesus says to warn us against the evil on the ground that it won't
work. It may. That's what made him shudder.

But now let's press beyond all these questions of the rough and the
smooth. What is really upsetting is that life itself is the crisis we are
up against. And that doesn't often occur to us. Life is the one precious
thing we have in common. It is the rough and the smooth that matter;
nothing's the matter with life. You'll come much closer to the truth
here in the twenty-first chapter of St. Luke if you'll stop long enough
to let this strike home: that it's your very being alive and in the world
which seems to close in on you as Jesus speaks. There is a NO EXIT
sign over everything you thought was a door. They tell us that the
only inborn fear we have is the fear of falling, of having all the sup-
ports withdrawn from under us, the props taken away. And that's exactly how it feels when all at once a lucid moment comes and we
realize what it means to have things so comfortably as they are, without any assurance that any of them will be there tomorrow. Kafka
calls it the knocking at the castle gate, very much like that knocking
in *Macbeth*. Something, maybe it's death, something I don't want to
face, is trying to get into my world, waiting out there; and there's no
security against it, none anywhere. Men say this and say that in order
to cover up; or they take what others say. Too many of us are at
odd times like some Charlie McCarthy sitting on our favorite ven-
triloquist's lap! When suddenly the powers of heaven are shaken, and

we feel again some nameless dread: our hearts failing us for fear, and for looking after those things which are coming on the earth.

"It's the instant when my throat seems to tighten," says Helmut Thielicke, "and I catch my breath at the unknown that has me surrounded." No use trying even to give it a name: it will come back when the name has worn off. You may call it the dashing of some hope, or the loss of someone you love; and that's terrible. But it isn't the Terror underneath that's forever pressing in. Edgar Allan Poe in one of his stories tells of a room with a bottomless pit at the center, and walls that keep crowding you toward it, no matter which way you turn. You are the cat on the hot tin roof, and you'd like to jump off— but where? The whole world is like a wasteland, and you've already begun to suspect that the wasteland is inside. The morning and the afternoon narrow like a bottleneck, and you are forced on into the evening toward the twilight of all the gods you trusted; and the flood which they had conquered for a while sweeps on you again, the sea and the waves roaring.

If we can get at least that far with this strange chapter, it may not seem quite so much out of focus as we thought it was. But we have to go farther! It isn't only that we are up against life. That isn't all Jesus had in mind. We are up against God! And you are not likely to find any "constructive solution" for that! You may want to object; indignantly, maybe violently. "That's an outrage," you say. "God isn't a problem. He's the solution." I have heard so, more often than I sometimes care to remember! But come now, let me put it to you. When you find out from the Bible, and not from any popular opinion, who it is that's going to be there when you arrive, and what he's like— incalculable, unmanageable, of whom men once said that he was a consuming fire, with the kind of compassion that's thoroughly capable of reversing everything you mean by the word and turning it upside down—when you find that out, does this business of taking off in his direction, so frequently recommended, seem to you like coming home to some dear shelter, or does it seem like setting foot on the shores of an undiscovered land, untamed, perilous, and wild?

Ugly as we know ourselves to be—and we know it most painfully when we are at our best—which of us wants to be beset behind and before, as we are in the Bible, by a God who knows too much? Knows our downsitting and our uprising, understands our thought afar off! Much better to say that he's good, and mean by it what we mean by good; we are altogether in favor of the good. And the true and the beautiful—that's what God is! We have to decorate him somehow! And we can't. The God of the Bible is naked God. He watched in Gethsemane when Jesus prayed; and did nothing about the cross when morning came. He left Stephen among the stones. He looked on and did nothing—so you would have said—as men and women and children sang their songs in the arena, with leopards leaping at them. And we can't stand it. So we set up in his place our little images, hoping they will run our errands for us and keep us safe. Certain it is you cannot prove we love God by the tricks we play to be quit of him. Waiting there at the end of the world, in the hour of death, waiting here now, not simply, as we try to believe, with "comfort and kindness, but with holiness and judgment."

And so at last, I think, we are plunged in where we've got to come, whether we like it or not. Now listen, as Jesus turns all common sense everywhere upside down: "When these things begin to come to pass, then look up, lift up your heads!" You can never get Christ's measure until you chart the distance, there from the edge of the abyss, to this utter about-face. Never will you understand what sense it makes until you see what nonsense it is, not because of anything that can happen to us in time, or when time itself is over; but because of what we are and what God is—with nothing now between him and us but the coming of a child in a manger, and the death of a man on a hill.

I read a parable once about a five- or six-year-old boy who was walking through a dark forest holding the hand of his father. It was a pretty picture. The moonlight shone weirdly through the trees, and in the shadows every bush took on some bizarre and ghostly shape, stealing by, or creeping up, reaching out its arms, clutching with its fingers. There were roots and holes, and the lad would stumble. There were terrifying noises. Branches cracked, night birds called and flapped their wings overhead. But he held fast to the "strong and knowing hand of his father," and marched bravely on. I wish it were that easy. Nobody has a right to make it so.

Jesus had to do more than merely to pronounce this vast *nevertheless* of God. He had to give it flesh and sinew and bone. When in the temple he sketched for his disciples that cosmic upheaval, and told them never to mind it, never to mind anything, do you think it would ever have been seared on their hearts, unforgettably, if Gethsemane hadn't followed it, and Calvary? Or if he hadn't been able himself to break through when at last they shrank from him in horror, and the wild beasts in Pilate's court began to howl for his blood? Would Peter have gone telling of his glory "a many hundred miles to Rome," or Paul "to the sharp sword outside the city gates, glad beyond words to drink of his sweet cup"? Leaving behind this triumphant thing: "Now the God of hope fill you with all joy and peace in believing, that ye may abound in hope, through the power of the Holy Ghost"! Jesus lived out and died clean through God's *nevertheless*. And there's more in it now than a lad's hand in his father's, swinging away through the dark woods.

"When these things begin to come to pass. . . ." What things? It doesn't matter, says the New Testament, as long as you don't put off what Jesus said, and think it meant some other time, not this time, not now. Beyond the smooth and the rough is life itself; but that isn't the crisis. God is. And he's trying the best he knows how—in us here—to invade this world of ours. From one of my classes comes a story of the day when the Allies landed on the beaches of Normandy. "Waiting in the stillness of dawn," ran the letter, "there was an oppressive silence. Eyes were straining at an angle above the water: the whine of landing craft pushing their burdens toward the shores of Europe, every man holding vigil at his station. Great expectancy was in the air. Here at last was the hour! We could look back at the blood and tears and the mighty planning which had brought it." Back to Bethlehem in the gospel, and Calvary! "And we looked forward to victory. On this razor's edge of time, our hearts beat with joy."

Can't Christ get any of us to do as he says? "When these things begin to come to pass, lift up your heads!"

Grant us, O God of the fire and the solace, of the purge and the healing, such strength as may stand fast now, in the peace of Thy steady purpose; through Jesus Christ, our Lord. Amen.

They That Wait for the Lord

O God, Who in Thy Son didst come among us, and in him wilt come again, of Thy mercy grant us not to shrink from Thy presence, but ever to rejoice in it; through Jesus Christ, our Lord. Amen.

ISA. 49:22-23—Thus saith the Lord God, . . . they shall not be ashamed that wait for me.

The Bible is very honest and outspoken about the times when God doesn't seem to be around at all, when everything would seem to indicate that he had gone off stage, returned to his own place. "Why shouldest thou be as a stranger in the land," Jeremiah wanted to know, "and a wayfaring man that turneth aside to tarry for a night?" And Habakkuk, as he stares out across the fields at the spoiling and the violence: "O Lord, how long shall I cry, and thou wilt not hear!" Every step of the way, from the beginning of the Old Testament to the end of the New, you would say that over here is a splendid, stalwart faith which refuses to die: facing it over there, a world that with ceaseless rebuttal tries to make a mockery of it. While in the place between, men keep asking of us, "Where is now thy God?" And there are hours and days and

weeks and months and years aplenty when we just don't know! If anybody should shout to him in the dark, as a sailor might shout, "Stand
by!"—why then that's what he does, and nothing but! The Bible makes
no secret of the fact.

The trouble is that to all intents and purposes the only thing it has
to offer apparently is this word "Wait!" So let's begin there, and say
right away that it's a disturbing word. It's disturbing because more
often than not it doesn't seem to get you anywhere. Nothing seems
to come of it. You wait, and decent hopes are still crushed, and whoever it is up yonder isn't near enough, or doesn't care enough, to do
anything about it. In those sad and disillusioned days after the Exile,
the Jews turned their waiting into a song on their pilgrimages to the
Temple. They were gallant enough to do that. "I wait for the Lord, my
soul doth wait. . . . My soul waiteth for the Lord more than they that
watch for the morning." But when the morning came, it didn't look
much like the Lord! Through the centuries that followed the only thing
that happened was that wave after wave of conquest swept over their
land. It was like being back at the beginning again, with all of it to
do over.

Finally of course the hour struck which the liturgy undertakes dramat-
ically to re-enact on the first Sunday in Advent, so that you too may
take part in it. Through the Introit runs the slow yearning of the past:
"Unto Thee, O Lord, do I lift up my soul: O my God, I trust in Thee;
let me not be ashamed." In the collect you hear it again: "Stir up Thy
power, O Lord, and come." As the Service of the Word moves toward its
climax, the Epistle is read, and you know for Paul, writing to the church
at Rome, something has happened which was like the clanging of an
alarm bell, rousing us all from sleep to cast off the works of darkness,
seeing that the night is so far spent, and to put on the armor of light, for
the day is at hand. In Luther's *Formula of The Mass*, the first Protestant
Service of Worship, that high-pitched monotone falls away into silence
when a procession forms, with its cross, and its incense, and its lights,
and the first confident notes of a chant are heard: "They that wait for
Thee shall not be ashamed. . . . Show us Thy mercy, O Lord: Grant us
Thy salvation." Followed by the stirring cadences of the gospel, when
men had once stood and unsheathed their swords. It seems that at last
the waiting is over. And for a symbol of it, through the memory of the

people of God, that curious pageant winds its way again down the slopes of the Mount of Olives and up the steep ascent of Zion to the sudden fluttering of palm branches, and the excited cries of "Hosanna to the Son of David: Blessed is he that cometh in the name of the Lord: Hosanna in the highest."

You might suppose it would be different now. But within the week, and Matthew's story of that pitiful triumph standing here at the very threshold of the Christian year reminds us of it, whoever this was that had come "unto his own" died on a cross. True enough, there were many who said they had seen him alive after that, and they spread their news all around the Mediterranean world, warning everybody that he would come soon again on the clouds of heaven, with power and great glory; but he didn't! Instead, they themselves were stoned, and sawn asunder, and slain with the sword, wandering in dens and caves of the earth, breathing out on the very last page of the record they left us, "Even so, come, Lord Jesus."

Sometimes you are almost ready to throw up your hands and say that the whole thing is the epic of a God, if there is a God, who goes on forever promising more than he can deliver! On the stage it was called *Waiting for Godot*, and it was an utterly idle and hopeless business. There was nothing to do except to wonder what to do next. That's what waiting was taken to mean. Nothing was ever done, and nobody ever came.

But that isn't what waiting means in the Bible. It doesn't try to calm anybody down, or get him to hold his horses a while. It's a disturbing word precisely because it doesn't mean that! We shall have to get more than the soles of our feet wet in it if we want to understand at least in part why so little seems to come of it. "Wait, I say, on the Lord," sings the psalmist. And we think it has to do with sitting down patiently in something, and letting the time pass—time that heals all wounds; whispering to ourselves, "Who knows? The chances are it's all for the best. Surely there's a silver lining somewhere. It can't go on like this forever. The night is always darkest just before the dawn"— with a great deal of the other pious nonsense we like to scatter abroad.

In the Bible this word "wait" is disturbing, not so much because so little seems to come of it as because it keeps hinting at something in us which we may not even know about, but which nevertheless every day we live insists on getting between us and God—something we want more or like better. What if the waiting had to do with that first and foremost! Not merely our sins. That's too easy a label. We are quite ready to confess that we have done those things which we ought not to have done. We make a ritual of it, tying up in a bundle like so many sticks the wrongs we've been guilty of; then throwing in for complete coverage those things we have left undone which we ought to have done. How much of that do you think it would take to make Bethlehem worth while, and the Calvary that's always alongside of it in the heart of God?

What if it were something farther down? "When thou passest through the waters I will be with thee." So God is reported to have said back there in Isaiah. What if the only peace we ever really seek were the peace of not knowing how deep the waters are! That might account for the New Testament! To have something in us or about us, unknown and unnamed, which makes us aliens in God's world, strangers to him, and strangers to each other! Kafka writes of it in *The Trial*. There it is K. himself who stands accused before a mysterious tribunal, but can't find out what he's supposed to have done. He runs over the past in his mind to discover what it is they know who have pressed the charges against him. He wants to defend himself, and can't. He can never settle on the quarter from which the attack is going to come. And it ends that way—with an execution which is a kind of blessed relief, because he doesn't any longer have to wonder what's the matter.

Maybe God doesn't seem to be around because down in our hearts, underneath everything else, there is something that doesn't want him to be, and couldn't stand it if he were. That might cost a crucifixion! Job had his moments when he hated God, called him a Watcher of men, and wrenched at the hand on his shoulder. So did the psalmist: "Whither shall I go from thy spirit? Whither shall I flee from thy presence?" He was trying to get away, scrabbling over hill and dale as fast as his legs could carry him. Luther was many a time just as indignant, and heard the blasphemy in his own soul. Nietzsche, so much better than his detractors thought him, said it out loud, tearing at the knowledge which hardly ever seems to dawn on us: that every man with his idol is bent on getting rid of the God who won't leave him alone! That might well cost God everything he has! And we think all we have to do is to relax, and say we're sorry for something we remember, and for much that we've forgotten!

It may even be that the waiting disturbs us because we don't believe any waiting is necessary. Do we not have God already? Is he not our private piece of American real estate, all staked out and entered upon and possessed? "This nation under God"—there's nothing so dreadful about that. Will he not act as we are sure he will, approve what we approve? It has to be that way. Nothing else will do. It's too difficult to endure a waiting which means *not* having him—in some doctrine, or in some church, or in some book. It's too disconcerting to live in a place where there is no shelter from a God we do not have and cannot utterly know.

But that's exactly where the Bible locates us! It's why the waiting has nothing to do with sentimental escapism, and nothing to do with the stoic fortitude which just grins and bears what it cannot change. It wants you to see a man stretched out and straining between his having and his not having. between his knowing and his not knowing. It wants you to see him turning and twisting, weaving strands together into a rope that's strong enough to hold. Now a prayer: "Hast thou utterly rejected Judah? hath thy soul loathed Zion? . . . . Do not abhor us, for thy name's sake . . . break not thy covenant with us." Then a Voice, and the sound of a great compassion: "O Ephraim, what shall I do unto thee? . . . . I taught Ephraim how to walk. Since I spoke against him, I do earnestly remember him still." Weaving all that together, until the people stand and pledge themselves, "We will wait upon thee." Is that what it means? No matter what happens, to know that God isn't engaging with you in a kind of hit-and-run game, always disappearing, as someone has put it, "to get ready for the next blow by the time you arrive at the scene of the crash"! To know that in the life and death and resurrection of Jesus Christ both God's judgment and his mercy have already found you out, overtaken you, shattered every bit of your fancied security—so that now you may only seek to understand what it is he wills for you, with a will more gracious than any you could ask of him; may only probe with your faith into the mysteries of his dealing, looking for him where you had never looked before, in everything that goes as you want it to go and in everything that doesn't, among people you never paid much attention to, in tasks you were sure were beneath you —confident of only this one thing, that while your search for him is always out around the circumference somewhere, and so in constant danger of being distorted into some kind of idolatry, his search for you is central, with the waiting that strains toward you, every muscle taut, like his muscles there on the cross. Nail his hands fast, and his feet; he will yet bring men home to God! "Wait, I say, on the Lord"!

But let's come away now to the issue. We weren't ready before. We should be by this time. This disturbing Word is a word with a promise attached to it. "Thus saith the Lord God, . . . they shall not be ashamed that wait for me." And it's no puny assurance. It doesn't say that you won't be disappointed; that you won't be lonely any more, for instance. He'll ask you why you're so lonely, with so many people around! That would be sheer gain! It doesn't say anything about feeling needed again, all at once, with life chock-full of meaning. You may begin to wonder why you feel so unneeded, with as much need as there is at no more than an arm's length from where you're sitting! And that's something! Nothing about quick answers, or knots that come untied the minute you start pulling at them, or problems that solve themselves while you're asleep!

The Bible operates at deeper levels. It never plays about in the shallows. It doesn't do much surface work. It's like the men far down in the mines that Job talks of, searching out "to the farthest bound the ore in gloom and deep darkness"; putting their hands to the "flinty rock," overturning "mountains by the roots." When it uses the word *ashamed*, it's thinking primarily of whatever it was that made Adam hide, back there in the third chapter of Genesis, the day the Lord God walked in the garden and kept calling to him in the cool of the evening, "Adam, where art thou?" It's thinking of what comes over a man when his eyes are opened by the waiting he has done, and he knows himself as he is, unable to stand any longer before God or his fellows without losing face. How much of life's loneliness and anxiety do you think comes of that sense of ultimate nakedness; how much of what Sartre calls its bitterness and irony and resentment and dread of death? Arthur Miller's story of Willy Loman in *Death of a Salesman* tells of how it can drive a bare, plodding, desolate nobody, who can't put up now with what he sees in the mirror, from one pathetic deceit to another, until he's so far away from his sons that they can only despise him, so far away from his wife that her love can't reach him, so far away from himself, from what he truly is and might be doing, that there's no reason he can find anywhere for going on with the rotten lie his life has become even in his dreams, and there's nothing for him but that rendezvous with a gunshot, and a grave, and a woman's tears.

Well, to be free of that is what the Bible is thinking about. Not just to feel free. The Bible wastes very little time on the way we feel. It's thinking of a fact—not in here, out yonder; and not just the fact of forgiveness—though you can document from many a modern drama and novel what goes on where there is none. Not even the fact of the virtue that can get in now where the vice was. It's thinking of the fact, for anybody who will take hold of it, that you can stand again, whenever you want to, where life once stood before it was soiled and knew that the only thing for it was to hide: that you can stand there where Christ is, that very inmost citadel and self of yours ravaged and under another flag—lest living without him be a chattering emptiness, and dying without him "a cold horror"! That you can stand there with him, free of the past and open to the future! In a world where nothing is yours, but you are Christ's, and Christ is God's, and so life and death, and things present and things to come, all are yours! I know it sounds like rhetoric; but it's Paul's rhetoric! And five times he turned it into prose, with the forty stripes save one; three times with rods, once when he was stoned, three times in shipwreck, in hunger and thirst, in cold and nakedness. Poetry for us, God pity us! Prose for him! A pageant in overalls! "They shall not be ashamed that wait for me."

But there is something else. When the Bible talks of being ashamed, it's thinking not only of that nameless weight of guilt which brought even Jesus to cry out "My God, my God, why hast thou forsaken me?" He did that so that we might never have to! When the Bible talks of being ashamed, it's thinking too of being defeated, driven off in headlong flight by the odds. And it keeps saying that that doesn't have to happen either! It says there isn't anything we can't whip to a standstill now on its own ground. There would be no sense in saying so if times without number it hadn't been done. There would be no sense in saying so if you couldn't do it. Jesus once spoke, as men remembered it, of building his Church on the marshlands of a life which he called a Rock. Peter it was, and a more unlikely bit of shifting sand you could hardly have found! But Jesus said, in his "humble, outrageous arrogance," that the gates of hell would never be able to prevail against it. Maybe you thought he meant it was hell that was making the assault. He didn't! It was his Church that was storming the gates of hell, and the gates of hell couldn't hold out! What chance is there that he'll find altogether beyond him the odds which happen at the moment to be staring you out of countenance? "Now that"—can you hear him saying it as he looks at your outstretched hands?—"that is something I can't possibly manage." He has taken this vast, straggling company of his would-be kingdom, which is the Church, and written it large into the text of human history. But he can't do anything about this that you are up against. Not that! It was silly of you ever to think that he could!

Edna St. Vincent Millay tells of a day in her life when the world seemed to crowd in on her from every side. Even Infinity, she thought, came down and settled over her. All sin was of her sinning. She knew man's hunger for her own. All suffering was hers, and death. And at that strange word the earth gave way, to let her sink gladly, deeply into its breast. Yet there was still the friendly sound of the rain above, and she wanted to kiss its fingers. And the dripping trees, and all the silver of the spring, and the autumn gold. Who could bear never to see any of it again! If only she were alive once more! If only God would put her back! When suddenly, to the sound of herald wings like music, the startled waters plunged down the sky and washed her grave away! The winds blew, and thrust the miracle of breath into her face. Up from the ground she sprang, and hailed the earth with such a shout as is not heard save from one who has been dead, and is alive! She wound her arms about the trees. Like one gone mad, she laughed, and laughed, and hugged the ground. There was a God whose radiant identity no dark disguise could ever hide from her again. Never could he move across the grass but her quick eye would see him pass. However silently now he spoke, her hushed voice would answer him. Back on the hilltop she stood, where all of it had begun, and the world had crowded in; but with a heart now that could push away the sea and land: a soul to split the sky in two, and let the face of God shine through!

"They that wait for me." What is it that's stacked up over against you? Put your finger on it and listen. "They that wait for me shall not be ashamed." It's very hard to make out what God is doing anywhere, at any time. Where would you have liked to live, and when, just to be sure? When Jesus stood before Pilate? When Paul died outside of Rome? When Augustine lived and watched the Roman Empire crumble? When the Reformation cracked Christendom wide open? God alone knows how it's going to turn out. But beyond his knowing, and the willing that brings it to pass, what more do you want?

Show us Thy ways, O Lord; teach us Thy paths: Thou who art always the same in Thy coming, yesterday, today, and forever. On Thee do we wait all the day long. Amen.

Scandals of Faith

Grant us, O God, to hear Thy voice; and in what we think is Thy silence, bring us still to listen; through Jesus Christ, our Lord. Amen.

MATTHEW 8:2—Lord, if thou wilt, thou canst make me clean.
8:10—I have not found so great faith, no, not in Israel.

These Gospel lessons, as a rule, seem so neat and simple. And they aren't at all. So often they turn out exactly as we want them to turn out. Jesus cures the leper, then heals the centurion's servant. He tells wonderful stories, says matchless things; and we love it. It's out of this world. And that's just the trouble with it. There are cruel pages, of course, which seem somehow to belong in the world we know; but then comes the Resurrection, and everything is simply splendid again. The result is that to profess a faith like ours seems about as easy as one could wish. There is so much here for weakness and guilt and loneliness and anxiety and despair. There is something here even for death. And what I want to say is that there is nothing here for anybody, unless we are ready and willing, before we do anything else, to run headlong into what the New Testament calls the "scandal" of the gospel, the stumbling block which is hidden away for us in almost every passage. It's at that point that the gospel comes alive. We cannot so much as hear God's good news, to say nothing of accepting it, until we ferret out in each case not so much what pleases us as what offends us, face it squarely, come to grips with it, and somehow, instead of falling down flat or throwing up our hands, climb on it.

Take for instance what this leper says. Let's start with that and dig into it a little way. "Lord, if thou wilt, thou canst make me clean." There is no reason to suppose that he had any misgiving about Jesus' willingness to heal him. What he was saying was simply "I know you can if you want to." But there's no getting around it, that does take the power for granted and leave the will in the realm of the uncertain. As if we should say, when life goes all awry, and the world turns topsy-turvy, and nothing gets any better, everything keeps getting worse—as if we should say, "God could do something about this, if only he would!" It's the first hazard we've got to deal with here; and never think that it doesn't get in our way. We like to fling about the "could," and postpone all serious grappling with the "would" until we see how things are likely to go with us. The power is there. God is almighty, isn't he? But what about the willingness? He could if he would.

Our ancestors felt that way about him in the primeval forests of Europe. The Jews should have known better, but often enough they felt that way too. Why else were they forever trying to get on the right side of him? He was omnipotent, that's why, and they didn't want to be on the wrong side, out where the judgments were about to fall. So they prayed and worshiped and fasted and offered sacrifices. The whole Old Testament is nothing but the long record of how God tried his best to get people to quit that. And at the end, Jesus—the hugest effort God ever made or could make to get them to quit it. Only to have us still "lobbying around in the courts of the Almighty," as another has put it, looking "for special favors." We want something, and you may be sure we shall go on plucking at his sleeve, pestering him for it. He can if only he will.

It isn't the special favors which make our persistence such a dubious practice. Peter and James and John had special favors, and Thomas, and the Magdalen, and the two disciples on the road to Emmaus. Children are always after them, and God is a Father. We expect them partly because we hope to be treated as persons, and not as humanity en masse. What calls it into question is that as we see it every bit of added pressure we can bring on God is all to the good, will not hurt anything. What we've got on our hands is an almighty but reluctant God; and down here on our heathen levels we are out to persuade and cajole and maneuver him. There is a source from which all blessings flow, and we are in this business of being Christians not without some effort to turn it on if we can. The trouble is that just now, and we can't understand it at all, the faucet seems to be stuck!

It was an ugly picture as Job stripped it down to a kind of loveless power standing at the center of things. He understood as much about God's omniscience as his friends did, but it didn't bring him much comfort. God wouldn't answer his questions, and nobody could ever, ever answer God's, not one in a thousand. And Job knew about God's omnipotence. It made the omniscience worse. You could be as heroic as you pleased, but you couldn't hold out against the God who ripped the mountains wide open with his fire, shook the earth to its foundations, blotted out the sun with storm cloud and eclipse, trampled down the waves of the sea. What on earth could you call all that but the glitter and dash of some monstrous power? Never mind the wisdom, the love was gone! No wonder nothing was left for him but irony and bitterness and resentment and fear.

Not many of us here, I suppose, can come anywhere near such an intolerable conclusion as his was; not now, not when we read these stories about Jesus, certainly not so long as the world plays reasonably fair with us. But there was one dark moment even in Jesus' life when there seemed to be nobody anywhere who cared enough to keep his grip on things. And sooner or later we face it. The God of the mathematicians and geologists, the God of the astronomers and historians, can go hang then. We want help. Disaster strikes, disease, flood, hurricane, war; a very drunken debauch sometimes, from one end to the other, of poverty and homelessness and hunger and death: and we try to pray, but it does no good; so we try to read the riddle, and can make no sense of it. The psalmist looked up into the starry heavens one night and wondered about man, if any one there could possibly be mindful of him. How does it look now that we have to stare across aeons of light years into bleak, black distance? So—multitudes who can't quite make up their minds to give their minds over to mindless chance say, "If your God is almighty, he isn't good. There is no other way to explain it." And we undertake to smile bravely and answer, "O yes there is: God so loved the world"—until it comes our turn to remind him that we too are still here, and that things have gone terribly wrong with us, as well as with these other people, and will he not please do something—please! He could if he would. It's the scandal of what looks many a time like loveless power. How can you get along with that?

And the only way out of it is into another scandal on the next higher level. Let me lay it in front of you without any decoration. You say that if God is almighty he isn't good. What if I should come right back at you and say that if God is good he isn't almighty? What alternative is there in this crazy quilt of lights and shadows which we call life: poets and murderers, as Theodore Dreiser once described it, violets and armies, music, rats, the bacillus of cholera? You have to rescue God's power at the expense of his love, or you have to rescue his love at the expense of his power. And in that you'll come nearer the truth, shudderingly nearer! If there is anything at all in this Jesus, we shall have to say to him not what the leper said, "Lord, if thou wilt, . . ." but "Lord, if thou canst, . . ." There is something in him that looks far more like powerless love than like loveless power.

Two thousand years ago, the Jews in Palestine were faced with that dilemma, and decided not to put up with it. Power that seemed lacking in love was not so hard to understand; but love like this that was lacking in power—they couldn't swallow that. So they nailed it to a cross and wagged their heads and said, "If thou be the Son of God, come down!" And one of the malefactors railed on him, "If thou be the Christ, save thyself and us." And the scribes wrote love's epitaph, and God's, over the face of the whole miserable transaction: "He saved others, himself he cannot save." Quite so! It was the day that turned history upside down. Indeed, if there's any choice now for us between power and love, if these are the horns of our dilemma too, and there has to be an *either-or*, then we've got to take the love and let the power look out for itself. Who here is up to it? Of what use is such a friend?

And that's what the New Testament means. Loveless power isn't the problem there: the problem is powerless love. Give anybody just one glance at it, and that's what he would say. Whatever else God is, you can count on him, first, last, and all the time, to be willing, eternally willing, willing before ever we begin to worship him, willing when the prayer hasn't even formed itself yet in our thought. The prophets said it: "Before they call, I will answer." Jesus became it. When they asked him why he was like that, he told the story of a shepherd who had lost a sheep, a thoughtless sheep that had nibbled its way out of sight without ever meaning to, and could never have gotten back; but it bore on the shepherd's heart, and he found it. There was a woman too who had lost a coin, an unfeeling thing that could only lie where it had fallen; but it lay on her heart, because of everything that losing it involved, and she found it. Then there was a father who had lost a son, a willful lad who wanted to do as he pleased with his own; and did, until he had squandered it all, and tired, and ragged, and half starved was on the way home again, murmuring to himself the words he had learned, keeping time to the shuffling of his feet: "Father, I have sinned against heaven, and before thee, and am not worthy to be called thy son: make me as one of thy hired servants." Going over it once more as he crossed the brow of the last hill—when suddenly somebody began running toward him, somebody who had been waiting and watching the road; and there was the warm shelter of those arms, and a kiss that stopped the mouth of his poor little memorized piece, and a voice that kept whispering "My son, my son!"

Bethlehem and Calvary and all the dusty miles in between simply will not add up to power: they add up to an anguish in God's heart, with its marks still in his hands and feet. He will if he can. It's the offense of the cross. Captain Ahab, in Herman Melville's *Moby Dick,* caught a fleeting glimpse of it. "I know thee, thou clear spirit," he cried, looking up at the yardarms that seemed tipped with flame in the storm, "I know thee, and I know that thy right worship is defiance. I own thy speechless power; but to the last gasp of my earthquake life, I will dispute its mastery. Come in thy lowest form of love, and I will kneel and kiss thee; but come as power, and though thou launchest whole navies of full-freighted worlds, there's that in here that will defy Thee."

Bethlehem and Calvary, plus all the dusty miles between, mean that there are places in the human heart where power cannot come; only weakness can get in. Quarrels can't be stopped until we are ready to stop them. There are people who can't be made good, because they don't want to be made good. The wickedness of evil lives can't be kept from hurting the innocent, airplanes can't be kept from dropping bombs which fall on children, shells can't be kept from bursting and killing somebody we love. It is not God's might we need to ponder. We need to ponder his weakness. He has to put up with no end of contradiction in order to let you be a person, in a world where courage is possible, and choices are pretty grim, and faith is a clean adventure far and away on the other side of spoon-feeding!

It's the love of God that's unconditioned; we condition his power. "Lord, if thou wilt. . . . ?" Not at all! "I will. Wilt thou?" And to the blind man, "What wilt thou that I shall do unto thee?" And to the impotent man by the pool of Bethesda, who had enjoyed ill health for thirty and eight years, "Wilt thou be made whole?" And over Jerusalem, once more at the last, his lamentation: "Thou that killest the prophets and stonest them which are sent unto thee, how often would I have gathered thy children together, even as a hen gathereth her chickens under her wings"—he remembered that from when he was a boy in Nazareth, looking around on his way to the hills in the evening, seeing it happen, smiling and thinking of God—"how often would I . . . , and ye would not!"

So have we moved from the power which seems lacking in love to the love which so often seems lacking in power—and never is! The primary and ultimate scandal of the Christian religion is the power-in-love that will not devote itself to our ends: not to our American policy, not to the public welfare, not to anybody's private peace of mind. You can hardly expect us to understand it very well; certainly we don't like it much. Its one profound concern is with the faith in our hearts, that there may be enough of it to make possible whatever it is God hopes to do for us and with us. We want other things, and he wants that. There is so much else that matters to us; and nothing else at rock bottom matters to him.

Take for example the centurion in this same chapter. Let's turn to him now. Observe that neither his reputation nor what he had done came into focus for Jesus. What the Jews said about him made no impression. They said that he was worthy. And it wasn't just gossip. Luke tells us it was an official pronouncement of the elders of the people; their reasoned appraisal, if you please, of a foreigner, a Roman, and a soldier: quite as generous a thing as you will find anywhere in the New Testament. "Do go ahead. He built us a synagogue." So ran their request. "He's a good man, and deserves anything you can do for him." While on the heels of their urging came the centurion's own estimate of himself. He was a member of what I suppose we would call Rome's expeditionary force, an officer in it, as a matter of fact. And what is it he has to say to a Jewish rabbi, from over Nazareth way? "I am not worthy that thou shouldest come under my roof." He feels that he'd be embarrassed no end, shamed out of all countenance, by such a presence in his home, even if it was the best home in Capernaum. We don't feel any such thing. We want him to come by all means. Abashed? No. Uncomfortable? Not much. Just glad to have him as a guest—without ever stopping to think how he turns the tables on people when he comes. The centurion asked Jesus only to speak, to give the command, much as he himself did every day, saying to one, "Go, and he goeth; and to another, Come, and he cometh." His servant would be healed in that selfsame hour. He was sure of it.

And Jesus listened—"He is worthy," they said; "I am not worthy," said he—but paid no attention to any of it. Jesus was looking at something else entirely, at the only thing that mattered, and there was a light in his eyes. He had come upon a faith which was of itself enough to be almost a miracle in that land of timid and doubtful and suspicious folk, where he himself had grown so heartsick for it. He hailed it as if it were something he had been looking for everywhere, high and low, and suddenly in this out of the way place had stumbled on it: "I have not found so great faith, no, not in Israel." There was more that God could tie to in that rank outsider than anywhere else from Nazareth to Jerusalem and back again!

It's all he looks for in any of us; at times he seems unbearably careless about the rest: only something in you and me that will keep saying a resounding Yes to him every day we live, to him and to all the contradictions that life can throw in the way; pressing on as far as we can see, and when we can't see any longer, going it blind! Do you have an idea that it's easy for him to fashion that kind of faith in anybody? It won't take much out of you, you think? This ruthless love, which so often can do so little about the hazards without ceasing to be love, and so has to do something about you—or cease to be power!

And when he has wrought in you enough faith to receive whatever he has in mind, beyond there is the still costlier gift of the faith that will accept it; that can gaze straight into the eyes of some gray messenger of sorrow, as a friend of mine thought he could, and did the day his wife died, asking "What blessing then do you bring?" All along in Job, from the drawn-out bitterness of his heart, through the lurid flashes of blasphemy on his lips, you can watch that kind of faith being shaped by those great compassionate hands. And it hurt, and the hurt was an offense to Job. You can fairly see him losing his neat little God and coming up before that Other who himself would put the questions without bothering too much to answer any, except by being there and being himself. Until Job said, "I have heard of thee by the hearing of the ear." Good-by then to the God he used to worship! "Now mine eye seeth thee." And he laid his hand upon his mouth. That was no loveless power. It was no powerless love either. It was something else.

Read sometime in the New Testament the story of Peter, if you want to know how painful that something else is even under the terms of the Christian gospel, and how determined. One day on the lake Simon looked into the eyes of Jesus and trembled. "Depart from me, for I am a sinful man, O Lord." But it was to be harder than that. "Follow me." Now try to keep up with it. As the shadows of death began to close in, Peter could stand it no longer: "Be it far from thee, Lord." And Jesus turned on him. "Thou art Satan to me, Simon. Thou knowest not what thou sayest." Then at supper: "Thou shalt never wash my feet!" "If I wash thee not thou hast no part with me." "Not my feet only, but also my hands and my head." After a while breaking out again: "Though all men be offended in thee, yet will not I." And Jesus said to him, "This night, before the cock crow twice, thou shalt deny me thrice." A few hours later, as the cock crew, Jesus turned and looked at him; and he groped his way through the darkened street sobbing his heart out. The third day, early in the morning, running, overtaking John, stumbling into the tomb. And so on, blundering down the years—"Thou knowest that I love thee."—never quite forgetting, trying to understand. At last, in the legend, stealing away from Rome, only to be met by a vision, and to stammer, "*Quo vadis, Domine?*" "Lord, whither goest thou?" "Yonder to the city, to be crucified in thy stead." Ah well, you can't get clear of him! Back then to the soldiers, and to death. He asked them to set his cross head downward in the earth, we are told. "Because," said he, "I am not worthy to die as my Lord died."

That isn't loveless power, and it isn't powerless love. It's something more disturbing than either of them. It's the power-in-love—in love with us!—that spares neither itself nor its object, like a potter with his wheel, day after day, turning out a human soul.

God knows it isn't an easy gospel. I think we have never heard it until we've been offended by it. If by nothing else, then by its divine effrontery. Over against the vast mysteries of life it stands. Have you ever looked into the face of them? Thousands upon thousands of years back, millions of them, and other thousands—or millions—to come: and you here in the vastness of such a universe, touching the surface of that stream as with a swallow's wing! Over against the dark mysteries of life, only the love of Christ. Over against the ceaseless rebuttals of the world, only the power of one who keeps saying, "Behold, I stand at the door, and knock. If any man will open the door"—You do it of course at your peril! There's never any knowing. He may deny you peace to give you glory!

What we ask of Thee wisely, O God, do Thou of Thy great bounty bestow; with all that we so deeply need and know not how to ask: that in the knowledge of Thy love we may have the peace that comes not of our striving but of Thy gift; through Jesus Christ, our Lord. Amen.

THE LONGEST STRIDE MEN EVER TOOK

Exodus at Jerusalem

Grant us, O God, to hear Thy voice, and in hearing it both to love what Thou dost command and by Thy grace to do it; through Jesus Christ, our Lord. Amen.

The Old Testament selection for the second Sunday in Lent, Exodus 33:12-23, is a scene lifted straight out of a story about the exodus from Egypt; while the New Testament lesson to be read in connection with it, Luke's account of the Transfiguration of our Lord, speaks rather of an exodus at Jerusalem. "Behold, there talked with him two men, which were Moses and Elias: who . . . spake of his decease," says the King James Version; but the word is *exodus* really—"who spake of the exodus which he should accomplish at Jerusalem." So much of what Luke sets down, here in the middle of his ninth chapter, a touch now, a stroke then, sends the mind back to that hurried flight out of bondage: the "glory" in which Moses and Elijah are said to have appeared, like the pillar of fire by night; the cloud that overshadowed the disciples; the tabernacles Peter wanted to build—reminiscence after reminiscence of those days in the wilderness when a nation of fugitive slaves set out on its long trek toward the land of promise. It's a theme that runs through the Bible from beginning to end, history, prophets, Psalms, Gospels. There are half a dozen references to it in the first few chapters of Matthew alone. Until after a while as you read you begin to suspect that it is the central theme of the whole human epic: precisely this deliverance, genuine and vast, which keeps repeating itself, yet somehow seems never really to come off, not quite; not even when Easter shall have added itself to Good Friday.

Let's establish our position then deliberately. We shall not be standing in either the Old Testament or the New. We shall be looking back from this moment of our lives, looking back through the New Testament at the Old. If we are to take history with any seriousness, there's nothing else we can do. We shall be looking back through the exodus at Jerusalem, the death of a lonely man on a cross, by whom, Paul writes, and by his resurrection, God "hath delivered us from the power of darkness and hath translated us into the kingdom of his dear Son"—back through that, as if it were a kind of magnifying glass, at the exodus from Egypt. Together they spell out the drama of our lives.

To begin with, there is the Word of Command—in every generation; it's the Bible's first answer to the riddle of human existence: "Speak unto the children of Israel, that they go forward." And remember, if you please, that back there on the way out of Egypt the odds were impossible. They always are. We have to be very clear on that score. What is so disconcerting to me is that the children of Israel never seemed to get those odds located in the right place. Their prophets did, but they didn't. "Forward" seemed like a good word, with Pharaoh's host behind them; it was a sensible order. The only trouble was that the sea was in front of them. Pretty bad, wouldn't you say? They thought so. And without once having it occur to them what the real hazard was. Not the host behind them, or the sea in front of them; not even the wilderness which was to stretch out around them for forty years. The odds they thought were impossible—weren't! They themselves were the odds. They were the reason why only two of them got through. But of that hazard they took no account; just went on century after century, not to be awed by God's wrath, not to be won by his love; until the covenant he had made with them hung by the thread of a solitary life, and they snapped that on Calvary with their own bare hands.

But you can't finish anything before God calls it finished. Soon there was the sound of running feet, and you could hear people singing in the strangest places. If you had asked them why, they would have told you there in prison that they were free, as they never had been free in all their lives. It was something to sing about! While here and there and far away yonder men and women were setting off down the years toward the promise, like streams flowing into a mighty river; and where they went the face of the world was no longer sad. Partly because the odds were clearer at last. Never mind the Roman Empire, with its legions and its arenas; you couldn't stop God with that. But what was more now, you couldn't stop him even with this enormity inside the human soul. Did you see it that day at the cross—intent on going its own way, blind, and deaf, and dumb, except for the shouting and cursing it had to do? Well, nothing would come of that either. The only power it could have over you was the power you were willing to give it. Hell and all damnation couldn't finish off what God had not finished.

Can't we then at least get the odds located? They were on the stage, in *The Dark at the Top of the Stairs*. They were in *Endgame*, with the meaningless litter of ashcans in an empty lot. They were in *West Side Story*, and *Peyton Place*, and *Long Day's Journey into Night*. If preachers won't talk about them, dramatists will. And novelists. In Faulkner, there's a gleam of light maybe, on the horizon; but under a leaden sky is the falling spire of a little Negro church, just to show what it is that's going on in the world! The danger lies in not understanding what the odds are and where. It lies in not getting them located where they belong. It lies in thinking there aren't any, except for the mess we're in; striding about with a thumb in each armhole, as if nothing were the matter inside and underneath, and we could manage quite well, give us time. You say that just now nobody could possibly be that silly; everybody, in his more sober moments, is pretty well scared to death. But how many are scared to death about the right things? Merely to look around, in a world like ours, and grow pale is sheer nonsense. It always has been. Not because dreadful things can't happen. They can and do. But because there is a word of Command, which is God's Word: and it starts out by writing all the dreadful things as a footnote. It will write them so even in our time, when a hammer and some nails are a bit naïve, and we have to reckon with the stench of battlefields, and crumpled bodies, and frightened, homeless millions, and nuclear weapons, and slums, and Negroes shoved out of the way, and all the comfortable damned that look on and do nothing! Every man of us has his Egypt, and the odds against breaking away from it are inside odds, not outside. What else does the cross mean? And in the shadow of it this word still: "Speak unto the children of Israel, that they go forward."

But the Bible has a second answer to the riddle of human existence. It says more than that God is in control, issuing his mandate. That could be cold comfort. It says unequivocally what the novelist and the dramatist never explore, that no situation is hopeless, precisely because in no situation is anybody ever helpless. "My presence shall go with thee." Nothing less could keep that straggling horde of runaway slaves from being ridiculous. So does the drama move from the Word of Command to the Word of Promise. Only—so that you may never think it a cheap promise—there is a Veil over it!

You remember how it was. Moses said, "Show me thy glory." And the Lord answered him, "Thou canst not see my face; for there shall no man see me and live." I suppose because the freedom which makes us men would wither and die at the sight. But the Lord went on to say, "Behold, there is a place by me, and thou shalt stand upon a rock." So God set Moses there, in a crevice, covered over with his hand, and caused all his goodness to pass by. One might see, so to speak, only his footprints, only the mercy and the long-suffering and the truth where he had been. Is that enough for you? The Promise, "My presence shall go with thee"; and the Veil over it, "Thou canst not see my face"?

What God has done is indeed, I have no doubt, the only evidence we shall ever have in this world of what he is, and of what he's doing now. But when the evidence is all in, he has done such strange things that it troubles me. There is more in it than the one-sided sweetness and light which I'd like it to be. It says more than one thing. And as I listen, I sometimes begin to wonder if I can risk having him around. We have to catch the sound of that too. It is here in this passage, and it runs all through the Bible. Nearly a thousand years later, during the Exile, into the void of those desolate years in Babylon, stepped first an Enemy! "When I bring the sword upon a land, . . . if the watchman see the sword come and blow not the trumpet, and any person be taken away in

his iniquity, then will I require his blood at the watchman's hand."
German blood, English blood, French blood, American blood—God, how
much of it there is! Whose head is it on? "Woe," cried the Voice: "the
sick have ye not strengthened, neither have ye bound up that which was
broken, nor brought again that which was driven away, nor sought that
which was lost." On to the very edge strode the Enemy. Then turned,
and his face was the face of a Friend. See him now, somehow he will do
it, retracing our loveless steps from that very farthest edge all the way
back home again: "Behold, I, even I, will seek that which was lost, and
bring again that which was driven away, and bind up that which was
broken, and strengthen that which was sick." First the Void, then the
Enemy; only after every bit of it the Friend. "And I will make them,
and the place round about my hill, a blessing."

It's a strange God who goes with us, rooting out and pulling down to
build and plant again, wrath and loving-kindness. "I will not go up in
the midst of thee," he had said to Moses; "for thou art a stiffnecked
people." He was afraid to get too close, lest he consume them. But
Moses besought him earnestly, saying, "Then carry us not up hence."
It was better, far better, to run the risk of being burned to a cinder
by that holiness than to be abandoned by it, without any of the
difference it would make between you and all the other people on the
face of the earth. So the Lord said, "My presence shall go with thee." But
it was a veiled presence. "There shall no man see me." And it was
still perilous! Is it any the less so for the tenderness on the lips of him
who got himself into the midst of the worst, very man of very man, and
fought it out, until he could seal the mystery of his austere holiness
with the sign of a cross, and the scars in his hands and feet? "Very
God of Very God." The Promise is the same, "Lo, I am with you alway."
With this to make it new: that here at last, in one unvanquished life,
anybody may see where God has been, the long-suffering and the truth,
and how they come out on the top of a hill into that same dreadful
steadiness which contradicts us here even as our hearts yearn toward
him; yet goes on forever beckoning to us, that we may be found of him
in every one of his judgments by some mercy that seeks us out, and in
every one of his mercies by some judgment that will not leave us alone.

The Word of Command, "Speak to the children of Israel, that they go forward," is the Bible's first answer to the riddle of our being here. Then the Word of Promise, "My presence shall go with thee"—and the Veil over it, "Thou canst not see my face." Nothing now but the human face of Jesus! That's the Bible's second answer. The third is more even than that, once you locate the odds where they are, inside of you. The third answer is a Word of Victory already won, if you can bear it, and square your shoulders under it, in the knowledge that nobody's life is shut out from it except by his own choice. I say "if you can bear it," because it works itself out sometimes into such painful patterns.

Pär Lagerkvist, the Swedish poet who won the Nobel Prize for literature in 1951, set down in a little novel called *Barabbas* the story of how painful the pattern may be. He tells of how this robber they swapped for Jesus looked on at the crucifixion, staring long into that face, a face "so strong that only in weakness could it have its way." It haunted him in the copper mines where he was sent soon after. It haunted him in the years that followed, over in Nero's Rome. Until at last he made up his mind to close with it. He would help these Christians and their Jesus, so he thought, to set the whole of that odious world on fire—only to find himself farther away from the face when he was sure he was nearest! They arrested him and crucified him with the others they had caught; but over there to one side, by himself, because they knew he did not really belong. The metal disc he wore carried the symbol of Christ, but the symbol had had a line cut through it, canceling it. Over there alone he waited for the sunset, and for the death he had always feared. As it drew near, he was heard to whisper into the darkness, as if he were addressing the oncoming night, "To thee I deliver up my soul." But you can't quite believe that he was speaking only to the darkness and the night. He had at least remembered the words—from Calvary! What a pattern it was for the Promise to take: "This day have I brought thee up out of the land of Egypt." And we seem to be listening once more to a man crowded with his disciples into a narrow room on a dead-end street, saying quietly in the face of measureless defeat, while the ghost of that Fear which had stalked them there began its chattering at the door, "Be of good cheer; I have overcome the world."

Why do we keep expecting the issue to be simple and clear-cut, looking for the kind of assurance a man can never find? We live on the narrow edge, a catwalk between confidence and misgiving, doubt and faith, between seeing and not seeing. Some of you may recall that moving sermon—it has been pronounced one of the best in literature—toward the end of William Faulkner's *The Sound and the Fury*, where you almost come to think that some kind of faith, even if it seems like a tale told by an idiot, will turn out to be the only thing that makes sense. The visiting Negro preacher, in his "shabby alpaca coat," stands in the pulpit, one arm resting on the reading desk. His voice with its nameless pathos consumes him, until men's hearts are "speaking to one another . . . beyond the need of words." "I see it, Brethren, I see it, the blasting, blinding sight! I see Calvary, with the sacred trees, the thief and the murderer and the least of these. I hear the boasting and the bragging, the weeping and the turned away face of God. . . . Then what is it I see? I see the resurrection and the light, and the meek Jesus saying, I died that they who believe might live again. Brethren, O brethren!" Whereupon you turn the page, and the vision fades, and Faulkner lays all the problems back in your lap.

And he's right. This far, at any rate: that there's a kind of confidence a man dare not rest even in God—if he thinks he can have it as his own. There is no place on earth that can be called "safe in the arms of Jesus"! None of my Sunday-School teachers ever told me how dangerous a place that was! Said a friend to me once, "I can't take it any longer, this beating about between what God wants and what I am. Why can't I give up the fight and just be myself?" Then back he went, every day he lived, choosing the hurt of the battle. Facing out toward the wilderness and the God whose own job has never gone as it should either; but it bears his signature now. "This have I done for thee. What hast thou done for me?"

So, every step of the way, it's the irreversible story of the Exodus—from Egypt to Jerusalem to this moment in your life and mine: the venture into a freedom which doesn't quite come off because we are the odds against it! First the Word of Command, "Speak to the children of Israel, that they go forward"; then the Word of Promise, "My presence shall go with thee"—with the Veil over it, "Thou canst not see my face"; and the Word of Victory, for all who can bear it—it never has depended on anybody's being sure of it—"This day have I brought thee up out of the land of Egypt": "Be of good cheer; I have overcome the world." Can you live with facts like that, shoving and pulling at one another everywhere you turn? Maybe it's more important to ask if you can live without them!

O God, who didst send Thy Son, that he who by a tree once overcame might likewise by a Tree be overcome, speak Thou in Christ Thy word to us, and in him go with us to Thy triumph. Amen.

Then Came Jesus
and Stood in the Midst

O God, Thou that wilt not flatter us who love flattery, and dost offer us toil who love ease, open our eyes that we may see what Thou wouldst have us see in all the world about us, and our ears that we may hear what word Thou wouldst speak in Him who is that Word, even Jesus Christ, Thy Son, our Lord. Amen.

JOHN 20:19—Then . . . came Jesus and stood in the midst.

That is really the theme of the whole Resurrection symphony in the Fourth Gospel. If we read any of it now on any of the shallower levels of history, we misread it. One is deliberately refused the luxury of setting it down in the simple category of the past, and so in a sense being rid of it. That first morning in the garden Mary had said, "They have taken away my Lord, and I know not where they have laid him." Why do you think they cherished the story through the years, these little Christian communities scattered about in a hostile world? And this that came of it: "When she had thus said, she turned herself back, and saw Jesus standing, and knew not that it was Jesus." So with the account of those men in the evening, hand-picked to upset things, but huddled together now for fear, shut up with a memory; and Thomas, who called the whole thing nonsense when they told him: only to be confronted himself a week later by that haunting figure of a man— "Then came Jesus and stood in the midst"—the words repeat themselves. And once more he said, "Peace"—*Shalom*—and called Thomas by name, and held out his scarred hands! It wasn't just something that had happened once, any more than that the whole Bible was just something that had happened once: it kept on happening; and whatever keeps on happening is hard to refute! Maybe even then you trudge back dispirited to the old routine tasks, as Peter did still later, up in Galilee. "I go a fishing," he said. Why not? It was all over wasn't it? And the others joined in, "We also go with thee." But there in the dawn stood Jesus on the shore; and "the disciples knew not that it was Jesus" until he gave them the old familiar sign: "Cast your nets."

Now there's a pattern in all that, and I want to see if we can follow it through. As these stories unfold, there's always something about Christ's coming back from death that everybody likes very much—if I am not putting it too mildly; so much so that you wonder now and then if our faith at this point isn't what a good many people say it is, a bit of wishful thinking! I'm sure that the pulpits on Easter were full of everything about it that we like! And indeed half the gospel does run that way. But I wonder if we're aware that the other half, so to speak, runs the other way? It keeps hinting at things about Christ's coming back that we don't like. And both halves come to their point in the quite inescapable fact that whether we like it or not we have to do something about it. It's all there, I believe, in these last two chapters: the pattern of a past which is forever strangely present.

Let's be quite blunt then: What is there about the Easter gospel which says what we want it to say? A Columbia student once remarked of the sermons he had listened to in New York, that most of them left him thinking, as he went out of the church, "That isn't true; but I wish it were." Well, Thomas belonged to his party, and there's no counting the thousands in every generation that also belong. But it's a risk we have to run here in the New Testament: the risk of coming to grips with what the disillusion that begets cynicism, and the cynicism that begets a proverb, would insist on pronouncing "too good to be true." Perhaps "too good not to be true" fits God's world better.

What happened that evening in the upper room, or wherever it was —it may have been a larger meeting than we have thought—what happened that evening, and goes on happening, was on the face of it, precisely what everybody there very much wanted to have happen. It was God's way of saying something that desperately needed to be said about this place we live in.

It's a place where nobody can be hounded and victimized, forced by circumstances into a kind of straitjacket that's enough to choke the breath out of him; a place where now in sheer fairness to ourselves we have to raise the question about *God*'s knowledge of his universe, and *his* "infinite resourcefulness," instead of just trying to capitalize on our own. How much more is a world which is pliable to the scientist pliable to the God who shaped it—with how much less danger of his making a total wreck of it! Pliable because he knows about it, and cares about it, and as someone has said is of "endless ingenuity." If we are aware of that, we shall not be growing so undiscourageably despondent every once in a while, as if nothing could ever get in from the outside. If we aren't aware of it, we may believe in as many miracles as we please, provided we keep them safely shut up in the Bible, and it will make no difference.

God's world, no matter how it looks, is not the kind of place where you can finish off the Sermon on the Mount with a hammer and some nails. It isn't the kind of place where D. H. Lawrence can write in a postscript to Katherine Mansfield, "Don't worry, Kate: Jesus is a back number"—and appear to be anything but incomprehensibly silly! A good deal more was going on under the sun than "a tale told by an idiot"; and death couldn't stop it. They needed to hear that, there under the rafters behind the locked door. We all needed to hear it in Tennessee Williams' *Cat on a Hot Tin Roof*, in *Long Day's Journey Into Night*, in Colin Wilson's *The Outsider*, but nobody did; so everything added up, act after act, page after page, to no more than the grin on poor Yorick's skull. It was "very early in the morning, the first day of the week," that God said No. And in one way or another he has made it stick. He said No to the judgment hall where they tried Jesus. He said No to the hill where they crucified him. He said No to the grave where they buried him. And the No meant that you didn't have to settle down in grim facts—the cross was the worst of them—or in any of these spotty little anecdotes that seem to make up our life: not in a world where Christmas comes out of a stable, and the Son of God out of a smelly little village, and twenty centuries of Christianity out of a tomb!

Moreover, God's No meant something that the disciples wanted it to mean about themselves. You remember what Philip Wylie thought of us in his *Generation of Vipers*—claws and jaws and stomachs, not much else; and how he undertook then to write a book about the kind of moral life we had to build with that for a foundation. In the face of all the evidence available to us and more, Jesus laid everybody out on such a different blueprint! Have you ever seen those massive figures there in Florence, still bound in the crude stone from which Michelangelo's chisel has only here and there released them? You'd think they were writhing to be rid of the unshaped marble, trying to throw it off with their hands, struggling to get their feet out of it. Jesus saw Mary Magdalen that way, and Peter on the shores of Galilee, and Zacchaeus down in Jericho. He knew that none of us could ever safely be treated as less than we are, our hunger and our thirst, our eternal destiny drawn out in every straining muscle. If the cross had been the end of it, I suppose men would still have remembered how he had flung his gallant promises around in the very teeth of the gale that whipped away his breath; calling out hopes that had long since been dead, getting them up from their forgotten graves: but if death had stopped his mouth, they would have known who the winner was, for all his fine language. Now he stood there looking at his followers as one might look out on the sea. Do you know what it did for them? They were such little folk, but his eyes were so sure they had it in them that their fear didn't matter any more, or their running away, or the poor showing they had made. By this undefeated life—what else could it mean?—they were as great that night as ever they could bear it, greater than they would have liked if they had known.

But that brings me, you see, to the other half of this strange gospel, the half that runs the other way. There's something about it we don't like, that keeps us from playing it down to the level of fish and chips and immortality. Maybe that's why there's so much dramatic excitement in John: people are fighting off a kind of life. They don't mind the length of it. "Everlasting" is all right. It's the quality which John calls "eternal"—that's what they can't stand. In one of Eugene O'Neill's plays, the Lazarus whom Jesus had raised from the dead laughs softly at the townsfolk there in Bethany, as out of a vision, like a man in love with God, saying, "There is no death!" His laughter makes their ears drunk, and they stagger after him for a while, groping for joy. The light in his eyes is a flame, and like moths they dart toward it, only to reel and turn—for they dare not come too near! Until at last very mad-men they rush upon him and put him away, and hide him in the grave again. How else can men forget the God in them, lest remembrance imply too high a duty?

It takes a touch of gallantry to live in a world where things are no longer as they seem, where every one of our perspectives, as in some modernist painting, has been tossed about by this incredible thing; and the big, with which we are so thoroughly at home, turns out to be uncomfortably little; and what we are sure is little, nothing more than a cup of cold water, seems all at once so intolerably big. And you are told how lightly you have to sit now by the poor things you're giving how much of your life to; and your goods are gone over, and everything you try to seem to others, while you yourself live far away inside with everything you know you are. Lazarus turned upside down everybody's idea of what was what and who was who in Palestine, and all the men and women who loved their solemn affairs thrust their fingers in their ears. Why can't we be left alone in the world that makes such good, hard sense, whose ways we understand, to hold fast our bargains? Maybe that's what we're doing anyway, because this gospel isn't the gospel we really want!

Do we want it to go on pitching things for all of us higher even than any one of us here has ever pitched them? Anatole France thought there was one thing of which we could be absolutely sure, that men were always smaller than they seem. The trouble with the Easter story is that it makes them bigger than they care to be. Some people say we betake ourselves to this faith of ours because it's a kind of antidote for our cosmic insignificance: it gives us some fictitious stature under the stars. But is it stature we're after? Watch the man who comes to any large city from the town back home, where he taught the adult Bible class, and all the customers in the barbershop marked his downsitting and his up-rising: watch him scuttle for cover as if he'd found him a rabbit warren where he could hide out from all the things he doesn't wish to be involved in any longer. Nobody knows him here, thank God; and nobody pays much attention to anything he's doing, thank God again! If we should start living as big as we are, we'd have to be brave enough to live even in London, New York, or Chicago as sons of God, even in the rush hour morning and night; and when we aren't loved we would have to go on loving without fear. Is that what we want?

"Then . . . came Jesus and stood in the midst." Half of it I like, and half of it I don't; and I have to turn it over now and then just to keep from feeling that I've been fed a two-pound box of sweet chocolates. The Columbia student whom I mentioned said he'd heard a few sermons that left him whispering to himself as he went out of church, "That's true, but I wish it weren't!" Meanwhile, whatever half is uppermost, whether the half I like or the half I don't, I have to go on doing something about both of them. It is the surest way I have of knowing that I'm aware, not just of life, but of God. Things keep reminding me of him.

In the entrance to the Jan Hus church, over in the East Seventies of New York, there is a photograph of what is said to be a dark hillside covered with patches of snow. And that's what it looks like—chance, meaningless, scattered globs of black and white; until as you keep staring at it, quite mystified, because the caption tells you there's more in it than that, you suddenly see in three-quarters profile a face, with highlights and shadows; and you wonder why you'd never seen it before. You can't ever again miss seeing it. It's the face of One who always has left men uneasy. Catch sight of it in the world, and you have to do something, if no more than to try to lose sight of it again! And losing sight of it isn't easy. Do you want to? Maybe the first bit of real evidence you'll ever have that you too have met him is just the knowledge that there has to be something more now.

But what? Not just the peace that Jesus uttered. It was too queer a brand to come just by his uttering it. The turmoil went on outside. Nothing got better anywhere. Things got worse. Nothing secure anywhere. Nothing certain. Do you call that peace? Ecclesiastes had swung off down every road looking for it; and he has left us the record of his search. He looked for it in pleasure; and could have found it in his heart to hate life. He looked for it in labor; and could have found it in his heart to envy the dead. He was like a blind man, wearying himself to find the door.

"Peace be unto you"—with the ugly sound of the present still in their ears, and the grim future they saw every time they took their hands away from their eyes. What sense did it make? Peace couldn't come that way. Not while they thought there was nothing left in the world worth doing. Might as well say, "Oh, come now, cheer up," to a child on a long rainy day with its nose pressed against the windowpane. Peace had to come this way—if you wanted it really—you decide!— "As my Father hath sent me. . . ." God had hurled him like a spear in the world's face, that's what the word means; and it hadn't been at all safe. There had been a cross there at the end. You had to make up your mind, for it or against it. "Even so"—those terrible words!—"send I you."

But perhaps we aren't ready for that yet. Peter wasn't. What peace came to him had to come later on, up by the lake, out of the agony of his repentance and the bitter mercy of God: "Lovest thou me?" It's enough to break your heart. Saying over and over, "Feed my sheep"—as if you couldn't tell any other way. Warning you too, perhaps, as he warned Peter, in the loving-kindness that was his judgment, of how life meanwhile, and death, still have you surrounded. Said he that day, "When thou shalt be old, thou shalt stretch forth they hands, and another shall gird thee, and carry thee whither thou wouldst not." Peace would come that way. You had to decide.

Date any of it where you think it ought to be dated. With this Love in here that has broken through—maybe it's the only thing that ever can—and that wide gesture toward the life out yonder. "As my Father hath sent me. . . ." Whatever the future holds it will not be dull on those terms. So he "breathed on them" that night in Jerusalem, and said, "Receive ye the Holy Ghost." Can you now date that too? There's no magic about it. It's just the assurance that God doesn't need to have you on his hands any more—you can have him on yours, if you prefer it that way, with more than the memory of a face and the echo of strange words that flout us with what isn't true, and we wish it were— or with what is true, and we wish it weren't. You say which it is to be. So often I'm reminded by this Easter story that in the ancient art of India the Buddha never appears: only the footprints which mark his passing. That doesn't have to be the tragedy of any life that's here.

Andrew over yonder in the corner; James and John by the table; Matthew, Bartholomew, Philip; and Thomas now. Figure out their chances sometime, then range them by the side of yours!

Still this day Thy steady hand is on our souls, Jesus, Son of Mary. Of Thy great might, keep us from falling; and of Thy deep compassion, never let us go! For Thine is the kingdom, and the power, and the glory, for ever and ever. Amen.

How the New Testament
Punctuates the Gospel

*Thou hast called us into Thy presence, O God. Give us therefore light
for our darkness and strength for every high purpose wherein we are
weak: through Jesus Christ, our Lord. Amen.*

MATTHEW 11:2-11; PHILIPPIANS 4:4-7.

These two passages, associated in the historic lectionary of the Church,
reflect in a vivid way the controversy which Christianity has always
been carrying on with the culture of which in every age it is a part. They
may indeed have been among the lessons used for the ordination of the
clergy, possibly thirteen, possibly even seventeen centuries ago; and
used quite defiantly, in the world's teeth, at those very seasons when
the pagan festivals of purification were at their height: hurled, so to
speak, at the heathen gods, with their poker faces, as they tried to
crowd in around Jesus of Nazareth to take his kingship from him.

The selection from Matthew tells of how John the Baptist, from his
prison down on the shores of the Dead Sea, sent his disciples to Jesus
with that master question of all questions: "Art thou he that should
come, or look we for another?" And as we hear it read we have time
to ask it for ourselves. Whereupon Paul's letter to the Philippians, from
another prison, this time in Rome, confronts us not with a question but

with a solemn assertion, an assertion much more momentous than perhaps we have ever understood: "The Lord is at hand." But we are not
allowed to stop with that. This vibrant little apostle, as he so often
does, insists that we carry it farther, into something which sounds as
much like a shout as a man can get on paper: "Rejoice in the Lord
alway: and again I say, Rejoice!" When you take them together, this
gospel and this epistle, they are the unfolding of a perpetual drama, the
reconstituting for us of the pilgrimage which Christianity wants us to
assume we are set here to make. It's a pilgrimage which moves from
a question—"Art thou he that should come?"—to a period—"The
Lord is at hand"—and on to an exclamation point—"Rejoice in the
Lord alway, and again I say, Rejoice!" So does the New Testament
punctuate the history of salvation.

Let's look at it. The question comes first. It always does. Life begins
that way, in the cradle, with a thousand questions—eyes, fingers, tongue,
exploring this strange place, trying to find its meaning. Science begins
that way in the laboratory; and I think God sees to it that our deepest
Christian experience begins that way, with a question. "Art thou he?"
It doesn't have to come first in point of time. It comes first in the sense
that nothing which God wants to have happen in your life and mine
can happen until we have asked it, and each in his own way answered.
It's forever lurking in the shadows. Follow it through the New Testament. You will find it in one form or another on almost every page.
Herod asked it of the wise men. "Go and search diligently for the
young child; and when ye have found him, bring me word." The devil
asked it of Jesus. "If thou be the Son of God, . . ." The disciples
asked it. "What manner of man is this, that even the winds and the
sea obey him!" Pilate asked it. "Art thou a king then?" Paul asked it
on the road to Damascus. "Who art thou, Lord?" I am not sure we
always have the courage to haul it out into the light, but it's there. It's
there when you stand for the order of worship, when you kneel for the
prayer, when you sit quietly in your place for the sermon. For the most
part we keep it tucked away out of sight and hearing. Until one day,
as we look away over the rooftops, or far down the street, at this
incredible business we call life, thinking of the world as it is after all
these centuries and of ourselves as we still are, so much wrong that
should be right, so much crooked that could be straight—one day it

breaks out on a man's lips like an agony, "Art thou he that should come, or look we for another?" (See pp. 61 f. context.)

All I want to say about it at the moment is this: Never be afraid of it; because, you see, God himself occasions it, simply by his strangeness, by reason of the fact that he doesn't fit into life as we know it. John had read in the prophets that Messiah would come with a fan in his hand, to send the chaff scurrying from the threshing floor, pitchfork and shovel, toward the blazing fire. But he came so gently, doing such compassionate, obscure things, walking up and down the roads of Galilee and Judaea, healing the sick, calling out of their graves people who had died long ago, stooping under little doors like a king, walking among the rich like a beggar, poorer than the foxes that had holes and the birds of the air that had nests. It wasn't right. How could such a Messiah be at home in that harsh age? And so something in that lonely herald down by the Dead Sea was prodded to its feet, and he sent his deathless question.

And something in us, forlorn and wistful; forever frustrated because it wants so much to have its own way; its reach exceeding its grasp, today, and tomorrow, and on into the day beyond; never willing to make friends with God's sovereignty or with his reticence, with his lordship over the world or with his hiddenness, and the anonymity of his gifts; tormented by this freedom that we have to reject him, this awful freedom which we fear so much that we flee from it to make our own little rules and draw up our own little plans for his Kingdom. Who do you suppose is responsible for the turmoil? Who brought Jean Paul Sartre to cry out from the depths of his heart into the abyss of his loneliness, only to say in the next breath that hell is other people? Who tore him apart? Why couldn't he rest? And Camus. Calling God the Death-Bringer—then with what irony dying that senseless death of his! Why were both of them at once so infinitely near and so infinitely far away from the Kingdom of God? Walt Whitman once stood for a long time watching a drove of cattle knee-deep in clover, telling us later how much he envied them. They didn't lie awake at night bemoaning their sins. They didn't turn over and beat the pillow because they weren't accepted, and had to live fragmented lives. But they were cattle, and Walt Whitman was a poet. What if that beating of the pillow at night, that *where* and that *what*—"O that I knew where I might find him!"

"What shall a man give in exchange for his soul?"—what if that *how* and that *why*—"O Lord, how long shall I cry, and thou wilt not hear!" "Why hast Thou forsaken me?"—what if all of it were fighting its way to the surface out of a kinship with God which we can deny and betray but cannot break, not with Christ there, trying to restore it; not with the hold he has on us which only he can assert and only we can thrust off! The questions are themselves the letters patent of our nobility. They are prompted by, and bear witness to, that vast encounter with the Eternal God in which you and I are now engaged, the vast encounter which faith is. The questions are God's questions, and he has so many.

Jesus understood that better than we do, and so sprang to John's defense that day when the messengers came. "You can stop nodding your heads to each other," he said to the scribes and Pharisees standing around, "snickering behind your beards. This was the man who called you a generation of vipers, and warned you to flee from the wrath to come. And he was right! You think now, because he doesn't seem to be doing so very well himself, that he never was anything but a reed, shaken by the wind. Only a softling at heart, like the fops that play about in kings' houses. I tell you he was a prophet. He was more! No man born of woman was ever greater than he!"

It was the same inexpressible tenderness that held out its arms to Thomas one evening, met him on his own ground, not half-way, the whole way and three-quarters more: "Reach hither thy finger, and behold my hands; and reach hither thy hand, and thrust it into my side: and be not faithless, but believing." Was it, in all honesty, anything he saw that convinced Thomas, anything he touched? Or just something that got home to him, something so like the Jesus he had known that he couldn't make head against it any longer, or keep the others from hearing what was in his heart and didn't have to be heard, because it was in all their hearts? "My Lord and my God."

So often it's what we think is wrong with this Christ that turns out to be right. Can we let that get deeply enough inside of us never to be forgotten? For Thomas, the crucifixion was wrong; today it's one of the no more than two or three reasons we have for calling ourselves Christians. Thank God for what was wrong, and for the right that came out of it! For John, "the gentle Jesus meek and mild" was all wrong; but it wasn't! Neither was it all right. The word Jesus sent back was that it was at least half right. John had to put the halves together for himself. The fan, and the chaff, and the fire, that was half of it, back there in the prophets he had read; but he had missed the other half, about the blind that were to see when the Messiah came, and the deaf that were to hear—the lame, the lepers, was there to be no room for them, or for the poor who so desperately needed some news of God's Kingdom?

And with that, I think, we have begun to move away from the question mark and are coming within sight of the period. Let me say at once, there have to be periods. This generation of ours has fallen so much in love with what it calls the open mind that it has begun to identify periods with ignorance and to mistake conviction for bigotry. I remember watching a television program for one whole stricken hour on a Sunday afternoon, while professors, reporters, and quite a number of experts in foreign affairs sat at a round table exchanging views, as they said, about Red China. The absorbing thing about it was that no view was ever exchanged for any other. And the name of the program was *The Open Mind!* At the end of it I was merely confused on a much higher level. My mind was so open that you could catch cold in it—until I closed it by coming to the conclusion that I didn't know what was going to happen, and they didn't either. That was the period, and there have to be periods. But I want you to see how the New Testament arrives at them.

The scene is laid in the city of Rome, Nero's Rome. Paul had promised the church there that he would pay them a visit. Now he had arrived, though not exactly according to plan. Destiny, or whatever it was, had turned another of its somersaults for him, and he had been escorted up the Appian Way a prisoner, to be hurried off, when they reached the city, into what the Nazis used to call house arrest, with a guard to keep him company. It wasn't the happiest kind of setting in which to write the letter he wanted to write to the Christians at Philippi. But never mind the setting. All at once his mind was running swiftly ahead to the day when Christ should come again, to gather in his hands, sceptered hands now, every little bit of this "sorry scheme of things entire" and bring it to its consummation under God. There had been a period in his life when Paul thought that would be soon: but as the years passed, the time schedule mattered less and less; be-

cause what he had it in mind to say was always true. It always had
been. It had been true when he prayed about that thorn in his flesh
which he had never understood, and got only the answer, "My grace is
enough for you." It had been true there on the island of Malta, when
the viper bit him, and he shook it off, and was unhurt. It was true now,
right there in his prison. So he spelled it out for them. "The Lord is at
hand."

And at the moment something was happening to underscore it; something that must have reminded him of what he had said so long before
in his letter to this Roman congregation: "We know that in all things
God works together for good with them that love him." I can't tell
just how it was. Perhaps one day as he was writing he glanced down
at the chain clamped to his leg, binding it fast to the leg of the Roman
soldier; then looked up at the soldier—and smiled! What more could
an apostle want than just such a captive audience? When the other
frowned and asked what the smile was all about—life wasn't so very
pleasant, was it?—he little knew the risk he ran of being taken prisoner
himself. "Oh, I wasn't thinking of life particularly," Paul must have
answered. "I have known much worse than this. Five times I've had
thirty-nine lashes with the whip. Three times I was beaten with rods.
Once I was stoned. I wasn't thinking of that, or of this chain. I was
thinking of something that took place many years ago, far across the
sea, in Palestine: and of how it changed everything for me, turned the
whole thing into a pageant. And now these people of Philippi have
thanked me for telling them about it; because it has changed everything
for them too. And they have sent me their love. That's worth a smile,
don't you think? Come here and see what I've written them. That Greek
word means 'the Lord.' You know very well who your lords are. They are
your masters. I have only one. He loved me, and gave himself for me.
Did any of yours ever do that? And this word means that he is at hand;
here, while we are talking to each other. That's why I smiled. Let me
tell you about him." And Paul was off! With two or three fresh guards
every day to listen to him, no wonder he could write to the Philippians,
"Don't you worry. These things have fallen out rather to the furtherance
of the gospel. Men all through the imperial city are preaching now more
boldly than ever they did, taking courage from the very fact that I am
here in prison for Christ's sake. And some of them are in the very house-

hold of Caesar!" "The Lord is at hand." It was the period which the apostle set to every circumstance of his life.

"In all things—God." Hidden away on the other side of every riddle, poverty, pain, humanity's countless sorrows, "the heavy and the weary weight of all this unintelligible world"—on the other side, or at the heart of it, as the riddle keeps teasing you like a mischievous child, plucking at your sleeve: "Give up? Give up?" If you nod your head and say "Yes," it won't tell you the answer; it will just laugh, and point its finger at you, and run off to look for somebody else. God can never find you in that "Yes"; he can find you only in the "No," as you turn back to the place where you were about to stop, and the Presence which beckons to you from deep inside of it, wanting you to follow even when it's darkest, and there seems to be no sure footing anywhere. "In all things—God."

Hidden away among your private troubles, the things you complained of this morning so bitterly. There was something, wasn't there? Perhaps it was yesterday. Emerson used to cover up his embarrassment at not recognizing people when he met them again by holding out his hand and saying, "Well, well, I am glad to see you. Tell me—how is the old complaint?" Everybody had one, and so everybody was certain that he had been instantly and intimately remembered. "In all things"—there's room in that for the dreams you once had that won't come true now, not as you dreamed them; for the illness that has laid its iron grip on somebody you love; for whatever it is that's so wrong about your life that it festers, and you long to be rid of it—the sin that doesn't know it's beaten, and comes crawling back as if it could defeat God, and it can't. It has no power but the power you are willing to give it. What do you make of this offer? "In all things, God."

Never tiptoe by any of the facts, treating them like locked and haunted rooms, scarcely daring even to glance their way. Samuel Johnson once remarked to Boswell, speaking of some gay resort in London, "It went to my heart to consider that there was not one in all that lively company who was not afraid to go home and think." Never just grit your teeth, either, and plod ahead in the face of it all, tired brain, aching muscles, clenched fist, from one commandment to another, like slaves under a whip carrying bricks. Not while all the way along this music keeps rolling from the life of one whose eyes were looking no more surely than yours can look now into the face of the Son of God. He writes down the score of it for us: "The Lord is at hand." Then pulls out the great diapason stop: "All I had gained was loss. And all the loss I have suffered is rubbish, if only I can lay hold of that for which Christ laid hold of me." How I envy the man his gift of seeing the road while he was traveling it! He didn't have to wait until his hair turned gray, and he could look back over his shoulder to find what God had been doing. There used to be a hymn, "Some time we'll understand." We sing more heresy than all the councils ever condemned. For the sake of this that God offers us, his own life in Christ, "perilous and untamed," both hands full—let's understand now! "In all things—God." Period.

But there, there indeed, we get to the hard part. We'll go along with the question, "Art thou he?" We've wondered about that ourselves. We may even go along with this period which Paul sets to it: "The Lord is at hand." There may well be unexplored possibilities there which we have all too often overlooked. But how on earth, with everything it plunged him into up to the neck, did Paul turn the period into an exclamation point? Something that even in cold print reads like a shout from the heat of battle? "Rejoice in the Lord alway: and again I say, Rejoice!" That we can't manage.

Maybe somebody should tell you that you aren't supposed to. I may just as well do it right now. Here isn't something you can manage. Nobody can entice you into it, or advise you into it, or exhort you into it, or command you into it. It's something that has to happen to you. And it happens when you are rid of enough of yourself to make the difference. This is precisely why all I'm saying now is so very hard that I need your help. No sooner do we come to talk about rejoicing in the Lord than we quit rejoicing! And you know why. It's because all at once we've got ourselves into the middle again. We are feeling our pulse. The apostle says "Rejoice." Let's see now how I'm doing—and we finger away at our wrist. That would take the joy out of anything, painting a picture, playing the piano, preaching a sermon, anything. A psychiatrist once told me that in our present-day almost psychotic passion for psychiatry, students in certain medical colleges are taught that when they are confronted by a patient, they are first to ask themselves "Who am I?" Then "Who is this person?" Then "How does this person feel toward me?" Then "How do I feel toward this person?" Then "Why do we feel toward each other as we do?" That, I suggest, would do more than take the joy out of practicing medicine; it would be likely to take the patient out too! The only ghost of a chance any of us have is in starting to forget —starting to forget ourselves into the freedom of the sons of God.

I have read somewhere that the slaves in Jamaica, when they knew that on a certain day they were going to be set free, spent all the night before getting ready: moving by twos and threes out of their huts into the village lanes, joined by others in the forest and on the plain, climbing the highest hill through the darkness, crowding together at the top, straining toward the sunrise. As the first faint streaks of the dawn began to show on the horizon, a ripple of laughter spread through the crowd like the murmur of waves. Then a shout went up, and they began to sing, in their own peculiar rhythm, everybody with his arms around somebody else, paying no attention to the tears on their cheeks, falling to their knees at last and lifting their wide open hands to heaven, crying "Free! Free!"

That's what the gospel promises; and that's what it delivers. You won't take it for no more than a pleasant prospect, will you? Why do we have to twist every promise there is in order to make that out of it? It has very little to do with getting out of trouble. Every time Paul got out, he hurried right back in again, with a doxology on his lips! Whenever there is anything in our lives that's like an ecstasy, and sometimes there is I know, it springs from the most unlikely soil. It springs from the very fact that Christianity isn't at all what most people think it is. They have an idea that the Christian is always warming his hands somewhere in the neighborhood of the first Psalm. "Blessed is the man that walketh not in the counsel of the ungodly. . . . He shall be like a tree planted by the rivers of water. . . . Whatsoever he doeth shall prosper." That's what we have to let go! There was once another kind of tree entirely. "They took Jesus, and led him away. And he bearing his cross went forth." "He will not suffer thy foot to be moved." "They came to a place called Golgotha." "There shall no evil befall thee." "There they crucified him."

They say, these people, that the reason for the Christian's joy is that he has an Omnipotent Helper; and exactly that is what the Bible from beginning to end says you don't have: somebody to run your errands, to make the Church strong where she is weak, never mind the stubborn elders, the incompetent pastors, the men and women with no vision and tight purses; somebody who will bring religion back into Russia, and make Red China a little more like the United States. That's precisely what you don't have! All the Christian has is something that was said in Gethsemane. "Thy will be done." Something that Paul and Silas said in Thessalonica, and turned the world upside down with it: "There is another king, one Jesus!"

Then they hit on the secret, they are sure of it, these lookers-on who know so little and like to talk so much about what Christianity is. The joy of the Christian, they tell you, comes of giving back good for evil, in order to make the evil good; forgiving seventy times seven, to win himself a friend; turning the other cheek to influence somebody, going two miles when you compel him to go only one. And none of it comes anywhere near the mark. All the Christian can expect for his pains is his share of that bitter compassion which was placarded like a torn piece of paper on a cross. Strange to tell, queer beyond all telling, that's the way the joy happens: in some place beyond the self where peace is born and hope gets up out of its grave again. Like the fearless, almost gay abandon which found itself crowded one night into a narrow room on a dead-end street, only to draw its humble, arrogant line through all common sense everywhere: "Be of good cheer; I have overcome the world." The price hasn't been marked down any. But the odds are no greater than they ever were.

And there I leave it. It's the drama of human life in the grip of the Eternal God. "Art thou he?" "The Lord is at hand." "Rejoice in the Lord!" From a question mark to a period to an exclamation point. So does the New Testament punctuate the gospel. You'll not get them all neatly arranged like that, each one treading on the other's heels. They'll be jostling one another, slipping in and out of the hymns you sing, interrupting the Creed and the Lord's Prayer. But that's what faith means. What else could it mean, when you come to think of it, with lives like ours, and such a God as this?

To whatever Thou hast called us, O God, and at whatever cost, let it be. Only do Thou lead us, lest we stop anywhere when Thou art saying "Come," and by the gift of Thyself make us strong; through Jesus Christ, our Lord. Amen.

Creative Insecurity

O God, who dost ever seek us out not only at Thy peril but at ours too, calling us away from all that our hands can do to that great thing which Thine have done, look on us with compassion that we need Thee so, and as Thou wilt, send us each to his appointed place; through Jesus Christ, our Lord. Amen.

ACTS 9:15,16—He is a chosen vessel unto me . . . I will shew him how great things he must suffer for my name's sake.

We are told that the new kind of person who is just now making his appearance in history—post-Christian, post-individual, post-moral man, as he is called—finds it very hard to believe that there is a God; though if one were to judge from the plays and novels that he writes, with all their anguish of rebellion, the bitter emptiness which comes of being utterly without purpose, when the mask is off and the chips are down he finds it even harder to believe that there isn't. Life for him turns into a kind of foreign language, which as Christopher Morley once put it everybody promptly begins to mispronounce.

But none of that is really hard. What is really hard is to find that every time you open the Bible you have to reckon with another kind of believing altogether: the kind that will never allow you to manage your own life any more. The picture of a lovely girl, with a very lovely smile, was on the cover of a magazine some time ago, under it the caption, "I have earned the right to live as I please." It was exceedingly high pay for whatever it was she had done. Angels rush in where even fools are afraid. You'll say a long farewell to that sort of thing when you come face to face with the God of the Bible. It isn't then so much a question of "believing" or "not believing": in the Bible you run the risk of meeting him. You run the risk of finding out that he isn't at all the kind of God who will stay out there somewhere and let you look at him, or talk about him. He isn't so much occupied with being, he's occupied with acting. And that's what shatters a man's peace. He's forever coming, and at his own convenience, not ours. He's forever choosing, and for some purpose he has in mind: it may not jibe with ours in the least.

Take the story of Paul's conversion, there on the road to Damascus. What God had in mind for him certainly didn't jibe with what he had in mind for himself. Something familiar, something which seemed solid and secure, was finished; he was snatched away from it. Something which looked like nothing at all that was solid, something which looked like the last word in insecurity, had begun; he was headed for it. *From* something, *to* something: that's our cue. It's how the lines run for us as well, these lines of God's direction.

From what comes first. Did it ever actually strike across your mind with some little anxiety that Paul wasn't converted from an evil life, but from a good life; not from impiety, but from piety; not from irreligion, but from religion? Everything inside of him had been swept and garnished, not to say starched and ironed, for years. Every commandment had been taken down from the shelf, dusted off, and polished. There was not a demand which his devotion to the God of his fathers had laid on him that he had not done his best to meet.

Yet something was wrong. He doesn't seem to have had any overwhelming sense of sin. It wasn't his conscience that bothered him. It wasn't the boredom which comes of having nothing to do. He was doing a job at the very moment, and it was the job he thought God had given him to do; he was going through with it. But from what he said later, he had found it all rather disheartening. You could breathe out threatenings against other people who didn't believe as you did, that was your plain duty; but you couldn't strike up a tune about it, or hoist a flag over it, or break out into any doxologies because of it.

And he tells us why. It's no secret. It was because all the way along he had been trying to manufacture his own stock-pile of seemly behavior and righteous living; and that's tiresome business. I'm not so sure we ever get quite clear of it. For what other reason does Christianity turn out so often to be so dreadfully dull? You have seen what a universal phenomenon student riots have become during the last quarter of a century. How do you account for it? It's partly because the culture of which they are a part has lost its enthusiasm. I should hate to think that we now have to say the same thing of Christianity— when in fact it's a drama far more exciting than any other the human mind has ever conceived, unless indeed you look on it as a fairy story: the infinite and eternal God become man, to live as we are afraid to live, and to die as we are afraid to die. You may call Jesus anything you like, wrote Dorothy Sayers; but you cannot call him dull. It was because his enemies couldn't tame him that they had to crucify him. It's his friends who have decked him out in pastel shades and made a gentleman of him—chiefly perhaps by wanting of him no more than some sense of security, which in the end, we have to admit, almost inevitably turns out to be so insecure that even a bad cold can upset it.

Under such circumstances, what we like to think of as our religion can do nothing for us but hand us over to the tyranny of some good which is always just out of reach; but we have to go on clutching for it, like a drowning man, to keep our heads above water. Only to find ourselves at last, like Paul, desperately far away from the Kingdom of God precisely when we think we are safely and squarely in the middle of it, and quite well, thank you; so well that we have no need of a physician, since we have grown used to the pride which we have learned to call humility, and are quite content to mistake our sober satisfaction with what we are for three hallelujahs and the sound of a great Amen.

Maybe you are saying to yourself right now, "Well, thank God, I am not like that." In which case, instead of thanking God, you must allow me to thank you. You have helped me to make my point. That's what the Pharisee said in the temple. And it's more than self-righteousness.

What frightens me is that it's blasphemy. It's the attempt to stake out a claim which is calculated to bind God's freedom. You have some little status with the divine bookkeeper, haven't you? You aren't like that publican. Job said he wasn't like the wicked, and said it out loud, shaking his fist at God. If he were any kind of God at all, he'd play the part, and quit pampering all those rascals, instead of the upright you-know-who. This way you couldn't count on anything.

And all of it comes of looking around in our shaken world for something safe, something to lean on and build on; but "around" is never the way to look. Nothing else so twists our judgments, or sends us off on such weird tangents. Peter one day looked around at the other disciples. They had come a long, hard road. And he said to Jesus, "We have forsaken all, and followed thee; what shall we have therefore?" He was sure it would be something special. If you couldn't spread out before God, now and then at any rate, the few decencies you have been able to bring off in your time; if you couldn't depend on his weighing them, and entering them where they belonged—then for pity's sake what kind of world was it anyway? What was the use, if you couldn't set them up and on occasion get in behind them for cover? And Jesus told him about the first who were last among the laborers in the vineyard, and the last who were first.

Which is only to say that there is no way at all of striking a bargain with God and holding him to it: doing this and doing that, so as to make these lives of ours shipshape, then expecting a smooth passage in return. Dickering is out. And by the same token tinkering is out too, on whatever scale, big or little. I remember a tiny insert in *The New Yorker*, a picture of that huge projector in the Hayden Planetarium. A stepladder had been planted against one of its great bulbous heads, and a wee mite of a man on top with a screwdriver was getting the universe fixed up a bit by adding a few sputniks. Is that what we are after, with our reform movements and one-man righteousness cults—getting the universe fixed up a bit? Nobody has a right to be cynical about what is sometimes spoken of as returning to religion. But if much of it adds up to nothing more than being afraid "for looking after those things which are coming on the earth"; and so, not knowing what to do, attempting to get in under what the Bible tells us to do, on the off chance of being able somehow to arrange matters a shade more in our favor—then God pity us! And I doubt that he will have any means of showing it. An acid comment on all such tomfoolery was made by a recent cartoonist. Some well-dressed fellow had just passed the sign which reads PREPARE TO MEET THY GOD and was standing now in front of the mirror on a cigaret vending machine, taking off his hat, brushing his hair, and straightening his tie.

Primping up for safety doesn't get you anywhere. Neither does scuttling around. What you are after isn't in the creed, it isn't in the liturgy, it isn't in the hymns, it isn't in the prayers. It just isn't "around." It may not even be up. And for a very simple reason. The faith we talk about as if it had to do primarily with believing something, or at least with relying on somebody, means being back again with Christ. It means that before it means anything else at all. Back with the Christ who laid down his life to bring us back. But back where? Back in the company of a holy God who is himself a kind of reckless pilgrim down the long reaches of his purpose, knowing his way through, never faltering any, yet always in the dangerous vanguard of human life; with nothing to clutter his going in our generation but those of us who try to dig our heels in the ground and hold out against the future which is on its way among the nations and among the races—because we think we can be safe that way. It's the one thing which most imperils our lives.

Why then can't we come to terms with what we can't dodge? It isn't safe to believe in the God of the Bible. Indeed it isn't safe to live! Security at its peak is little more than sterility. Only insecurity has some chance of being creative. It can never be overcome. It can only be resolved into some other brave risk for us to take. If your life is dull, you haven't been taking any. If it's uninteresting, you've made it so. And you are not likely to help things much by acquiring a few added "interests" in the shape of luncheons and lectures and book clubs. Life doesn't want to be safe. It doesn't want to absorb something. It wants to create something. It wants to breast some slope. It wants to be gallant. Insecurity is its heritage.

Richard Hughes has told somewhere of a lad in the last war; a shy and ineffectual lad who had never done anything worth while. Nothing had ever happened to him. Missing his breakfast once in a while was the only variation in the routine that he had ever known. But one night, in a front-line trench, just three minutes before zero hour, when everybody was in a blue funk, he climbed out on the rampart of sand-bags and sat there smoking a cigaret, with bullets whining all around. It was a crazy thing to do, against all orders; but as the others looked on, their nerves grew steady. Then he glanced at the watch on his wrist, flipped the butt of his cigaret away, and said, "Well boys, it's time. Let's go!" And there wasn't a man who didn't leap out at his word.

But at that point we've got to add something. And this is the second thing I wanted to say. Paul was not only converted *from*; he was at the same time converted *to*. *To what?* That's the other half of the picture we're thinking of. And by the way, don't let the word *conversion* upset you. It doesn't necessarily have to do with becoming either a saint or a Christian. It has to do very simply with turning around, which is a maneuver we engage in, I dare say, pretty much every day we live. Every-thing that through the centuries had made God God and kept him God had broken into the world again in Jesus Christ, and Paul had to right-aboutface from one kind of belief to another kind entirely. He was tossed bodily out of the security of what God had done into the insecurity of what God was doing; and he found it to be the insecurity of a manifold and unreckoning grace! A grace which kept giving him all he asked when he was at his best, and kept asking of him all it gave: trying for love's sake to get him clean away, as far as could be, from the old familiar pattern, into the courage to be different, when it was difference that life called for; courage to make, beyond each strict account, some incautious trial of that compassion which finds the good where others had found only the fault before. And if you think that's tame, try it!

You'll not be given a blueprint of what needs doing. Paul didn't get one either. He said, "Lord, what wilt thou have me to do?" And the Lord said, "It shall be told thee what thou must do." All you can count on is that it will be no craven thing: it will be a brave thing, some-thing that will take more than you have in your own right, something God wants to get done, something he has in mind now. Make no mistake about that. To say as much about him is to say no more than you have to say if you say anything about him at all. We may be willing to concede that he has a purpose for everybody in general. That's a comfortable platitude. Or perhaps we say he had a purpose for Moses and the prophets, for the "saints" and for "all the glorious company of the apostles." And that's a comfortable alibi. There has to be some back door by which we can sneak out of our own unique and individual, our own personal and particular responsibility for the Christian faith and human history. Only there isn't. All through the Bible, from Adam to Abraham, from Egypt to Canaan, from Babylon back home again, every judgment and every mercy, every threat and every promise, comes hurtling straight at you, and you know it. You read it that way yourself.

So why boggle? It's you that are chosen now for this thing God has in mind, a thing so fitted to your life that it won't get done in exactly that way unless you do it. At the point where the transition is made from all the choosing God did in the Old Testament to all the choosing he continues to do in the New, stands this violent apostle, talking of being hand-picked. And you can be sure he wasn't rationalizing some self-interest. Read the story of his life. He wasn't indulging any self-righteousness. All that belonged to his false history, and he was done with it. He was only saying something about himself which he insisted held true of everybody else: each at God's appointed post, "called to be saints . . . according to his purpose . . . in one hope of your calling."

He was well aware of the absurdity of it in his case; he was bewildered by it, baffled every time he tried to figure out the reason for it. Ananias had answered the Lord that day, "I have heard by many of this man, how much evil he hath done." Paul knew how much, and knew it better than anybody else. But he knew that this unreckoning grace which had beckoned to him wanted out, and it wanted out where he was. Nothing mattered but that. He knew he couldn't manage by himself. Who can? But he knew enough about the past, and had already plunged deeply enough into the present, to know how God works. He understood that whatever salvation there was, God had wrought it; but that didn't let him off. You couldn't think that if you had even the foggiest notion of what the love of God does when it gets hold of a man. It turns Sinai into Calvary, and as surely as there is nothing you *can* do, so surely there is nothing which at God's word you *won't* do!

And there was something more that Paul knew. He didn't have any special privileges now. Not any longer. He used to have, as a Jew, or thought he had; and he had done his best by strict obedience to hold on to them. The gospel had stripped him of them. That he knew. But he never let the obedience go. For all his vaunted freedom, he lived the Law; but he lived it as love. And that made all the difference. Once he had had to read all the others out, sinners and Gentiles alike; under the eyes of Christ he had to read them in, every one of them. The boundaries of God's Kingdom were not his to tamper with any more. God could alter them, he couldn't. And God would alter them if any of the elect began to figure they were the elite!

One of the most touching things I have ever heard was the reply of a Jewish scholar when he was asked why he had become a Christian. With obvious tenderness, and with a profound understanding of his own history as a Jew, he answered, "I couldn't bear to leave Jesus alone among the Gentiles." But that's just where Jesus is—always. That's where he's bound to be, alone among the outsiders, until we go there too. Not because we pity him, poor man, so far out of his element. And not because, as insiders, we pity them. A few years ago I sat with a group of ministers who were talking about the missionary enterprise of the Church in so-called foreign lands, and about the extent to which our support of it had fallen off here at home. Everybody was exhorting everybody else. And everybody, it seemed to me, was incredibly mistaken about the why and the wherefore of the whole undertaking. We had to save these people. They were lost. We had to pluck them like brands from the burning. And nobody said what I am sure has to be said, that we've got to quit fooling around with labels. Jesus mixed them up so thoroughly that they are of no use to us. Who are the saved? You can hide from God himself behind that label. Who are the lost? Everybody who thinks he isn't! Leave the labels to God. We've got to go and do simply because the compassion which holds out its arms to us in Christ won't let us sit on the front porch and rock ourselves to death. If that isn't it, we'd better resign from the entire project, at home and abroad. We go because that's what the grace of God has chosen us to do. Can't we get that straight? On the left hand of God in Jesus' picture of the final judgment, nobody seemed to have any inkling as to why he was there. On the right hand, nobody could make any sense of it either. But the secret wasn't long in coming out. "Inasmuch as ye did it not. . . . Inasmuch as ye did it. . . ." It's the *inasmuch* that matters, and "the least of these my brethren," and the Christ who only in them is to be received or rejected.

But there was still more. And this Paul did not know. There was the "how great things he must suffer for my name's sake." Are we willing now, in the shadow of the cross, to listen to that? C. S. Lewis, in *Till We Have Faces*, tells the story of Cupid and Psyche, and writes of how bitterly Psyche's sister cries out, "Do you think we mortals will find you gods easier to bear if you're beautiful? I tell you . . . we'll find you a thousand times worse. For then you'll lure and entice. Those we love best—whoever's most worth loving—these are the very ones you'll pick out . . . I can see it happening, age after age . . . growing worse and worse the more you reveal your beauty: the son turning his back on the mother . . . the bride on her groom, stolen away by this everlasting calling, calling, calling of the gods . . . We'd rather they were ours and dead than yours and made immortal."

This it is precisely that's all changed now. Mr. Lewis, as he wrote, was no stranger to what had happened on a little hill outside the walls of Jerusalem. Ever since then we have been better able to understand that God, like the kings of old, can do us no higher honor, show us no greater hospitality, than to give us of his cup to drink. We may at times draw back, and try to remain spectators. Matthew describes it: ". . . sitting down they watched him there." Maybe we should first investigate some of his claims. Couldn't he have spared himself the thorns and the reed and the nails and the spear, and at least have looked a bit more like God? But the New Testament goes on quietly taking it for granted that here is the very flaming center of life, and that we'll be back, as someone has said, to flutter furiously around the intensity of its burning!

"How great things he must suffer for my name's sake." Paul found out. And I have more than just a twinge of conscience when I say it. It hasn't been given many of us. We have only to face the disciplines of life. Sometimes they are hard, yes. We have to face its uncertainties and its insecurities, the devotion that's without any safeguard; death, when it comes to us, or to some one we love. Shall we resent them? Can't we manage, with all we have, to bear redemptively what we shall have to bear in any case? The greatest joys the world has ever known have come that way out of its sorrows. It's the grace of God, that incredible, gallant thing, that wants out; and it wants out where we are!

You have seen Millais' painting of the boyhood of Sir Walter Raleigh.

He is sitting on the sands of Devon by the shore, his knees clasped in his arms, gazing far out across the water. His friend lies beside him, chin cupped in both hands, while from the sea wall a sunburnt, stalwart Genoese sailor, back and bronzed shoulders towards us, points with his right arm southward, telling them romantic tales of the Spanish main; and about the wild hurricanes—that's my guess—how the ship would dive nose down into the trough of the waves and shudder up again, with the water spouting from her scuppers, shaking her bow clear, and rolling on into the next fearful plunge. There is something in God like that. And unless there is something like it in us, what can he lay hold of? "Saul, Saul!" Something that will come at his signal, never mind what happens. It may be that we shall have to pay more heavily than we thought, in a Father's house, for being that Father's child!

There was a youth, wrote a great Scottish preacher, who once sought eagerly for the court of King Arthur. When he came at last to the ancient gateway, there an old man stood. "Dare you?" the old man asked, glancing sharply at him. "Once past this arch, and our royal lord will lay vows on you which it were shame not to be bound by, yet the which no man can keep." What if we could answer, things being as they are, "Sir, write my name down!"

Beyond everything we have seen and known of Thee, O God, there is more. Create in us now that readiness which Thou dost require, and fashion our lives into that obedience of love which Thou dost command —in so far as by Thy grace Thou wilt grant us to go; in the name of Jesus Christ, our Lord. Amen.

AFFAIRS ARE NOW SOUL SIZE

As Free—as the Servants of God

Grant us, O God, such knowledge of Thee as shall illumine our minds, and cleanse our hearts, and establish in Thee our going out and our coming in; through Jesus Christ, our Lord. Amen.

I PETER 2:16—As free, and not using your liberty for a cloke of maliciousness, but as the servants of God.

If it's Peter himself who is saying here that you are not to make your freedom an excuse for doing anything that's wrong, it's because he has learned the hard way that Christian freedom always has its limitations: you are only as free as the servants of God; no less, no more.

And that's a strange sort of freedom. It may seem to some of us even stranger still that all of the appointed lessons for the four Sundays in Advent, which look so steadily toward Christmas, should celebrate that strange freedom in one way or another as the greatest of God's gifts in Christ. So does the hymn we sing, "Come, Thou long-expected Jesus, Born to set Thy people free." But what about these people to whom Peter was writing? They might very well have signaled to us in the middle of that first stanza and shouted "Stop that! You know nothing whatsoever about it. Ask us! We are 'free'—to die at the stake! 'Born thy people to deliver'? We are being 'delivered'—to the wild beasts!"

With the flames all around them, or perhaps they were trudging through the bloody sands of the arena—just how free is that? Once in a while we should come to grips with it.

What does it mean in the Bible to be free? Back of the word, of course, and back of a dozen kindred words, lies the thought of humanity's terrible wrestling with some kind of bondage. It makes you think of the Laocoön group, the priest and his sons held fast in the coils of the serpents Apollo had sent. A dozen variants of the theme provide the subject matter of the Greek tragedies. For the Jew, the symbol of it was that faraway hateful slavery in Egypt. Every year at the Passover, as the story of the Exodus was handed down from father to son, God's mighty act of redemption kept repeating itself, buying a man back from under the lash of his taskmaster, striking off his shackles, bringing him up out of his exile and home again. He couldn't forget it, or ever stop talking about it. It was the very pattern of his history, and it would go on being that forever. Without it life never had made or could make any sense!

So he killed the thing he loved. It's the undying tragedy of man's existence. The privilege he had by God's gift, he tried to possess. Like an ancestral estate, it had come down to him from his fathers: what was to keep him from building a fence around it, and posting some rules, and living on the inside of his heritage with the Almighty? The New Testament tells what happened when God broke through. It wasn't easy to understand a man who paid no attention to the fence and went around outside as well as inside healing the brokenhearted, preaching deliverance to the captives, and setting at liberty them that were bruised. Certainly you couldn't call the Jews any of these things. They were the children of Abraham. Then get this fellow out of the way! He was an offense. They weren't safe with him around.

And that's exactly how it is from beginning to end. Here is the secret of the only freedom the Bible knows anything about: it comes of an appalling insecurity! You destroy it when you try to acquire it; you lose it when all you want to do is to keep it! It doesn't mean that suddenly, in the twinkling of an eye, you are rid of anything on the day's agenda. You haven't been snatched away from the blood and the sweat and the tears, on the beaches, across the fields, and in the streets. There hasn't been any Shangri-La for anybody I know, where the tumult and the shouting die. There's nothing but the eternal faithfulness of a God who offers himself to you in Jesus Christ, up to the head of the nails! Then what kind of business would you suppose might be afoot if that's what it is that happens? Nothing but a skirmish somewhere off among the hills, or a bit of a scuffle in a back alley?

What if the essential pathos of our situation, indeed the central irony of human life, were simply this: that at a time when progress seems to consist in keeping just one jump ahead of disaster, and in a world with the kind of business on its docket that it takes God to handle, we are free with such a freedom as all the ages have found too "awkward and dangerous," so that the only way there is of making it safe is to refuse it. While the very issues of history turn on what we do with it! Certainly we miss the point with almost supernatural accuracy when, by abusing it and doing what we like we rationalize it into bondage again, or because we have been disillusioned—we should never have had any illusions in the first place about what freedom means!— chuck it in the pigeonhole with the other ideals we used to cherish when we were young. We are grown-up, hardheaded realists now!

Perhaps it would be well to get some of our ideas straightened out. Of course we are not free as we have wanted to think of freedom. We shall never be stepping altogether out of this shadow which the self is, for example. Nor shall we ever be anything more than forgiven sinners. If we are going to have any peace of mind we'd better get used to that. We may try to pull away, God knows we do, from the things that cling like barnacles to a ship's hull; but they are still there: thoughts we'll not boast about publicly, any of us; tempers that flare up, the prejudice that never sleeps very soundly, and the indifference that does. While this innocence of ours, once every so often, still has to accuse everybody else, even heaven itself. Secure in the knowledge that only our modesty helps us to shine, as Camus has written somewhere, that nothing but our genuine humility helps us to conquer.

When the Bible insists that whoever you are, whatever the past, you are this day set free, it means that for the first time in your life perhaps you are free to fight your way through all that, rid of everything that would narrow your life down to what it has been or hem it in with what you call its possibilities. Give the enemy what name you like beyond flesh and blood, speak of principalities and powers: but know that the odds are no longer over there; they are over here, where you are. It's a battle that's been won, and that you never have to lose. The question is, do you realize that, and do you ever thank God for it? Paul knew it, as he looked out on the tragedy of a world that didn't:

> Only like souls I see the folk thereunder,
>   Bound who should conquer, slaves who should be kings,
> Hearing their one hope with an empty wonder,
>   Sadly contented with the show of things.

To be bound without knowing it, while you're free, and could yourself storm the gates of your prison!

We sometimes talk about our literature of defeat, and would like to have you understand that it's far too pessimistic. I submit that it isn't pessimistic enough. It's only half the picture. To be caught in a steel vise is bad; it's worse to be caught in a steel vise without having to be! We are sufficiently familiar in our day with men and women, not always on the stage or in some novel, who are desperately unhappy, laboring under some anxiety, weighed down by some sense of guilt, wanting to be what they are not and are afraid they never can become before death overtakes them; and we are asked on all sides to believe that they are typical of our generation—people held fast in the grim jaws of Fate, or in what one Broadway play represented as *The Dark at the Top of the Stairs;* condemned to spend their lives in that dungeon cell of the Middle Ages which was so appropriately known as the "little ease," because you couldn't sit, or stand up, or lie down in it. It's bad, no use saying it isn't. Nothing but the other half of the picture could make it worse: that no living human soul has to be like that.

The first chapter of a book I've been reading is entitled "The Country of the Blind," with twenty-six stricken pages about the novelists and playwrights who have of late been making that country their permanent address. While I read something kept haunting me, and I pinned it down. It was a man who once squared his shoulders on the desolate frontier of that country of the blind and wrote, "I also suffer these things: nevertheless I am not ashamed: for I know whom I have believed." Chapter 2 was headed, "World Without Values"; and that voice kept clamoring on the threshold of it, "I count all things but loss for the excellency of the knowledge of Christ Jesus my Lord: for whom I have suffered the loss of all things." After that came a chapter on the romantic literature of the last century and how it tried to find a way out, only to satisfy nobody. Then another on "The Attempt to Gain Control." Step by step the whole table of contents was the biography of our time. You could take your pick of images as you tried to figure out what it was like to be alive in the modern world: Kafka's "Fasting Showman," who died at last quite forgotten, not because "he had any tremendous will power to abstain from food," but simply because there was "no food he ever liked"; or that Eastern fable of a man clinging "to a shrub on the side of a pit to escape an enraged beast at the top and a dragon at the bottom," while "two mice gnawed at the roots of his shrub," as he reached out for a few drops of honey on the leaves and licked them.

You call that pathos, say it's the irony of human life, write it down as the tragedy of our existence? Is not the tragedy rather in this, deeper than pathos, more bitter than irony: that around all of humanity's "frozen misery" is the vast freedom of the New Testament, with the way through to it wide open. Paul stretched his arms and legs in it. "Of the Jews five times received I forty stripes save one. Thrice was I beaten with rods, once was I stoned, thrice I suffered shipwreck." Quarters like that could never be cramped as things now were with him! So he looked back at what he had written and put an asterisk there, with a footnote: "God hath made of my life a constant pageant." The world is nineteen hundred years older, and no measure has been set to that freedom!

But right here the Bible holds up its hand, like a traffic officer at the corner, and the light turns yellow, then red. In the lessons for the second Sunday in Advent we are brought face to face with two very specific situations which seem to limit still further this already strangely limited freedom of ours, even to negate it. Let's look at them. The epistle is taken from the fifteenth chapter of Romans, the fourth through the thirteenth verses. The one point which Paul is driving home throughout the letter is that nothing can hamper us now, no law that has to be obeyed if we are to achieve some status before God, no rules that have to be followed if we want to share in this new order of things under the lordship of Christ: when suddenly here toward the end he seems to throw everything into reverse! Just when we are about ready to say that we have begun to understand something of the freedom that is ours in the gospel, he appears to reach out for it and take it all back. "When the friendly lights of the harbour seem so invitingly near," writes Karl Barth, "there comes a final command—'Halt!'" And to our surprise the Epistle to the Romans begins to dispute its own point of view. The freedom of God begins to provide us with chains. Listen! We who are strong are to bear the burdens of the weak. There it is, cramping our style. We are to be like-minded, one toward another, receiving one another as Christ also received us; not to please ourselves, because Christ did not please himself. What does that do, if it doesn't hedge us about? It reads like the denial, the utter impoverishment of the self. It reads in a word like the bankruptcy of freedom.

But wait a minute. The burden that's being laid on us is the burden of love; and what if there were no freedom for you anywhere once you get out from under that? In his play, *No Exit*, Sartre says that hell is—other people. And the New Testament goes on saying, "Ah, God pity us, but there is no other heaven!" It's the simplest fact of all and the hardest, that what seems to hedge in these little selves of ours is the only thing that can enlarge them. The very lives around us which so often we feel to be closing in upon us are many a time the only offers of escape that are held out to us. And never think you won't be reminded of it, over and over again.

In almost any bookstore you can find a paperback on *How to Get Away from Yourself;* while over there on the counter opposite is another which has long since given that up as a futile pastime and concentrates now instead on *How to Live with Yourself.* I wish people could make up their minds! Both books will devote whole sections to the subject of making others your hobby. I heard a university professor recommend it as one of the best ways in which we could deal with the crisis in American education. Albert Camus, in *The Fall*, satirizes it with just the right smell of sulphur! Help that blind man across the street, and when you leave him, tip your hat: not to him, he can't see it, but to the public. Why shouldn't you take a bow? Give directions to that stranger on the bus. Lend a hand in pushing a stranded car. Buy flowers from the old peddler, even if you know he stole them from the cemetery. When a beggar comes down the aisle of the subway, exult in it!

Only be sure none of it will work. Nothing works if all you want is to have it work. To be free is to plunge into human life "up to the elbows," without looking at the price tag, or wondering about the pay-off. To take inside what's outside, never mind how much it hurts; and to see fewer things out there and more faces. Something had happened to the inside of the poet who on an autumn evening "saw the ruddy moon lean over a hedge like a red-faced farmer," while all about "were the wistful stars with white faces, like town children." The moon and the stars were a farmer and the village teacher's brood!

If ever you begin to see the world like that, it won't be because you've been trying to get away from yourself, or putting through a few exercises in learning how to live with yourself; it will be because the God who reached out to you on the cross has begun to break through the shell of your hiding place. Maybe the faces that haunted him that day on Calvary will never let you go either, not now: a boy, stumbling along home from a far country; a rich man striding up to his own front door without ever once looking at the poor bundle of sores and rags lying at his gate; or that other, with his barns full of wheat, and the whisper in the night, "Thou fool!" And Judas, and Peter, and the scribes and Pharisees grinning and shaking their heads. While in his mind there as he died was the incurable sadness that came of listening "night after night" to the "voice of Rachel weeping for her children and refusing all comfort," the children who long ago "had been killed for him." It wasn't the pain that broke his heart. It was the faces! It may even have been the faces—in what deep sense?—that made him cry out, "My God, my God, why hast thou forsaken me?" Do you want to travel that road? Freedom has to, if it's to be the freedom that belongs to the servants of God.

And there once more the Bible holds up its hand, and the traffic we've just got going again grinds to a full stop, this time in front of the Gospel that was read. It's a magnificent panorama: "And there shall be signs in the sun, and in the moon, and in the stars; and upon the earth distress of nations, with perplexity; the sea and the waves roaring"—to the Jew that was the symbol of primeval chaos—"men's hearts failing them for fear, and for looking after those things which are coming on the earth: for the powers of heaven shall be shaken." No doubt the disciples thought Jesus was talking about his coming again at the end of the world. And some people, when they get to this twenty-first chapter of St. Luke, want to know if they can believe that even by clenching their fists and gritting their teeth and trying ever so hard! But who can believe in God at all, and at the same time believe that what he's about is going to end—"not with a bang, but a whimper"? For me the more meaningful question is this: When it's a matter of believing, why try to stop with the Second Coming, when Christ comes again in every event that overtakes human life? In any case, to get back to the point, what we have here is something surely which negates everything that even looks like freedom. When all that's steady in your world reels round like a drunken man—and that does happen: there are times when you don't have to press the figure very far, if indeed it is a figure. When all that's solid enough to lean on dissolves, who on earth can be free? That cancels everything!

Why then at the precise moment when this unbelievable tumult rises to its climax does Christ assert that by the right arm of God instead of canceling everything it establishes everything? "When these things begin to come to pass, then look up, and lift up your heads; for your redemption draweth nigh"! You have run into that *nevertheless* of God which is the very ground of your freedom. Where else will you come upon it if not in the hour when you realize that all this which we name life is under the shattering, reshaping hand of God? What else did Jesus mean when he broke off that catalogue of terror to tell his disciples of the fig tree, and all the trees: "When they now shoot forth, ye see and know of your own selves that summer is now nigh at hand. So likewise ye, when ye see these things come to pass, know ye that the kingdom of God is nigh at hand." It isn't winter when a man's arrogance is humbled and he knows himself once more to be what he is; that's spring! Even Sartre found that "it was during the war, working in the underground resistance, in constant danger of betrayal and death, that he felt most free and alive." "There shall be signs in the sun, and in the moon, and in the stars."

How else can God protect us, asks Karl Barth, than by reminding us constantly of death; and so just as constantly directing us toward life? How else can he protect us from the kind of faith which smugly hails the "breakdown of secular thought" as the one sure way to religious revival? How else can he protect us from beliefs that "you can put in your pocket"? From a religion that wants to buy all the "promises cheaply"? How else can he drive us out of the "petty trivialities . . . in which men are normally imprisoned," and so make us "free to apprehend what is certain and living and eternal"? "When these things begin to come to pass, then look up." Here is no negation of any man's freedom; this may well be the final affirmation of it: when he finds out for himself what it is he cannot lose.

Only then can the meaning of this text come whole—not one half of it, but both halves: "As free—as the servants of God." What is strangest of all is that Peter found it no hardship any longer to end the verse like that. He wasn't pulling out a sword now to hack his way into freedom, or denying his Lord in order to break his way into it. It didn't seem to be just a gift either: you couldn't "butter your toast with it." It had arrived down a long, hard road. But as he got ready to sign his letter, with martyrdom perhaps not too far off, there was a benediction on his lips. Shall we let him pronounce it on us, let it settle down on our hearts wherever it will? It isn't for people who are any longer in prison.

The God of all grace, who hath called us unto His eternal glory by Christ Jesus, after that ye have suffered a while, make you perfect, stablish, strengthen, settle you. To Him be glory and dominion for ever and ever. Amen.

The Love That God Defines

*Direct us, O God, in all that we say and think, that from the knowl-
edge which Thou hast of Thyself may come our every word and thought
of Thee; through Jesus Christ, our Lord. Amen.*

The text you will find in the fourth chapter of the First Epistle of
John, at the eighth verse, and again at the sixteenth: God is love. But
we must be very careful not to import into it any ideas of our own;
above all else never to get it the other way around. It has nothing to
do with the notion, current in some quarters, that love is God. It has
nothing much to do with any of our notions. Before we can catch
even a glimmer of what it's talking about, we have to understand
that in John's brief sentence, as Dietrich Bonhoeffer has pointed out
somewhere, love does not define God: God defines love. That's why the
Greek word used here is not at all the familiar word of the streets, but
agape, a word which in the New Testament carries with it all the highlights, and the nearly impenetrable shadows, of Biblical faith and
Christian experience. C. S. Lewis comes close to its meaning when he
calls it "the lord of terrible aspect."

Let me read the text then as it should be read, putting the emphasis
where it belongs: not God is *love,* but *God* is love. When you say it

that way, and I want to begin with this, you are saying the costliest thing that could be said of God. You are not talking any longer simply of affection, or kindliness, or tender regard. Maeterlinck one day was sitting in his armchair looking on with quiet amusement as a litter of very young puppies played on the hearth rug in front of the fire. He said later that it made him think of how God must feel, up there in heaven, presiding over our ridiculous antics. On occasion a man of letters can indeed succeed in being ridiculous, if not downright wrongheaded! To say as the Bible says, "God so loved the world, that he gave his only begotten Son," is precisely in that measure, by all the width of the sky, different from saying that he is either fond of it or mildly amused by it. Look back over the long story for yourself, and tell me what you make of it.

In the first two chapters of Genesis, God is billed quite obviously as a friend. You remember the theme which runs through the whole magnificent symphony of creation: "And God said . . . and it was so . . . and God saw that it was good." Somebody, to have written that, must have seen how things are underneath the way things seem: somebody who loved the sunset and the dawn, the vast expanse of the ocean, the soft light of the stars, the blazing glory of the desert, the shadow of a rock, mountain and valley and stream, with all their teeming life. Surely he was not one to ask, "Why on earth was I ever born? What's the sense of it all?" The fish of the sea, silver streaks in the green water, every winged fowl; cattle and creeping snail—and over it all, man! We know what's going to happen, that this is where the trouble will soon start. But not yet. Still "God saw every thing that he had made, and, behold, it was very good."

In the third chapter it went wrong, and God began to act for all the world as if he were an enemy. That may not be the first authentic experience we have of him, but being what we are it comes right early! Adam and Eve, these little people of his, wanted to be gods themselves. The serpent put it to them in just those terms. There seems to be something very familiar about it. You come on it all through history. We still fall for it. They wanted to know as God knows, and to do as they liked with the knowledge, not as he liked. So he drove them out of their Paradise. He has been doing it ever since. What else would you say this world means? They always seemed to have some vague memory of it, but they could never get back. He had set his angels to guard it, with a flaming sword which turned every way.

Because once the evil got started, nothing seemed able to stop it. When "the wickedness of man was great in the earth, and every imagination of the thoughts of his heart was only evil continually," God sent a flood. Some benign gentleman said over the radio a few years ago that he couldn't think the Almighty would let men burn themselves to a cinder, not after all these tired centuries. Perhaps he should have tried a little harder. He may not have been well enough informed by the facts. Certainly whoever it was that entered into a covenant with Abraham and Isaac, with Jacob and Joseph, got them into all manner of trouble. He had chosen them for a purpose that wasn't always theirs; and when they made up their minds not to go along with it, he had to set himself against them. He herded them like slaves into Egypt, swept them away into exile, captives trudging across the burning sands toward Babylon: but always he was like a man biting his lips, doing something he didn't want to do, but had to; against them only because from start to finish he was never anything else but for them. Listen to him in Hosea, trying to argue it out with himself: "Ephraim is joined to his idols: let him alone . . . I . . . will tear . . . and take away, and none shall rescue him . . . O Ephraim, what shall I do unto thee? . . . . I taught Ephraim how to walk, taking him by the arms. . . . How shall I give thee up? . . . . I am God, and not man."

Keep turning the pages of the Bible, and see how contrary all of the prophets are, every mother's son of them. What else could they be? Whenever the majority thinks it has things well in hand, they go over to the other side of the House and speak for His Majesty's Loyal Opposition! Everybody says Yes, and they say No. Then when everybody is willing to say No, they say Yes. They must have been quite impossible to live with. You can't understand any of them—Elijah, Isaiah, Jeremiah—until you come to grips yourself with this God who is always coming to grips with the world that he loves. They had no idea that he was fond of it, smiling affectionately and shaking his head! From morning to night he was trying desperately to do something for it, anything to make whole again the life that men had taken up in their hands and broken into bits. That's what all genuine love is about, never mind the price. It cost him all he had.

It cost him that radiant life which the very people who should have stooped to kiss the hem of its garments hated and hounded and struck in the face, while a few poor peasant folk looked on. They wished they could do something about it, but they couldn't really. They knew that what this man had said was true, grander than any dream, and meant so tenderly. He had gone about with his compassion, reminding them of God every step of the way. Nobody had ever seen his like before. Nobody would ever see his like again. And Calvary had come of it. Where on earth was God? Was he anywhere? Why had he gone off and left it all, with that torn body against the sky?

But in that face, with the lined and ageless mercy on it, first one and then another saw the face of God; in those eyes which looked so far ahead with such humble and outrageous assurance, the peace that passed all understanding. The wonder of it was that at a place of public execution they began to read for themselves this riddle of human life, this monstrous drama, as someone has called it, of human cruelty and human pain. Where else can anybody read it now? They began to hazard the guess that all along God had been weaving a pattern with his fingers that had never been more than faintly glimpsed: as you might stare at the knots on the under side of some vast tapestry, catching only a hint here and there, yonder in the middle, along the edge, of the grandeur and color of the master's design. What if this end had been God's from the very beginning? What if for them this were itself a strange and new beginning? The mystery of it grew upon them, until at last they were ready to set down under everything they had seen, dark and forbidding as so much of it was, under and over all the turbulent centuries that had passed, this story of the scarred hands that had been trying to set it right: *God* is love. When men rejected him, his very judgments were his loving-kindness.

Giovanni Miegge, in his book, *Christian Affirmations in a Secular Age*, writes of the "realist," the disillusioned man of our time who thinks that the only truth is biological truth, the only master of our destiny the give and take of economic pressure, where there is always more take than give—Miegge writes of him: What if it were "the love of God which upholds him, whether he will or no, whether he knows it or knows it not, like the ground on which he stands and the air which he breathes"? A love that will have him for its own, "stronger than his hostility and his doubts, stronger than his coldness and his rebellion and his failures"; a love which is the clue to all of life's enigmas, this immense and changing panorama on "the cold and ever colder surface of a dying earth": "the supreme reality by which we live," whether we take account of it or not; its symbol the cross, where God has come to meet us under the very burden and weight of all our sin and suffering, in order that just there, by paying down on the counter of human life and human history the price of his own coming, he might give us the pledge of victory.

Only so, because he has imposed his own meaning on the word, did the gospel come to say the costliest thing that could be said about God: *God* is love. And when you say it that way, it becomes, too, the costliest thing that can be said about us. It follows, don't you think? You can't quite suppose that nothing more is expected of us now than the "little deeds of kindness," the "little words of love," which "help to make earth happy like the heaven above."

In the twenty-fifth chapter of St. Matthew Jesus tells of the day when "the Son of man shall come in his glory, and all the holy angels with him." It's like a huge canvas. All the nations of the earth stand before the throne of God, some on the right hand, where the light shines, picking out all the brilliant colors; others on the left, multitudes of them, where the storm blowing up from the horizon throws its purple shadows—everybody where he belongs, and nobody who knows why. When suddenly, either with glad recognition or with a terrible knowledge, it comes to them that they have all seen the face of the Judge before: somebody who was hungry or thirsty, a stranger with nowhere to go; somebody who was naked, or sick, or in prison—and a Voice is heard under heaven, "Inasmuch as ye have done it unto one of the least of these my brethren," reaching out your hand to them, or turning your back and looking the other way, "ye have done it unto me."

That was whittled down almost to the vanishing point once in a dream which is said to have disturbed the sleep of a famous preacher. He thought he had died, and St. Peter had glanced up from the books only to ask his name. He was surprised that the Office of Information had done such a careless and sketchy job; but he answered stoutly, "Ian MacGregor," or whatever it was, as if that would make all the difference in the world, and out of it too. And he was met by nothing but a blank look and the shake of a head. "What?" he asked. "Have you not heard of me? Of how the boys from the University used to line up outside my church in Edinburgh hours before the doors were opened?" "No word has come of that," said St. Peter, leafing through the pages. "Well then," the minister went on, trying to hit on something, "how about the time when in her shabby lodgings down in London I sat the night through with a humble serving-girl who was dying and had sent for me? There was a meeting in my church the day before, and I should never have missed it; but I went right away, and at my own expense too." Because no word had come of that either, the gate remained fast shut. Sadly bewildered, he was on the point of giving up, when all at once St. Peter did seem to find something in the record, and called out to him, "Wait a minute! Are you the Ian MacGregor who used to feed the sparrows on Princes Street?" And upon the poor man's no less bewildered acknowledgment that he was, swung wide the gate, with a sweeping gesture, and said heartily, "Then come right in! The Lord of the sparrows wants to thank you!"

It won't do, you know. The tally of Israel's bitter struggle, and of all the Christian ages since, red with the blood of martyrs even in our day, cannot be written off as a sort of "Be Kind to Sparrows Week"! Maybe our little is indeed God's big—and that, I dare say, is what the story means—and our big his little; but that isn't the point of the gospel. The point of the gospel is that God asks of us only what he gives; but what he gives moves in along more sober lines than that: not something he owes us for anything we have done, big or little; something he owes himself, because he is the kind of God he is. What he gives, the New Testament calls "the grace of our Lord Jesus Christ"; the length of his patience, the height of his power, the width of his compassion, the depth of his mercy—all that God is, from tip to toe, the whole reach of his love in action. And what he asks is the kind of unreckoning response which comes of such a gift. To say the truth, it isn't a response at all: it's part of the gift. It's the sharing of his life with you!

I wonder if you see how that makes a hash out of all our calculations, and puts an end to our bookkeeping? It pulls the chair out from under you just when you are about ready to settle down and let things go, upsets the accounts you have hoped to enter on the credit side of the

ledger, spills the ink, and throws the ledger out of the window. Erich
Fromm says that "to love is to commit oneself without guarantee." God
is willing to risk it. The question is, are we? There's the rub! We think
we are afraid of not being loved; we are afraid of loving! Afraid of
putting ourselves out. Did you ever really think of what that means?
Putting ourselves out of the picture, and doing it just as thoroughly as
we can. We are afraid of laying ourselves open, exposing ourselves,
without any guarantee at all that we shall not be hurt. That costs too
much. And the cost of not doing it keeps mounting steadily through
the centuries toward disintegration and death—toward the panic of
utter isolation and separateness.

In the gospel, this committing of oneself to God and to each other
is what comes of being forgiven. When the psalmist says, "There is
forgiveness with thee, that thou mayest be feared," he means that God's
forgiveness fills a man "with a sense of his own unworthiness," transforms his "anxiety about himself and his world" into "trembling adora-
tion of the transcendent Holy Lord"; but it doesn't just leave him on
his knees, with face uplifted. That kind of acceptance—whether it's a
mother's, a father's, a friend's, a husband's, a wife's, or God's—which
holds out its arms to you no matter what, such acceptance lets you in
for something. Have you ever found that out? Something more than a
deep sigh, as if everything were all right now. It lets you in for what
may be the first really adequate understanding you have ever had of
how much there is in this world that's all wrong. When you quit thinking of love as if it told you what God is, and begin letting God tell you
what love is, you will be driven across the frontier of a strange country,
where you are in for the kind of caring that has learned from him,
never mind the cost, to stand ready with your help—"when others expect it of you, and when they don't; when they need it desperately,
and think it's nowhere near, and when they think they have no need
of it at all; when they ask for it, and when they forget to ask for it,
and when they fall out of the way of asking for it." It's the kind of
caring that refuses to let you rest in a place where there is so little
as Christ wants it, and no promise at all of that peace of mind which
comes of having most things as you want them. Make no mistake about
it: if this text never turns anything upside down, never stirs any deep
discontent in your soul about the way you treat other people, what you

say, and what you neglect to say, what you do and fail to do, what you give and what you keep for yourself, never keeps tugging at you until it becomes a nuisance you wish you could shake off and can't—then perhaps you'd better stop fooling with it; it has nothing to say to you!

God is love. It's the costliest thing that has ever been said about him, and it's the costliest thing that can possibly be said about us. If it should ever lay hold on you, I don't know what the upshot will be, and you don't either. What really matters is, have you ever got up close enough in the crowd around Jesus to "buy" it, as we say, at any price? The hymn wants you to believe that

> He will not suffer thy foot to be moved:
> Safe shalt thou be.

And the Psalm, "There shall no evil befall thee, neither shall any plague come nigh thy dwelling." Will that be the way of it? It wasn't for Jesus. What can they have in mind, the hymn and the Psalm, if not this: that the wholeness of God's love, austere and shieldless, will move in whenever we let it to make whole these broken lives of ours? That's the only safety there is. God is almost intolerably careless about crosses and swords, arenas and scaffolds, about all the "evils" and all the "plagues." His caring doesn't mean that he goes in for upholstering! Not only before everything else, but even at the cost of everything else, he wants to bring back into our divided world, where people speak to you without having their voices "pay you any attention," some knowledge of our oneness with him and with each other: so that none of us may have to be solitary and desolate any longer—like that pelican of the wilderness, that owl of the desert in the Psalm, that sparrow alone upon the housetop, which provided the Hebrew poet with the best image he had of a soul in trouble because the face of God was turned away; so that none of us need any longer be split right down the middle between this and that, between love and hate, between being something and being nothing, between wanting and not wanting.

Even what we call love, poor and drab and warped and twisted as it so often is—and this is the theme of how much of our modern literature, novel and drama alike: *East of Eden, Tiger at the Gates, Tea and Sympathy, All the King's Men, The Sound and the Fury, Cat on a*

Hot Tin Roof—even what we call love is the only thing in the world that can break through the self, if just part way, tear down a few at least of its walls of separation, overcome some measure of the terror of its loneliness; a loneliness where, as someone has said, there is no loss and no gain, and victory is as meaningless as defeat. Love, with no other dimensions than those we give it, can do that; there is nothing else in the world that can: the trouble is that the novel and the drama never seem able to get anywhere outside of the world, where there is another love trying to break in, to which ours bears only its blind and groping witness. Mr. MacLeish's *J.B.* started out in its company magnificently, only to get away at last, and so to end by fizzling out like a Chinese firecracker!

God is love, and there is no other love that knows how to do what love has to do, none that knows how to shape human life. Yours doesn't, mine doesn't—that isn't our business. When we make it our business, trying our best not to maneuver anybody, or manipulate anything, the dearer the life is we try to shape, the more likely we are to bungle everything we undertake to do about it. There is a love that can stand by and hold its peace, and keep its hands off, never making things out of persons; and persons grow in it instead of dwindling. It looked on one day as a young man whose name was Mark turned back from traveling with Paul. The mountains were too forbidding, and the rivers were too cold. And it kept whispering, "O Mark, John Mark, what I could have done with you!" Until somewhere, somehow, it happened, and Mark sat down and took up his pen in his crippled hand, with his poor crooked fingers, to write, "The beginning of the gospel of Jesus Christ, the Son of God."

Bestow upon us, O God, all that Thou dost ask of us, that in asking life of Thee we may be ready to share Thy life, and the weight of it, which is Thy love in Christ Jesus. Amen.

The Moving Edge of Time

Thou hast brought us to this hour, O God, by all our several ways. Unfaithful as we have been, Thou hast nevertheless kept faith with us. Go before us still, we beseech Thee, by Thy Word and Spirit, leading us wherever it shall please Thee; through Jesus Christ, our Lord. Amen.

I SAMUEL 7:12—Hitherto hath the Lord helped us.

That was the key which for Samuel unlocked the meaning of history; which is the basic, prophetic function of all true religion. It can do as much for us. The scene is laid out on the hills of Canaan, three thousand years ago. Israel was in a desperate situation. True, in this later story, she had won something of a victory over her enemies; but it was no whacking great affair in any case. Yet Samuel was sure—so the narrator wants us to believe—that what was going on in the teeth of all the odds was a good deal more than met the eye. So he took a stone, and set it up, and called its name Ebenezer, Stone of Help; for he said, "Hitherto hath the Lord helped us."

The psalmist was saying it: "God is our refuge and strength, a very present help in trouble." Paul was saying it, while a world was falling into ruin: "If God be for us, who can be against us?" On another of life's perpetual frontiers, Luther was saying it: nailing against the door of a castle church his theses against what was then pretty much the whole of Western civilization; facing the emperor and the court and the princes of the Church, giving his answer without horns and without teeth, as he put it, straightforwardly, captive to the Word of God: "Here I stand. God helping me, I can do no other"; and when the threat of the Turks had been rolled back from Vienna, writing his hymn, "A mighty fortress is our God."

Always somebody on that moving edge of time which we call the present—gone before you can finish a sentence about it—confidently reading God into the past, never mind what it looks like, and just as confidently reading him into the future, never mind what it seems ready to hurl in his face; toiling up desperately through the light and the shadow to speak of an unfailing presence, then sloshing on into what's left of the mud and the dark as if listening to music, with nothing but the music to matter! "Hitherto hath the Lord helped us." It's like an echo. You can fairly hear it carom off the years. What right has anybody to say it?

There are times when reading anything into the past is hard enough; reading God into it sounds like saying to yourself, "Go to now, I shall put together this picture-puzzle as I choose. I shall make it spell out for me what I want it to spell out." And that, the skeptic will tell you, is precisely what faith is. Just deliberately to read God in is nonsense. But then, just deliberately to read him out is nonsense too! One of Camus' characters, after he had looked on at the agonizing death of a little child, said, "I will never love any scheme of things which permits that." Surely it should be of some significance that it isn't a scheme of things the Christian loves. That's why such words make such a strange sort of noise on Calvary. "And when they were come to the place, . . . they crucified him, and the malefactors, one on the right hand, and the other on the left." Now let's try it: "I will never love any scheme of things which permits that." Christianity concerns itself with a Person, not with a pattern.

Besides, what loving a Christian does, he doesn't do because he has scraped together all the evidence he could find in favor of it, and chucked out the rest. Nobody has ever fallen in love that way, and nobody ever will. You don't read God in on "the credibility of Joshua," or on "the edibility of Jonah." And when you read him out, you don't read him out simply on the evidence. Shakespeare once undertook to document divine Providence by finding "tongues in trees, books in the running brooks, sermons in stones, and good in everything." But what do the tongues say when the tree blows down and falls on you? If you slip in the running brook and drown, what's the title of the book? As for stones, David took one and put it in his sling, whereupon Goliath got it right in the middle of his forehead; but there was no sermon in it. How dare you talk to me about the "good in everything"? I can throw enough at you to turn such piety into a maniac's laughter! (P. 25.)

Before you say anything at all, you've got to make certain that I can listen with a knowledge of God in my heart which was already there when you started. Is that so odd? Have you never realized that you can say nothing and do nothing so as to be recognized by anybody who doesn't know you? Neither can God. Samuel could talk about God's help because these wandering tribes long years before had felt that compelling hand on their lives as they struggled up out of their bondage in Egypt. And their past had become his past! "God helping me, I can do no other." Luther could say it because he was held fast in the grip of a man who had come out of Nazareth with such bitter compassion. Gethsemane, Calvary, the past of the whole Christian community had become his past. So does the Bible reconstitute what it records. You don't have to look around to see what you can make of life, then look up for a little help. Moses looked around one day and killed a man! You look up first; after that, you look around.

"Samuel took a stone, and set it up." He didn't just decide one Tuesday to read things that way in order to make sense out of them. If we find ourselves unable at this point to look back and say "God," it will not be because we haven't heard enough or seen enough or read enough or studied enough or thought enough. It will be because for one reason or another we have never been anywhere in God's company, not anywhere that mattered. There used to be a TV program called "You Were There." You looked on while they captured Major André, or when Admiral Farragut steamed into Mobile Bay and damned the torpedoes; it was usually fighting of some sort. But no matter how often the announcer kept saying "You were there," he could never quite bring it off. God does! One day, as you read the third chapter of Genesis, it dawns on you that like Adam and Eve, you and I and all of us have been shut out of Paradise, because we have taken things into our own hands and set out to *be* God! Eden becomes then the most real place of all places on earth. We do so want it back, and look for it everywhere, as Auden says, and find nowhere anything but a kind of desert. Our way, like Israel's, lies across that desert. So does the way of all human life, every stage of the journey: Egypt and bondage, Exodus and freedom, Kingdom and rule, Exile and alienation, on toward Calvary—where, far out of earshot on the street, or at some party—but you hear it!—the old Negro spiritual wants to know, "Were you there when they crucified my Lord?" And in your heart of hearts you know that's exactly where you were!

Now let somebody rush in and try to wipe out all that past which has so strangely become your past. Let him tell you it means nothing—it would all have been the same if there had been no God; not one iota, not one jot or tittle or scrap of it would have been different—so that even the language which speaks of God, he presses it upon you, has no factual content. Let *me* tell you something: instead of being afraid to admit that, we'd better begin insisting on it. We knew what he knows before he found it out! Faith is response to a person, it is not compulsion by a fact. And our language about persons has another kind of content entirely. It doesn't begin, and it doesn't issue, simply in facts; it both begins and issues in a relationship which interprets the facts. There is a relationship with God which sees the very hiddenness of his purpose, its silent concealments in a world where nature and history alike say both Yes and No to him, and with equal vehemence: sees them all as the ceaseless beckoning of One who refuses to write out his name so that you can't betray him or deny him; yet hopes you will never stop where he is saying "Come," and makes no other arrangement when you contradict him, except that with his love he will contradict you!

"Hitherto hath the Lord helped us." Samuel said that not merely to boast of a fleeting victory over the Philistines. He didn't do it because somebody had nudged him when he was discouraged, and reminded him of how it was with Abraham, and Isaac, and Jacob. He said it to get into words something profounder than any of that, something deep inside of him, at the "very marrow of his being." And he wasn't just thinking about some part of the past that was pretty; he was thinking about all of it, the pretty and the ugly alike—perhaps on the actual spot where Israel had lost to the Philistines the ark of God's covenant, the shining symbol of his presence in the midst of her! You'll not keep a man like that from saying God, not even when all of life cries out against him. So he took a stone, and set it up.

But now let's get on. "Hitherto hath the Lord helped us." The "hitherto" left out nothing, and it looked both ways. It read God into the past, and it read him into the future. What I here want to make clear if I can is how thoroughly disquieting a word it is as it looks forward. I do not understand what grounds we have for thinking so comfortably of what lies ahead. "Blessed assurance, Jesus is mine!" It was of course quite the reverse in New Testament times. Then it was "Blessed disturbance, I am his!" Nobody was as listless as we are. Everybody was forever getting into trouble, and everybody was incredibly happy, singing a song. They never for a moment supposed that God was somehow engaged to reduce the strain on their lives, possibly by paring down some of his harsher demands, making them a little less severe at any rate. With us it's different. We do have such a friend in Jesus! Why not act as the hymn suggests? "Are there trials and temptations? Is there trouble anywhere? Are we weak and heavy-laden, cumbered with a load of care? Do thy friends despise, forsake thee? Take it to the Lord in prayer." We'd like to be rid of it all in one fell swoop. Unload it! And that's no way to treat a friend! You don't read the riddles out by reading God in. Thousands upon thousands of disillusioned people go plodding along dully from day to day because they have never had that relentlessly drilled into them. Whoever learns as he looks back to say God, will gird up his loins when he turns around to look ahead. The Revised Standard Version says he will tighten his belt. Because he's moving now in turbulent company, across the frontiers of a strange country where the only "authentic" being is being on the edge of peril and disaster. If only somebody could have persuaded folk that the only peace available is the no-peace where Christ is!

Why is it that in prayers and sermons congregations are still being promised more than God ever has been able on his terms to manage? The ancient Litany of the Church runs, "From the crafts and assaults of the devil, from war and bloodshed, from plague and pestilence, from all calamity by fire and water, and from a sudden and evil death, Good Lord, deliver us!" I wonder how much of that is God's business, and how much of it is our own! On a Saturday morning not too long ago the *New York Times* announced that one visiting divine would preach the next day on "Getting What You Want." Which indeed may very well be the risk you run! And maybe the preacher said that, I don't know. Who nowadays could set about hawking such a luxury item seriously, as if getting what you want were still important, and civilization had nothing more the matter with it than a bad case of sniffles—like the actress of whom George Jean Nathan once said that she was the only Camille he had ever known to die of catarrh! It isn't a question any more of getting what we want: it's a question of being able to deal with what we get. And to get God may mean to get hurt—among your friends, on the job, in the office or in the church, by the very people you are trying to help; at home, or around the corner on a picket line, in the struggle for some decent justice where the only justice there is is indecent.

Come face to face with him, that great Disturber of the Peace, instead of dillydallying about with him on Sunday, and you may well have to limp into the future, as Jacob did. He wrestled with the angel all night long there in the old Bible story; and when the sun rose on what for him was a new day and a new life, he halted on his thigh! It's the kind of double talk that runs all through the Bible: men can't live without God, and they can't live with him. These chapters of Samuel, I dare say, were not intended to be humorous; but they are. No sooner had the Philistines run off with the ark of the covenant than they wished they hadn't. Wherever they put it down a plague broke out, and all the lords of the people said, "What shall we do with it?" It was too hot for them! From city to city they moved it—three times, and every time the local politicians wanted to know, "How on earth can we get rid of it?" So they sent it back to Israel where it came from; and even there it stirred up trouble.

You think it's a fairy tale? Then what do you make of this entry in Gamaliel Bradford's diary: "I do not dare to read the New Testament for fear of its awakening a storm of anxiety and self-reproach and doubt and dread of having taken the wrong path, of having been traitor to the plain and simple God. Not that I do not know perfectly well that no reading would make me believe any more. But oh, what agonies of fret and worry it would give me; for I should be able neither to believe nor to disbelieve nor to let it alone." Holiness does that in our kind of world. When God quits having you on his hands and you start having him on yours, you'll see! He won't let you take much time to count your many blessings: he'll want to know right away what you plan to do with them. That way you'll realize that he's somewhere in the neighborhood. You'll not just smile as you read him into the future. We talk so glibly about security, and there is none, except in that peril which he is. "My peace I give unto you," says Jesus; and proceeds to heighten the tension in every man's life between what he is and what he could be, though he may never yet have thought of being it. His elect are not the elite: they are the uneasy ones, with the crust broken!

Never had the scribes and Pharisees felt so secure as on the day when they brought him a woman taken in adultery to ask if she should be stoned as the Law would have them do. They were all dressed up for the occasion in as much piety as they could find, whole layers of it: otherwise, they could not have devised such torture, as someone suggests, jerking her out into the light of day and flinging her down there in the temple court. And Jesus didn't say anything. How could he? He stooped and wrote with his fingers on the ground, maybe nothing but lines back and forth, up and down. What else was there to do in the presence of that grim outrage, that enormous iniquity which these good men had manufactured? Then he straightened himself for as long as he could stand their leering faces and said, "He that is without sin among you, let him first cast a stone at her." After that he stooped again. Whenever was the invitation into the Kingdom of God put in such heartbreaking terms? And they which heard it went out, beginning at the eldest, whose crust perhaps the years had worn a little thinner: as I grow older, at any rate, I like to think that. Anyhow they went, and in that came nearer eternal life than they had ever come before: they went as you and I have to go, every man, one by one, on God's sheer mercy!

All we may know of the God we have met in Christ is that in every bit of it, sunlight and shadow, he means intensely and he means good. "Hitherto hath the Lord helped us." Can't we too get that into the record now and keep it there against the odds? Samuel did, with nothing to look forward to, you would say, but more of the same that lay behind him: still these scattered tribes in a land of promise where the promise never seemed to come true. A thousand years later Paul got it into the record again. For no reason except that he too was a man "scoured on the side facing eternity," thrown out of what God had done into what God was doing, with everything which through the centuries had made God God and kept him God breaking into the world through the sound of the hammers that nailed the hands and feet of Jesus to a cross. Fifteen hundred years later still, Luther did it. In the last scene of Osborne's play he holds his child in his arms, a tiny infant, talking to it quietly of the vast disturbance in history and in his own soul, saying that all of it had been God's proper work. Then as the curtain begins to come down he looks off into the distance and whispers, "I hope it's true. I hope so!"

"Hitherto"—with nothing but the face of Christ there in front of you! Can you manage? How on earth, in the strange radiance of all these haunted years, can we leave that "nothing but" standing to make fools and cowards of us? What more do we want than his face? A student told me of the evening in Carnegie Hall when Toscanini walked over to the podium for his last concert. I am sure it was a romanticized version of what really happened, but I liked it. The tough old taskmaster was over eighty, and they had built a slender railing for him. Lightly he touched it with the fingers of one hand as he raised his baton. After a moment of almost unbelievable silence, the orchestra, a hundred pieces or more, stole softly into the first quiet movement of the symphony. On and on, until as the volume grew, first one and then another lifted his eyes from the notes and fastened them on the maestro there, with the wistful smile on his lips. And all the music they had in them swept up—toward that face! There is a face which I never have to romanticize. It does things to me that hurt and heal.

For every mercy of the past, and for Thy presence still, we praise and bless Thee, O God: be Thou yet our guide and our one sure hope forever. Through Jesus Christ, our Lord. Amen.

Through to the Better End

Not our thought of Thee, O God; let Thy thought for us hold our eyes and keep us steadfast; through Jesus Christ, our Lord. Amen.

II CORINTHIANS 11:19–12:9.

My subject is not misprinted, though I did hope that the possibility might occur to you. The story that was read—of the thirty-nine stripes five times over, the beating with rods, the stoning, hunger and thirst, cold and nakedness—always has made me think of that expression which we so commonly use, "seeing it through to the bitter end." But only a short time back I came across Don Marquis' suggestion that if you stroke a platitude long enough it will begin to purr like an epigram. So I tried it, and found out that "bitter end" was not the original form of the phrase at all. When the captain of a sailing vessel wanted to keep his ship from foundering, from being driven on the rocks by a gale in some narrow passage, he dropped her anchors to the wind; then, running out her cables to "the better end"—the end which was secured so far within the hull that it was not often used—he let her ride the storm head on.

The text is in II Corinthians, the twelfth chapter, at the ninth verse. It tells of what happened to St. Paul as the cables of his life kept running out toward that better end where a word whispered itself down through the silence out of heaven: "My grace is sufficient for thee; for my strength is made perfect in weakness." The lesson from which it is taken is the longest in the Church year; and that's not an accident. Fourteen centuries ago it got into the lectionary at a time when the outlook for the Christian Church seemed almost hopeless. The Empire, west and east alike, was falling apart, and there was nobody to hold it together. On the north the hordes of Europe, with one wave after another of barbarian invasion behind them, were pressing down on Rome. In Italy were famine and pestilence, with an ever-growing company of men all around the shores of the Mediterranean finding in monasteries a refuge from the world. One can see why these Sundays with their long Latin names were set aside just before Lent as seasons for special supplication, and why such opening sentences as "Why sleepest thou, O Lord,"—"Wherefore hidest thou thy face?"—got together with that ancient collect, "Mercifully grant that by Thy power we may be defended against all adversity." You know what came of it: the Empire didn't ride the storm; the Church did—her anchors to the wind, and her cables played out to the "better end."

Against the background of that long-forgotten crisis in history, I want to take St. Paul's experience for what it is, a parable of the Christian life. You know as I do how often it seems that we too have come to the bitter end of things: of a friendship, of some plan or hope or ideal which we have cherished. But I wonder if you know that nothing can ever alleviate or transform that bitterness until we understand what the source of it is? And for that we've got to look inside, not outside.

The ultimate threat to our existence is not necessarily greater when everything outside seems all wrong; it may be just as great, far greater perhaps, when we are so sure everything outside is all right, north, east, south, and west, that it takes God himself to show us how much of it is indeed all wrong. It goes without saying that each of us is surrounded by his own quota of difficulties. We'll tell you that. We'll tell the world! Who doesn't have just about enough—at home, with his friends, in the work he is doing? But just leave us alone. It may be bitter, but it isn't the end. We'll iron it out. We'll get together a few more facts and go over them carefully. A man once set down all the facts he could remember about his wife, and spread them out in front of me. Whereupon she gathered quite a good many about him, and in due time spread them out as he had done. They thought they could no doubt set it all straight if they brushed up a little on psychology. Possibly there were strategies which they had never tried. So it is with most of us. We have an idea that maybe if we can just figure out a new approach or another technique we'll be able to muddle through.

When along comes the good news of this gospel, but always with the bad news which we have to hear first: that even when everything outside seems all right, matters inside are a good deal worse than we think. The gospel tells us what we do not know about the real source of all bitterness, about the real threat to our existence, come sunshine or shadow. It talks to us about the serpent in Eden, worming its way into the heart of every paradise we stake out for ourselves, turning it into a fool's paradise. And the name of that serpent is I, alias me, alias my or mine—a self so busy with its own claims of priority, its own ceaseless demands on life, that it has little time to do anything more than to look around in the rush, and shake its head in deep perplexity about you and yours, about him and her and it—as if something were unaccountably wrong with the whole structure of the universe! The bitterest thing about the end is the bitterness of the defeated and frustrated self which has brought up there.

Paul saw at last that this was precisely what had corrupted the Jewish religion of his time; and the Jewish religion of his time was the best religion there was. It had corrupted what knowledge he himself had had of piety and virtue, and all his practice of it: until he was caught off his guard at noon one day on the road to Damascus. What was wrong was no more than the self, curved in on itself, and so trying by hook or by crook to establish itself, whether in man's sight or in God's, it was all the same, asserting its primacy somehow; and if anybody undertook, not to disallow its rightful claims—that would be to annihilate it—but only to sweep them off to one side of the board, as Jesus was trying to do there in his Sermon on the Mount and in most of his parables, it would crucify him as the first order of business on its roster of religious duties.

That's why sin, which preachers talk about so much less nowadays than novelists and dramatists, has to be defined as man's "attempt to attain life through his own efforts." There is no inevitability about it, other than the inevitability which the self gives to it when the self gets out of bounds. One young theological student in the Middle West, during a course of lectures I was giving, had got pretty well fed up with it. He leaned over and whispered to me just before the third lecture began, "But aren't there times when I can say to myself, 'I'm not sinning now'?" The troublesome fact is that when you think you aren't, or say you aren't, or act on the supposition that you aren't—you are, in thought, word, and deed, as the liturgy has it: you are curved in on yourself at the very moment you happen to be saying the Apostles' Creed, or praying the Lord's Prayer, or singing a hymn in church.

But even that is by no means the ugliest face of sin that the self wears. What you and I think is ugly is only the mask which sin puts on. If the mask were ripped off, we could see what God thinks is ugly. He sees sin as more than the self's perversion of some human good: he sees it as the self's perversion of his good. And God's good is the fullness of his grace, his power, and his love pressing in on us; we live under that, and move by it, and have our being in it. So much so that the withdrawal of it would make all the difference between being and not being. It is by his grace that we keep his commandments, if we ever do. By whose grace then do we break them? The angry word that yesterday put somebody in his place, and the grudge that keeps him there today; the pride that sets on its feet some claim of mine, to dispute your claim, or to write it down, or to write it off—all the scars across the face of human life—are they only as wrong as wrong can be, or are they as wrong as right can be? Do they not mean that God is letting us do with his love and with his power what we will, because he doesn't want to force us, and so turn into nobodies even those among us who think we are somebodies? "By the grace of God I am what I am," writes Paul. Is it not equally by the grace of God that the liar is what he is, and the thief? "There, but for the grace of God, go I," said Richard Baxter, or so the story runs, as he saw a man led away to execution. But is it not by grace, misshapen and misspent, that the murderer is what he is? The grace that keeps the breath in your nostrils and provides the strength for your arm, whether you raise it to wield a knife or to pronounce a benediction? Only by God's own power can a man make a hell out of what was intended to be a paradise.

I am afraid of the "cheap grace" which we think we can have for nothing, and can keep even when we make no use of it; but I am more afraid of twisting God's grace and distorting it. To be what we are from one week's end to the next by his love and leave is to twist that grace out of all recognition. To count our many blessings, one by one, only to make bigger and better tailfins out of them, or to sell more cigarettes, anything for a little payola, more profits in the public interest—never mind the strikes, and the dirty rivers, and the slums, and the state of public education—that is to distort God's grace into a sheer horror. To cherish our freedom of the press, only like some paranoiac to help bring on with it the disasters we fear, insisting that all the West needs is to get out ahead of Russia where we belong! What else is there to talk about day in and day out, in the newspapers and on television, if we want to alienate a few uncommitted friends and inflame quite a number of people?

Not cheap grace, twisted grace! When you take that for a clue to the meaning of history, you see how hard it is for God to have his way, and what it's bound to cost, from Calvary on "to the last syllable of recorded time." I do not wonder that all his life Camus kept affirming his "vision of cosmic absurdity," and by his death seemed to prove it. The wonder is that in the same breath he could keep passionately avowing, beyond the absurdity, his belief in "human creativity"—with all the evidence we have that human creativity apart from God serves only to provide more cosmic absurdity. The only justice it achieves is the injustice which comes of a grace that shuts itself up, like Camus' Caligula, in the demonic sovereignty of its own freedom, piling tragedy on top of tragedy in the "emptiness which passes understanding." What cosmic absurdity there is can scarcely be blamed on the cosmos.

Well now! I'm through with "the bitter end." It's the place where the self, in order to affirm its primacy, overplays its hand and turns in on itself, distorting not so much the grace that God has promised, as the grace which he has already supplied. The "better end" is the place where the self has learned to renounce the priority of its claims. Let's talk no nonsense about it. You can no more renounce all of the self than you can renounce hunger and thirst. But you can renounce the self that keeps setting itself up at the center of the picture. You can renounce the self that gets out of line, once you know where the line is.

And just this is the point of the story Paul tells. And he tells it in some detail. It must have been very hard for him to get out of his own way. He was that kind of person. Half a dozen times here he sneaks out in front, and is on the edge of boasting. He's a Hebrew, and speaks God's own language. He's an Israelite, and is of God's own people. He's a child of Abraham, and is heir to God's own promise. Then half a dozen times he calls himself a fool for it, and a madman. And of course he's right. When, all at once, without any warning, his thumbs are in his armholes again: labors, prison, stripes, and peril of death—they were his badge of credit; only to remind himself what a business it was when the bubble burst, back there at the very start, and he was let down by the wall, like so much meat in a basket. Caught up into Paradise—the account reads like a kind of fever chart— where he heard unspeakable words. He might well have stayed up in front on that score if God hadn't outflanked him and sent this messenger of Satan to buffet him: a thorn there in the very sinews of his apostleship, and it wouldn't budge. Why in God's name couldn't he be rid of it? But all he got on his lonely island of discontent was the hint and murmur of the sea; God's completeness around his incompleteness —around his restlessness, God's rest. He had written in days gone by to these people at Corinth about the weakness of this world that had been chosen to confound the wise. But being what he was, Paul could scarcely have found it easy to settle for weakness. It never has been easy. Many a preacher finds that out, when one day his old winged words come home to roost. "You have my grace; that's enough. You have my strength; it's being made perfect in your weakness." A man has to fall pretty far out of his own esteem to land there.

But then comes a question which is more important still: if he has to fall out of love with his own image, how in the name of common sense does he go about it? You must learn to "think highly of yourself," says some peddler of slightly old and somewhat warmed-over chestnuts. He thinks you'll get well that way, and being what you are, you get sicker trying. An inferiority complex doesn't come of not thinking as highly of yourself as you ought to think. An inferiority complex is the seatbelt we use when we have to fly slightly lower than the stratosphere where we are sure we rightly belong. Whoever can't tell the difference between that and this that Paul had—"most gladly therefore will I rather glory in my infirmities"—can't tell the difference between anything and anything else.

Just don't make the mistake of supposing that it was trouble which maneuvered him out of his self-esteem into the arms of God, where the power of Christ could rest upon him. Trouble alone can't do it. You might suppose it could—pain, or loss, or loneliness; broken hopes, the ashes of burnt-out fires—whatever it is: your share of that vast sum total of human suffering which drags the weight of its feet along from daylight to dark and never says much. If only it did speak up, any one of us perhaps could be to another what Isaiah called a hiding place from the wind, the shadow of a great rock in a weary land. But it doesn't. Peevishness is what's vocal: not the deeper anguish that like some timid wild thing goes off into the woods with its hurt to be alone. Yet for all that it can never bring anybody to write the self off as Paul did, and write God in! You don't get as far along as that simply by being beaten about from pillar to post by the winds of adversity.

And you don't get that far along because you've suddenly been frightened by the shape of things in the world. "It's all pretty bad. You aren't up to it. Better try God!" There are too many alternatives, too many other live options. There's aspirin. Or a tranquilizer, like the one Julian Huxley offered to sell the general public. On the one hundredth anniversary of Darwin's *Origin of Species* he told a group of eminent scientists, gathered in Chicago from I don't know how many nations, about the disappearance of sin, the sloughing off of tragedy, the withering away of all our superstitions, if only we'd keep on evolving. It would work wonders. In my book it already had worked wonders by turning out a man in our kind of world with enough foolhardy courage to say that! Paul had to reckon too, among these very Corinthians, with the wisdom of this world, which in our day God has made so foolish that we can set dates to it—1914, 1939. He told them it wasn't knowledge they could count on, and it wasn't anything they could do. No use trying to fling yourself with the Greeks into the struggle after virtue, or with the Jews into the hope of earning salvation by slogging down the road from one duty to another. You had to fall out of love with yourself. As far as he was concerned, that was the only way for it to happen.

And he set down very clearly the how of it: "I knew a man in Christ above fourteen years ago." What do you make of that? Mysticism? It was Paul's experience of the patient and holy love of God. If there is any such thing at all, what's so mystical about having it brought home to you? That's how it happened: Christ had got in, to wrestle with his weakness and his pride. So it was with Raskolnikov, in *Crime and Punishment*. So it was with the Grand Inquisitor, in *The Brothers Karamazov*. You remember how Christ kissed those bloodless lips, even as they pronounced the sentence of death on him there in the dungeon; and how the kiss lingered on in the old man's heart. Unless the long epic of human life in the Bible, with God feeling around in the middle of it to find some Jacob or some Amos, some Peter or some Zacchaeus or some Magdalen, and getting crucified for it that day they made a man trudge along carrying a sign down the windy street, "Jesus of Nazareth, King of the Jews," then nailed him to a cross, and the sign with him—unless from beginning to end every bit of that is some kind of weird vagary, you don't have to argue that being found can't happen to you. You don't have to inquire where the road to Damascus runs, and wish you could get up and walk down it. It runs through your home. It runs wherever you want it to run. "Lord, what wilt thou have me to do?" Ask that, and you're on it. You have come to the place where the self can get itself written off in the margin and God can get himself written down in the text. Call that "mystical" if you like, but you can't be quit of it that way. It is as solid a fact as any of the facts that have sprung from it.

Let me put to you now two of those facts as Paul does, and leave them. They are both right here. One of them, and you can handle it as you'd handle any other, is this: "My grace is enough for you." I suppose there are people who read those words and are far more sure than they ought to be that Paul actually heard them spoken out loud. They say, "We could manage too, on such terms. He prayed once, and what he wanted didn't happen; so he prayed again, and it didn't happen then either. We'll go along with that. That's exactly how it is. But the third time he got an answer, and we haven't had any." I can't help wondering about that. It's the silence, the terrible silence, that says No to us. I wonder if it wasn't the silence, only the terrible silence, that said to him, "My grace is sufficient for thee?" He carried that burden of the thorn his whole life, you know. Some physical blemish, was it, that would make a Jew ashamed? The spiritual pride and the passion, maybe, that kept nagging at him all his days. Perhaps the secret of it lies hidden away somewhere in the agony of that seventh chapter of Romans: "The good that I would I do not: but the evil which I would not, that I do . . . O wretched man that I am! Who shall deliver me from the body of this death?" Then the doxology for a victory that had been won, yet hadn't: "I thank God—through Christ our Lord!" You can almost hear him in the chapter which follows working out for himself, among other things, this business of the thorn: "If God be for us"—won't you ever count that in, instead of leaving it out?—"who can be against us? He that spared not his own Son"—because caring was God's business, it's your business, it was Paul's business too; will you never get into it as he did, instead of wondering what life is all about, with the furrow in your brow, and the pencil you are ready to fling down, sure that the only thing to do is to give it all up?—"How shall he not with him also freely give us all things?" Isn't it a bit too late for God to start failing now—with you? When you don't hear anything, isn't there something you ought to hear—in the terrible silence? "My grace is enough. . . ."

And this fact too: "My strength is made perfect in weakness." In weakness it comes into its own, nowhere else; accomplishing even in you what it's meant to accomplish. That's what perfect means: rounding itself out, full-statured and complete. It was like the long gesture forward that the cavalry officer used to make when he led his men toward the battle. It was like the first moving up along the beach of "a huge in-rushing tide with the whole sea behind it." What happens to you then doesn't have to look like strength. There are places in your heart where nothing that looks like strength can get in—only something which seems weaker than any hand you can get to drive a nail; but in spite of that shows itself stronger at last than all the generations of mankind. Whatever else the cross means, that's part of it. Maybe we'd better quit casting around for evidence, peering about on top of everything and under everything for proof: wishing there were some other sign than the signs we have—some stone turned into bread, some wild leap from the pinnacle of a temple, some gathering up of all the kingdoms of this world, and the glory of them.

But that's the devil's technique. It never has been God's. "My grace is enough for you." "My strength is made perfect in weakness." What a sorry sight Paul must have been with nothing more than that to count on, as the gale whipped its way along, tearing the crest from every wave. Nothing but those anchors to the wind, and the cables running out—to the bitter end! Maybe we should after all be calling it "the better end." The Roman Empire didn't weather the storm. Paul did. And the Christian Church.

Now may God bless you with all good, and keep you from all evil: illumine your heart by his presence, favor you with the knowledge of his grace and lift his merciful face toward you for eternal peace—Father, hallowed be Thy name!—Son, Thy kingdom come!—and Holy Ghost, Thy will be done!—that as it is in heaven so may it be on earth. Amen.

Adapted from *The Manual of Discipline,* The Dead Sea Scrolls

Life All the Way Up

Grant us, O Lord, to hear Thy Word while Thou stretchest forth Thy hand: that if there be any splendor of our faith which we have lost, it may be restored, and we may together again be strengthened in the way of Thy purpose; through Jesus Christ, our Lord. Amen.

Ernest Hemingway, in his early novel, *The Sun Also Rises*, writing of the frustrations which so many people of our generation seem to suffer, has one of his characters pack it all into the remark that nobody but bullfighters ever really lived "life all the way up." I suppose you could say that the whole Bible, end to end, deliberately sets out to refute that. Certainly the author of the Fourth Gospel in particular makes the refutation of it by all odds his chief business. When he says, over and over again, there in the fourth chapter, "Thy son liveth," that's what he's doing. He isn't just insisting that the nobleman's prayer has been answered, that the lad is no longer lying at death's door, that the boy is quite well again, all right now. You aren't to stop with a temperature chart and a cardiogram. You are being put on notice by the very repetition that something is happening which is far more significant than anything on the surface. It's being suggested to you, and you are to understand, that in this Jesus of Nazareth a whole new order of life has erupted into history from within: "life all the way up"—in a sense far deeper than Hemingway ever intended. And it's not some bull-fighter that's living it. It could be you.

But we are not supposed to get that far along all at once; not, so to speak, right out of the blue: we are supposed to get there by the road which John travels. There are two other stories that serve him in his Gospel—and he trusts they will serve us—as milestones along the way. One is about Nicodemus, a member of the Sanhedrin, who came to Jesus by night; the other is about a Samaritan woman who met him one day by Jacob's well. And please remember that none of it is just flat history. "Flat" is the one thing that history couldn't be as John saw it. He thought of it rather as a kind of ceaseless give and take between God and human life, in which some eternal reality is embodied in every event of our daily experience. He would have you watch these people coming up before Christ: a ruler of the Jews, a woman of Samaria, and a nobleman from Capernaum whose son's life is in the balance. But he would really like to have you ask yourself which of these is you. By some strange circumstance could it be that you are all three at once?

"There was a man of the Pharisees named Nicodemus." It's a familiar story. You know how it went between them, back and forth, there in the shadows that night in Jerusalem. For Nicodemus the first sharp word turned everything upside down. It was like having all the props knocked out from under you, because the things you'd counted on were the wrong things. All you thought really mattered was finished, and you had to start over. "Except a man be born again, he cannot see the kingdom of God." Perhaps we should just take the whole account up in our hands at once, and say to ourselves right away what John wants us to say: that "the old-time religion" isn't good enough; what has been won't do. And that's bewildering, if you should ever begin to deal with it seriously. It's bewildering because we were brought up in this faith of ours; the Christianity we know is part of the climate. It belongs to our way of life, and little by little, ever so gradually, we have settled down in it. It's a Good Thing for the community and for the nation. It gives life meaning. God knows it's comfortable, like the well-worn jacket and last year's slippers you put on in the evening when you're going to stay at home and jolly well mean to feel at home.

Something of the sort had happened to the religion of his fathers, and Nicodemus wasn't content with it, or he wouldn't have been there that night; but he didn't want to let it go either, or he wouldn't have kept asking, "How can these things be?" And as you listen to the wind that "bloweth where it listeth," you begin to wonder maybe if it has ever really blown through your own soul. What about the ruts all of us have fallen into? What about the way in which somebody over here, says Colin Wilson in *The Outsider*, starts chopping off the arms and legs of the Christian faith to make it fit life, while somebody over there is just as busy whittling at life to make it fit his faith: most of us bent on arranging enough compromises with things as they are to enable everybody inside the Church to get along all right pretty much as he is, and everybody outside at all times to feel welcome. It's the kind of religion that on almost every page of the Old Testament keeps running into the wrath of God, and in the New defies his wrath and does what it can to tear his love to pieces.

I hope we are beginning to see in our generation with terrible clarity that it won't do: the prayers that go around and around these selves of ours without disturbing them, so that they remain the one fixed point which doesn't change much; and the sermons that go around them and around, the hymns we sing. None of it seems very likely to rescue anybody. It has altogether too little to say to human life. It can scarcely redeem even the triviality which in Mr. Eliot's poems measures itself out "with coffee spoons," or "on Margate sands" tries to "connect nothing with nothing, the broken fingernails of dirty hands." We've got to understand some time before it's too late that we aren't just "baffled idealists" who could really get ahead if the Russians weren't so desperately unpleasant and life quite so frustrating. We too are people who like Nicodemus have to be stopped dead in our tracks every day we live by the radical demand which Christ always makes. We are people who if anything that matters is going to happen in God's disturbing presence have to be shaken free of everything else we've relied on, even religion. Whoever doesn't want this to happen, let him quit meddling with Christianity and go on about his "usual nonsense"! "Except a man"—but what if a man is spiritually numb; not what you would call really bad, not dead inside, just numb, grown used to the old that isn't enough—can he bear the pain of it? "Except a man be born again. . . ."!

Nicodemus spoke up once for Jesus in the Sandhedrin, so John says, a few chapters farther on; but he soon learned to hold his peace. And John says he was in at the death too, with his spices, his myrrh and his aloes, a great lavish heap of them—seventy-five pounds, I believe it was—maybe to make up for something, I don't know. But that's John's story, and that's the end of it. "There was a man"—it isn't clear that he was able to "take it"!—"named Nicodemus." Or was it you?

Simply to put that question turns the page for us, and brings us on to the woman of Samaria, with her effort to escape. I dare say that's the next step for all of us. We'd like to get away somehow from this shaking of the foundations, which is always God's first assault on the human soul. We'd like to be spared the hurt and the sting of any serious upset. Perhaps in one way or another we can draw back, as she tried to again and again, a little out of range.

The conversation began quite naturally, with nothing much to distinguish it from any other. Jesus asked her for a drink of water. God often starts that way when, as someone has phrased it, like a sailor rowing around an island he has a mind to land; and he always lands on some sensitive spot. In an instant she was on the defensive. I'm sure that says a great deal about her. She wanted to know why a Jew should ask water of a Samaritan. The Jews had no dealings with the Samaritans. And besides, a rabbi had no business talking to a woman! When in the next breath he offered to quench her thirst with a very fountain of living water, that was too much. Where would he get it? The well was deep, and he had nothing to draw with. God save the mark, would she then never have to trudge out here any more in the heat of the day with that heavy jug on her shoulder? Was he making himself out to be greater than Jacob, whose well this had been? It's the kind of shadow-boxing, the sort of preliminary swordplay, in which human life always indulges, by the very first law of its nature, which is self-preservation. It's fists are up, it's on guard, every time it finds itself cornered. It's sure that something is crowding in on it steadily, it doesn't quite know what, maybe God! Something that calls for an answer, refuses to go away and leave us alone.

When without any warning at all, like the quick glint of light on a blade, came the thrust, and there was no hope of parrying it. As John remembers the story, Jesus asked her, apropos of nothing, to go and call her husband; and she told him she had none. "Thou hast well said," answered Jesus; "for thou hast had five husbands; and he whom thou now hast is not thy husband." Very well, you say; but obviously that has nothing to do with you. Perhaps there was no exit for her; there's plenty for you. Wide open. All this talk about five husbands and a paramour leaves one singularly uninvolved. Why not merely take it at its face value then, and do no more than say, "My goodness!"—possibly because we know of no greater goodness we could call on to witness what a shameful business this was. That way we can get off without a scratch.

But let's cultivate the habit here in John of moving a little more slowly. From time immemorial marriage and adultery had been to the Jew symbols of the true religion and the false. Without pressing the analogy at all, the woman herself must have been such a symbol to the evangelist. It would have been almost impossible for him, as he wrote, not to think of the way in which the worship of God there in Samaria especially had been corrupted, mingled with all sorts of pagan practice, until on any reckoning it must have seemed to a pious Jew scarcely more than an adulteration of the ancestral faith with a secular culture.

And there, I'm afraid, it catches up with us. We'll not come away now lacking scars, as if we hadn't been anywhere. Whenever the Christian gospel insists on getting too close for comfort, there's no refuge so ready at hand as some combination of it with any one of a dozen popular cults: the cult of peace—how would that do? Let's talk about the way in which we can get rid of our inferiority complex, even though the New Testament, on the whole, talks much more about the importance of having one! In the Church, the cult of bigness—membership, budget, ecumenical organization. The cult of economic prosperity, of national interest, of white supremacy. Let's have a go at the godless Russians. How else shall we man the walls, and steady the ark, and keep God safe in this boisterous world? Let's preach sermons on the faith that ventures, and let's not worry too much about segregated churches. If the first part of Acts 17:26 is embarrassing, "God . . . hath made of one blood all nations of men," let's hurry on to the second part, "and hath determined . . . the bounds of their habitation." How does that make the ruling of the Supreme Court look? If Christianity isn't supposed to keep inviolate all this that we have built up over the years with blood, and sweat, and tears, then what is it supposed to do? And no Christian conscience can be satisfied with the cozy answer that it's supposed to right the wrongs which mar the face of human life. There are all too many who sidestep the intolerable pressure of the Christian gospel simply by plunging in to right them. That's how subtle our dodging is. Anything to avoid the cutting edge and keep the self secure.

So in the story the woman tries to fend off the truth by raising another issue entirely. Because Jesus had touched her to the quick, she shifted her eyes, and made a great show of changing the subject. There was Mt. Gerizim in full view. It would do as well as anything else. He was obviously a prophet, and so a theologian of sorts. Why not then put him this time a theological question that he could get his teeth into? "Our fathers," said she, turning away and pointing, "worshipped in this mountain; and ye say, that in Jerusalem is the place where men ought to worship." You won't read that either as no more than plain, prosaic fact, will you, such as that three and one are four, and Washington did cross the Delaware? It's too live an option still for all of us, this running off on some theological enterprise, just to get out of God's strange country, and away from the Invader! Talk to me about Bultmann and existentialism, or about realized eschatology, or something—and I'll feel much better. Deplore our unhappy divisions for a while—Lutheran, Presbyterian, Episcopalian, Methodist, Baptist: that will positively put me back on my feet!

But it's no good. She couldn't get away from those steady eyes. Everybody knows about the eyes, but not everybody calls them God's. Albert Camus, in *The Fall*, has a Parisian lawyer ask in a shady bar in Amsterdam the one question we all ask: "When you don't like your own life . . . what can one do to become another?" Just so. There was a time, he went on, when religion was "a huge laundering venture, for exactly three years, only it wasn't called religion. Since then, soap has been lacking, our faces are dirty, and we wipe one another's noses." It isn't a sense of sin that's missing in our generation. The sense of sin runs all through our modern literature, novel and drama alike. What's missing is the sense of a God who can tell you more about it and more about yourself in one revealing flash than you can learn from

Eugene O'Neill or Tennessee Williams in a month of Sundays: and with this greater difference, that he won't stop there. He'll answer your question, "What can one do to become another?" That's why you mustn't miss the little touch of irony here at the end of the story, as John gets ready to write about the nobleman's son. All the while the woman is away, telling everybody excitedly of a stranger who's manifestly some kind of prophet, Jesus is sitting there by the well, talking now to his disciples, making it clear in everything he's saying that he's so much more than she thinks. He isn't a prophet, he's a Savior. It isn't just knowledge he has to give, it's life—if you want it, not liking your own, wishing for another: "life all the way up"!

Then at last we are introduced to it. "There was a certain nobleman, whose son was sick at Capernaum." These stories taken together could be your autobiography: Nicodemus, and the old that wouldn't do any more; the woman by the well, and her futile attempt to get away; after that, a father who keeps pleading, "Sir, come down ere my child die." And the refrain that goes on repeating itself over and over, "Thy son liveth." Again I urge you, don't go plodding through it verse by verse, knee-deep in prose. Nowhere so much as in the Fourth Gospel are you made so vividly conscious of the timelessness of all that Christ says. Yet I cannot call it timelessness; because it has everything to do with time. It has to do with all of time—forever. Like that other sentence away back in the history of the Hebrew people: "The Lord our God made not this covenant with our fathers, but with us, our very selves, today, here, alive, all of us." "Thy son liveth."

It's the rescue, from afar off, of somebody who is at the point of death. And you know where that is. It's the point where life ceases to have any meaning for you. This father, you will remember, was an official of Herod's court, in all likelihood a Gentile—maybe Chuza, the steward, whose wife Joanna is later found ministering to Jesus. Suppose there were a love that could reach across such a void and set you on your feet again—to live each new day as a gift fresh from God's hand, and find in it a glory you'd never seen before, and a purpose you'd never dreamed of? What the early Christians saw in the story that so endeared it to them was simply that boundless mercy of God, tearing its way through, leaping over walls, breaking down every barrier, Jew and Greek, barbarian, Scythian, bond and free—a love which could reach that far, across any distance, as far as any man; as far as I know I am, in that hour and on that day when I feel myself to be an alien in Christ's world, not wanting to be as he is, not caring for what he has.

How far are you? Did it ever occur to you that you could measure the distance by asking yourself how strange it seems to come in off the solid streets of the city and listen to all this? "Except a man be born again, he cannot see the kingdom of God." "Whosoever drinketh of the water that I shall give him shall never thirst." To be told how much the meek will inherit, and the merciful, when all you have to do to refute it is to take a look at them. To hear of the eye that ought to be plucked out, and of the enemies that have to be loved, and the angels that sang lullabies at the carol service around a manger. How far from it do you live? And as if we didn't live far enough, what long sea miles have we not all put between ourselves and God by our very effort to find him? He says the search belongs to him! If there is a Love which means to reach that far, it has only one place to go before it dares to say anything at all about what it wants of me. And you may read of what happened when it went there. It went to Calvary and lay down on a cross, and waited for the blows of the hammer, and for the cumbersome thing to be jolted into the ground. Does it have no right to speak to you now?

When this story of the lad and his father was written, that had already taken place. Looking back John remembered that there had been no touch of a hand that day, only the word, "Thy son liveth": and a man had believed and gone his way. So it was still as the generations passed. There was a voice that kept overtaking people from the place where you would have said it had first been silenced with good stout nails, then buried away quite out of hearing. And every time through the centuries it comes somebody's length—Paul, Augustine, St. Francis, Luther—there is a miracle of life that answers to it.

Maybe the only difference it will make in your case at the beginning will feel like nothing so much as a sort of strange uneasiness. It's the pain of coming alive. If there is a loving-kindness of God anywhere, it may well arrive first as a judgment on all that you are and have been. But in every judgment some hidden mercy waits. As on that day when you said of your faith, "I can't tell you what I should do without it":

when suddenly you began wondering if it had no other hold on you than just the comfort it brought; and all at once whatever there is about Christ that condemns all shoddy bargains became for you the mercy which rid you of that one. Or shall I say there was a time when the only religion you knew anything about was forever trying to domesticate you here in a life that's open at both ends, with the winds of eternity blowing through it: a religion which hoped to make you feel at home and secure, as you went about your business humming a quiet tune, "This is my Father's world." And it's the world where Christ was crucified! A religion that in the teeth of every ugly thing kept on attempting to pull the wool over your eyes and keep you fooled. Like the sheep in the Eastern fable—let me borrow from Colin Wilson again: they knew that the magician to whom they belonged wanted their skins, and this they didn't like. But he hypnotized them, and got them to believe that they were immortal, and losing their skins would really be good for them; in any case it wouldn't happen right away, so they didn't have to trouble their heads about it yet. Besides, they weren't actually sheep at all, when everything was said and done: they were lions, or eagles, or men, or even magicians. So they stayed quietly where they were. Until the day came when you found out what nonsense it was, and the judgment in those steady eyes of Christ that condemned it became for you the mercy that rid you of it.

"Thy son liveth." It's rescue, but it's more than rescue: it's the ground of every claim God lays on us. He first gives the life that he then asks of us; and only what he gives will he ever ask: but he asks all of it. You can be sure we shall have more on our hands than simply improving the old. That isn't the language the gospel speaks. The New Testament says nothing of transforming what has been, or rising on the steppingstones of some dead self to higher things. It's too pessimistic for any of that, simply because it's intent on being far and way more optimistic. It destroys all our illusions of both optimism and pessimism. It talks of a new creation which Christ himself shall fashion, delivered from the cheerless enslavement of little things, of mean resentments and crippling fears, of memories that are too bitter and sorrows that are too old; of the disappointments that hold us back from trying because somewhere we failed; of the barren, futile victories we have won because somewhere else we had our way: we the loveless whom he has loved, we the unfriendly whom he has befriended, we the pitiless whom he has pitied, to stoop now under some corner of the weight that rests continually upon his heart, of this world's evil and its pain, lest any life, shoulder to shoulder with our own, should yet feel itself forlorn, or by lack of our compassion desolated, as if stripped of his. There is no hint in that of what somebody has called the loathsome smugness of an Abou Ben Adhem: "Set me down as one who loves his fellow men." Instead, the mark of the cross is on it. And that's as near as God ever came to writing his name. It's his sign and seal.

"Thy son liveth." Where's the profit then, tell me, in trying to get away: when it's not only love, but that Love, from which we keep holding back, asking, "How can these things be?"—warding it off, "Art thou greater than our father Jacob?" Are we afraid because of the threat it seems and the claim it makes? They are the way God has of saying that life is at stake—life "all the way up." And what do we come to him for, any of us, if it isn't for that? With the long years of Christian history that whatever the cost have continued saying Yes to him, and to the peril of his being here!

O God, our Father, we thank Thee for the revelation of Thyself to us, thou who at sundry times and in divers manners didst speak unto the fathers by the prophets, but in these days hast spoken to us by Thy Son. Show us Thy glory, whose face we may not see save in him whom thou didst send; and in him deliver us, not just from peril, not just from pain, but out of the bondage of our narrow, selfish ways into the freedom of Thy love—for his name's sake. Amen.

Index